In everlasting memory of my late paternal grandmother Fatma Dağlı, who introduced me to and inspired my love and passion for cooking.

For my late mother Fahriye Dağlı, who encouraged me in all my endeavors. For my late father Ahmet Dağlı, who taught me to be myself and prepared me to face life with all its beauties and difficulties.

My heartfelt thanks to Baki, my dearest husband and best friend, and my beloved children Murat and Beste, Mehmet Can and Deniz İlkin for their endless support and encouragement.

I dedicate this book to my darling grandsons Çem Baki İlkin and Ali Yiğit İlkin, whose arrival brought immense joy to our family and who have already given us the first indications that they enjoy my cooking.

—Nur İlkin

As always, to my family—Barry, Debra, TJ and Kaleb, Jeffrey and Marjorie and their new daughter Penelope—and my many wonderful friends who supported me along the way. For my mother, Roggie Weinraub, who started me on this culinary journey when she taught me to bake at a very young age.

We wish to thank Leyla Moushabeck, Naomi Tropp, Aliza Green, Paula Jacobson, Amy Riolo, and Sharon for their wonderful editing; Paula and Sharon for testing recipes; and Eileen and Barry for eating them.

A special thank you to Aliza Green, for sharing all her wonderful food knowledge. We wish to thank Semra and Fuat Yildiz, Zekeriya Torgut and Zuleyha Biçakçi for their great help in preparing and tasting these recipes. And a special thanks to the wonderful family members and friends who gave us recipes, and for their great help in making this book possible.

—Sheilah Kaufman

foreword

I first visited Turkey in 1974 complete with backpack, one jacket, a pair of jeans, a long skirt for dress-up, and very limited funds. I will never forget that plateful of mussels stuffed with rice, a typical mezze—small, tasty appetizer bites—from Marmara, because the waiter spilled a carafe of red wine all over that lone skirt! My vivid memories of the varied and delicious food that I ate at street stalls, bakeshops, and small, working person's restaurants finally brought me to Turkey again in 2007. Two weeks cooking, visiting markets, and eating in restaurants only whet my appetite and I wanted to know more about Turkey's complex history and imaginative cuisine.

Luckily, I met Sheilah Kaufman and Nur İlkin, two writers who have become friends though our mutual love of Turkish food. Kaufman is an experienced and prolific cookbook writer who has traveled extensively in Turkey and has also written about Sephardic Jewish cuisine; İlkin, native to the Turkish culinary capital of Gaziantep and wife of the Turkish ambassador to the United Nations, is an expert teacher and lecturer specializing in Eastern Mediterranean Turkish cooking. The two wrote their first collaborative effort, *A Taste of Turkish Cuisine*, in 2002, a fine introduction to the country's varied cuisine meant for a western audience working with western products and kitchens.

Five years later, the two have written a second book intended to present Turkish cuisine in more depth, not as a single broad entity but rather as a collection of regional cuisines—each based on the particular climate, history, produce, and people—joined together by the Turkish love of bold seasonings, and rooted in culture and family. Kaufman and İlkin lovingly depict the distinctive character of each region's cuisine, making dishes that are meant to be shared and enjoyed by people of all ages. According to Turkish tradition, a stranger at one's doorstep is considered to be "a guest from God" and should be welcomed accordingly.

In the words of the authors, *The Turkish Cookbook* shows "a love of good, healthful food, rich in variety and flavor, in a cuisine that can be traced back for more than 1,400 years." İlkin has collected a slew of appetizing recipes from her many friends, relatives, colleagues, and Turkish home cooks. Kaufman and İlkin have organized and written the recipes to suit the needs of today's on-the-go cooks looking for home-cooked, great tasting, and healthful meals. Like me, anyone that has been curious about Turkish food and culture will find that this meaty but down-to-earth book is not only packed with tempting recipes that I, for one, can't wait to try, but also gives an overview of Turkey's fascinating history and cuisine by region. From this book, I learned that one must understand Greek and Chinese to Mongolian, Persian, Arabic, and Georgian influences to know about Turkish food.

Although so far I've only visited the Aegean and the Marmara regions of Turkey, reading *The Turkish Cookbook* has made me want to get right on a plane and start exploring other parts of this vast and fascinating land—after making a whole lot more of the recipes, that is!

—Aliza Green, cookbook author and food consultant

introductions

My paternal grandmother, Fatma Dağlı, was a petite lady with a large personality and great flair. She was from the provincial city of Gaziantep in southeast Turkey but lived with us when I was a child. Gaziantep is known for its fine food, especially desserts and sweets, and my grandmother mastered the local cuisine. Since my mother worked, my grandmother did most of the cooking and everyone in the family was very happy with this arrangement. By age 6 or 7, I became curious about my grandmother's cooking and would hang out in the kitchen, following her every move and asking many questions. Only later did I realize just how much I had learned from her, and to this day, I chop vegetables exactly as she did. As I grew older and because I was her only granddaughter, she graciously provided me with more formal culinary instruction. She passed down both her methods and her philosophy; it later became apparent to me that her cooking often reflected the story of her life.

During World War I, she struggled to find enough food to feed my father, her only surviving child. Those years of hardship had a permanent impact on her; for the remainder of her life, she was careful never to waste anything and taught me to do the same. In her eyes, it was a sin to leave food on the plate. Grandmother stressed that a good cook was someone who could make a delicious meal from whatever ingredients were available. I gobbled up her advice along with her dishes.

I didn't start to put those priceless lessons to full use until I was married. My diplomat husband, Baki, was posted to Athens on his first assignment. I had come to the marriage with the knowledge of how to prepare family recipes and with a Turkish cookbook that my father had given me before our departure. Over the years, that lone cookbook grew into a library of books and magazines about Turkish cuisine as my father continued to send me whatever was published.

So, there I was in Athens, without my grandmother, cooking and starting my own family traditions. I began with simple dishes and progressed to more sophisticated ones. Some of my earlier attempts were mediocre at best. Baki kindly complimented me on everything I made and that encouraged me to keep trying. My cooking slowly improved. This could not have been easy for him as his mother was an excellent cook. She was well versed in Turkish and Arabic cuisine and Baki was used to her delicious meals. When we returned to Turkey for our vacations, she became my new cooking instructor and taught me a lot, even sharing her secrets for preparing Baki's favorite dishes. As with my grandmother's lessons, the more I learned, the more interested I became.

In 1974, Baki was posted to Moscow, where there was a dearth of vegetables and fruits. Since my grandmother had taught me how to be creative and prepare delicious dishes with a minimum of ingredients, I was able to adapt. I began using the dried beans and vegetables my mother sent us and learned to dry my own herbs (mint, dill, tarragon, and parsley) using my grandmother's methods (which I still do today). Everything I made tasted fresh and flavorful!

Our next assignment was London. I was delighted with the extensive variety of fresh foods. I continued to develop my knowledge of international cuisine and started sharing what I had learned by doing Turkish cooking demonstrations at the Anglo-Turkish Society.

It's a good thing I was developing into a good Turkish cook because the ultimate test of my skills came when we were transferred to Pakistan, where Baki had been appointed ambassador. Until then, our entertaining consisted of small dinners for close friends. Now we were Turkey's official representatives and we were expected to entertain on a much larger scale. Intimate dinner parties were replaced by large formal gatherings. I felt it was my responsibility to introduce our Pakistani guests to the pleasures of Turkish cuisine.

Since Baki was ambassador, I assumed that a chef would plan our official functions and that I would only have to provide some guidance. I was shocked to discover that our chef was a recently hired Pakistani who knew nothing of Turkish cuisine. I found myself back in the kitchen preparing family recipes. For four years, the embassy kitchen ran under my guidance. I learned which Turkish dishes really appealed to the Pakistani palate and prepared menus accordingly. My grandmother's words rang in my ears as I made the most of the situation. By the end of our stay, the Pakistani cook had become quite proficient in preparing Turkish food and I had expanded my own abilities in the kitchen.

We were then off to Copenhagen where we had an excellent Turkish chef. I was no longer needed in the kitchen, but would sometimes join him for my own pleasure and we exchanged many recipes. It was delightful to be in a completely different culture; and as I developed relationships with Danish friends, I learned how to prepare some of their wonderful dishes and shared some of my Turkish recipes with them. I was surprised to discover that lentils, chickpeas, and fava beans, which are basics in Turkish cooking, were readily available in Danish health food stores. However, most Danes did not quite know what to do with them! After joining us for a dinner at the embassy, the food editor of the Danish daily *Jyllands-Posten* asked me to share my recipes with the newspaper. I provided some Turkish recipes to give the Danish people some insight into how to prepare the previously puzzling foods.

After a brief posting in the Netherlands, my husband became the Turkish Ambassador to the United States and we lived in Washington, DC. Later we were posted to the United Nations in New York City. Living in Washington and New York was quite a culinary adventure, where there is a rich diversity of ethnic cuisines. My knowledge grew in leaps and bounds.

After living in and experiencing so many different cultures, I was inspired to start integrating Turkish recipes with other cuisines, developing my own fusion cooking. I started with the basics and have progressed to more sophisticated recipes. As guests have enthusiastically enjoyed the results and offered their appreciation, I have been encouraged to keep moving forward with my efforts. I try to keep abreast of the latest trends through new publications on Turkish and international cuisine. Although it has been my privilege to be exposed to the cuisines of many countries, Turkish cuisine remains my favorite. I'm sure that this is in part due to early associations with home and my grandmother's delicious dishes and in part because the cuisine is rich in variety and flavor and is delicious and healthful.

All of my experiences combined have led me right back to my childhood in the kitchen with my grandmother and the recipes for traditional Turkish dishes that you will find in this book. At the heart of Turkish cuisine are beans, grains, fresh fruits, vegetables, herbs, and yogurt. In fact, yogurt is one of Turkey's most important contributions to international cuisine. There is also a significant emphasis on the use of a wide variety of vegetables, which are often used as a main course. The vegetarian entrées are generally accompanied by rice or bulgur and served cold or at room temperature.

Most of these recipes require no special equipment and are easy to prepare. Those few dishes that are more challenging are so delicious that you will find it well worth the effort. You can fill your own kitchen with the tantalizing aromas and tastes that I experienced in the kitchens of my grandmother, my mother-in-law, and embassy chefs and bring the long tradition of Turkish cuisine to your own friends and family. As those fragrances fill your home and you accept the compliments that the dishes generate, you will become a part of my extended family. Welcome!

—Nur İlkin

It has been a joy for me to discover Turkish cuisine and culture. Nur and I met when she threw a Turkish luncheon in Washington, DC to introduce Turkish cuisine to the ladies in a diplomatic organization we belonged to. Having already been exposed to Turkish cuisine while in Turkey, I loved every single one of the (more than two dozen) dishes served that day. Unfortunately, I loved them too much, and had second helpings of a number of them, especially the desserts!

It didn't take very long for Nur and me to discover our mutual love of cooking, which in turn led to a wonderful friendship, and my begging Nur to teach me the recipes and techniques her grandmother had taught her. I wanted to learn everything I could, so I could prepare the dishes for my family and friends. Then I realized how much I wanted to share what I had learned so that everyone, everywhere could prepare and delight in these recipes.

I had just finished writing *Sephardic Israeli Cuisine* and realized Nur had enough wonderful recipes for a book. Happily, Hippocrene Books agreed with me and we began working on A *Taste of Turkish Cuisine*. We had a lot of fun working together in the kitchen and I was very excited about repeating the experience while working on *The Turkish Cookbook*. Writing this book was like going on a great, virtual adventure, and a fascinating one at that. The range of dishes that we tested and tried, finding the ones that really represented the seven regions, came in a large part from people who shared their family recipes with us. Turkish cooking is like a giant, colorful mosaic and Nur was once again teaching me the different components. I am the voice of the book; when you see "I" in the recipe headers, it refers to me.

—Sheilah Kaufman

history of turkish cuisine

Geographically, Turkey straddles both Europe and Asia, but most of the country lies in Asia in an area once known as Anatolia (or Asia Minor). The rest lies in Thrace—the Balkan part of Southeast Europe. Turkey's boundaries include three major bodies of water—the Black Sea to the north, the Aegean Sea to the west, and the Mediterranean Sea to the south. These are connected by the Bosphorus and Dardanelles Straits. Turkey shares its borders with eight countries: Bulgaria to the northwest; Greece to the west; Georgia to the northeast; Armenia, the Azerbaijani enclave of Nakhichevan, and Iran to the east; and Iraq and Syria to the southeast.

There are more than 30 ethnic groups living in Turkey. Other than Turks, the country is home to Kurds, Armenians, Albanians, Bosnians, Arabs, Azeris, Turkmens, Jews, Greeks, and Assyrians, to name a few! This ethnic diversity enriches the culture and cuisine of the nation.

This book is organized by Turkey's seven regions (Black Sea, Marmara, Aegean, Mediterranean, Central Anatolia, Eastern Anatolia, and Southeastern Anatolia). Each region's chapter includes geography descriptions, culinary highlights, the foods of the region, and recipes.

the origins of turkish cuisine

It is said there are four major cuisines in the world: Turkish, Italian, Chinese, and French. Each is based on local ingredients and flavors. As Neset Eren said in *The Art of Turkish Cooking*: "While many well-known national cuisines rely on one basic element (i.e., French cuisine is based on sauce and pasta forms the essence of Italian cuisine), there is no single dominant feature in the Turkish kitchen. Meats, fish, vegetables, pastries, and fruit are cooked in an infinite variety of ways." Turkish food is based both on geography and the creativity of the home cooks. Eating habits vary from region to region; each region has its own specialties and cooking style. Each of Turkey's seven regions boasts indigenous agricultural products, cultures, customs, traditions, and local dishes. In addition, the variety of climates in Turkey allows the cultivation of a wide diversity of crops.

The history of Turkey goes back to Stone Age settlements in 7500 BC. Over the centuries, parts of Turkey have been under the control of the Hittites, the Persians, the Romans, and the Ottoman Turks (among others). This fascinating part of the world has played important historical roles. For example, part of Turkey's southwestern shore was a wedding gift from Mark Antony to Cleopatra. Lasting over 600 years, the most powerful and long-lasting empire was that of the Ottoman Turks, who gave the country its name.

The history of modern Turkey began with people who migrated from the Altay Mountains in Central Asia. As they traveled, they encountered different culinary traditions, which they assimilated into their own cooking. Some traditions were based on animal products, such as the milk and meat of their horses as well as the wild animals they hunted. "When they reached Anatolia, they found a rich heritage based on beans, wheat, lentils, salt, and foods cooked with oil extracted from plants. As each group of peoples—Hittites, Romans, Byzantines, Arabs, Mongols and Crusaders—crossed Anatolia from east to west, they added to the culinary pool, thereby enriching the indigenous Turks' own cultural characteristics and cooking techniques," notes Ghillie Basan in *Turkish Cooking*. The cuisine that developed is the result of a rich historical experience.

The recorded history of Turkish cuisine is thought to have begun in the 10th century when the Turks came into contact with the Islamic culture under the Abbasid caliphate of Western Asia. The Abbasids were a Muslim dynasty based in Iraq who traced their lineage to the Prophet Mohamed's uncle, Al Abbas. During the Abbasid caliphate, education and scientific knowledge spread rapidly throughout Islamic society.

The Abbasids placed great importance on cooking and the philosopher Al-Kindi began to write about it as an art form. As their system of government began to emulate Persian models, so did their recipes such as the stews of meat

interesting facts

* Turkey is a land with a history that stretches back over 10,000 years and is best described as a mosaic.

* Anatolia (Asia Minor) was producing wine as early as 4000 BC.

* The city of Istanbul is uniquely located between continents and was the capital of three great empires—Roman, Byzantine, and Ottoman—for over 2,000 years.

* The Turks introduced coffee to Europe and also gave the Dutch their famous tulips.

* Turkey provides 70 percent of the world's hazelnuts; the nut in your chocolate bar was most probably grown in Turkey!

* An oral history of Turkish cuisine began in biblical times. According to legend, Noah's Ark landed on *Agri Dagi* (Mount Ararat) in Eastern Turkey and the last meal that was served aboard the vessel was a pudding made from nearly 40 leftover ingredients.

and fruits and vegetables. This laid a rich culinary foundation for future dynasties to build upon. The Abbasid kitchen also adopted native Turkish ingredients. When the Islamic alchemists perfected distillation, rose water became an indispensable ingredient in Turkish cuisine as well as a widely popular perfume and home fragrance. Other new foods—fruits, vegetables, and herbs—that had been nonexistent in Central Asia were introduced to Anatolia. Arab cuisine contributed many spices, including hot peppers and dishes based on wheat and mutton. There were also new sources of olive oil and seafood. It was not long before these ingredients were combined with the established foods—such as breads, dough products, and kebabs—to yield many new dishes. Though they learned pilafs (rice dishes) from the Persians, the Abbasids created a great variety of their own.

In the 11th and 12th centuries, much of the Abbasid power was transferred from Baghdad to the Seljuks, a Turkish Sunni Muslim dynasty. During their nomadic life, the early Turks depended on agriculture and on the breeding of domestic animals. Central Asian Turks consumed mutton, goat meat, and beef. The meat was prepared in a *tandır* (an underground oven), or grilled over an open wood fire as kebabs. *Kavurma* (small cubes of meat cooked in their own fat, salted, and stored in large earthenware containers to be consumed during the winter months) was another favorite. Meat was salted, spiced, and dried in the sun to make the preserved meat, *pastırma*. These foods are still a very popular part of Turkish cuisine.

Milk and dairy products also had a special place in the nomadic diet; milk and thick cream were the basic elements of the Turk's breakfast. A very important component of the early Turkish diet was yogurt, queen of the dairy products, and regarded as one of the most significant Turkish culinary contributions to the world. Mare's milk, high in vitamin C, was valued over sheep's or cow's milk. The nomads simmered the milk in large shallow pans, allowing the cream to rise to the surface where it formed a crust. The crust was eaten and the remaining milk dried in the sun and stored as a powder.

When available, fresh fruits and vegetables were used in season and dried and stored for the winter months. Fruits were soaked and cooked in water and a molasses was made from grape juice and used as a sweetener. Grape molasses is still a common ingredient in Turkish cooking.

Lastly, the basic diet of the early Turks included grains—primarily wheat and barley. Bulgur (wheat grain that is hulled, steamed, cracked, and dried) is still an important cereal in the diet of Turkish people. The typical bread of the nomadic early Turks—*yufka ekmek* (yufka bread)—is still made in the same way today. The dough is made of flour, salt, and water and is rolled out into thin, large, round layers and browned on a thin iron plate; it is then dried and stored.

The most significant impact on Turkish cuisine came during the rise of the Ottoman Empire and the reign of Mehmet II, who conquered Istanbul in 1453. The culinary arts played an important part in court life in Topkapi Palace, the center of the Empire and all culinary activity. Mehmet was a gourmet and the richest and most diverse flavors are found in dishes that were prepared during his reign.

At the height of its glory in the 16th century, the Ottoman Empire spread east to west from Baghdad to Tripoli and north to south from Budapest to Cairo. Once the Ottomans conquered, they rarely sought to impose their culture and there was no unifying language. It was a time when Christians, Jews, and Muslims lived relatively peacefully together.

By the beginning of the 1700s, the sultan's kitchen staff had grown to 1,370 people, all of them housed within the palace grounds. The preparation of each type of dish (soups, kebabs, pilafs, vegetables, fish, breads, pastries, sweets, jams, etc.) was regarded as a separate skill and each had a specialist chef. Ayla Algar, in *Classical Turkish Cooking*, notes "A list compiled in 1661 shows that 36,000 bushels of rice, 3,000 pounds of noodles, 500,000 bushels of chickpeas, and 12,000 pounds of salt were used in the palace. In 1723, the annual palace meat supply was 30,000 head of beef, 60,000 of mutton, 20,000 of veal, 200,000 fowl and 100,000 pigeons. Records also show that in the mid-17th century, 250 tons of bread were baked in Istanbul every day. A list of deliveries to the palace in 1660 notes the arrival of 2,000 pounds of cloves and nutmeg and 206 pounds of saffron, which were probably intended to flavor the fragrant pilafs that were the favorite food of the sultans."

Once the Ottomans controlled the entire eastern Mediterranean basin, they set about obtaining the best foodstuffs from the empire and beyond. They flamboyantly adopted and adapted the recipes they encountered in the Balkans, the Mediterranean, North Africa, and much of the Arab world. In *Turkish Cooking*, Ghillie Basan states that "During the reign of Suleyman the Magnificent (1520–66) the creations from the palace kitchens reached such dizzying heights of indulgence that dishes emerged with suggestive or humorous names such as 'young ladies breasts,' 'ladies' thighs,' and 'lady's navel.' Cooking was regarded as an art form and eating a pleasure, a legacy that remains at the root of Turkish cooking." These lavish dishes are still prepared today.

In *The Ottoman Kitchen*, author Sarah Woodward notes that "palace cooks plundered the markets for exotic ingredients to produce ever more ambitious menus, and to sustain this hunger more than 2,000 ships a year sailed to the Golden Horn laden with foodstuffs. The Ottomans themselves were not keen traders and tended to leave the actual business of trade to their conquered peoples." The 17th-century Venetian ambassador was shocked to find himself at a banquet of 130 courses! Where there was excess, there was also a true devotion to the sensual pleasures of the table and a continuing quest for the refinement of dishes. In the 16th and 17th centuries, the Ottomans traded with the Spaniards, who introduced many new products from the New World to Istanbul, including chili peppers, tomatoes, and maize. These products were quickly absorbed into the palace cuisine and thus out into the empire, shaping "much of what we today call the Mediterranean diet." Woodward calls the Ottomans "culinary plunderers, dedicated to the pleasures of the table; and in the palace kitchens, they perfected the recipes they had gathered from across their empire." Some of the earliest fusion cooking began with the Ottomans.

In every Ottoman city there was a shopping center, but since 1664, none has been more glorious than Istanbul's covered Grand Bazaar at the northern end of the Galata Bridge on the Golden Horn. It occupied 67 main streets and nearly 4,000 shops—a small town in itself. The Egyptian Bazaar, or spice market, featured spices from the east, caviar from the Black Sea, butter from Moldavia, olives and dried fish from Greece, fruits and nuts from the Balkans, dates from Egypt, and even live trout brought down from the rivers of Macedonia. Today, spices, dried fruits, nuts, seeds, Turkish delight (*lokum*), and other edibles still fill most of the shops, though jewelry and other high-end goods have begun to encroach on the market.

As time passed, due to outside influence and trade, olive oil gradually became an alternative for butter, and sugar replaced honey and grape molasses in many desserts. Flavors came from the spices cumin, coriander, cinnamon, mustard, pepper, and saffron; from the herbs parsley and mint (probably spearmint); and from onions and garlic.

the foods of turkey

Much as in the West, the people of Turkey typically eat three meals a day. Breakfast generally consists of eggs, a variety of cheeses, olives, fresh baked bread, a variety of homemade jams, butter, and black tea, the breakfast drink of choice. It is not uncommon to eat soup for breakfast, and in the hot summer months a bowl of yogurt.

Typically, families convene at home for lunch, which is traditionally a hot meal. Dinner is the main meal of the day. In winter, dinner usually begins with hot soup (an essential part of the Ottoman meal) or a selection of mezze dishes such as *Imam Bayıldı* (The Imam Fainted; page 99), followed by a dish of meat, poultry, or fish with vegetables or legumes, served with a rice- or wheat-based dish. Pickles are served as an accompaniment in the winter, and fresh salad is served in the summer. As many as two or three accompaniments may be served at one meal. When properly presented, these are often served and eaten on separate plates, since they deserve to be enjoyed individually. Bread is served alongside all dishes except *mantı* (Turkish ravioli, which was adapted from the Chinese dumplings) and boereks (filled pastries).

Seasonal tree-ripened fruits (especially those that are home or locally grown), puddings, or compotes are usually served for dessert. Syrupy pastry desserts are usually reserved for parties or as an occasional treat with tea or coffee. Cookies are not served after main meals. Instead, these are in a category of sweets served with tea or coffee, which is an important part of Turkish social life. These are often served in the afternoon when it is common to get together to socialize.

mezze

A selection of tasty morsels that precedes the main course is today a habit all over the eastern Mediterranean and throughout the Middle East. These dishes are meant to arouse the appetite before the meal and usually include roasted eggplant purée flavored with garlic and lemon; a thick yogurt dip made with garlic and dill; *dolmas* (grape leaves, cabbage leaves, green peppers, and other vegetables stuffed with spiced rice); the famous stuffed eggplant dish, *Imam Bayıldı (page 99)*; mussels; and a variety of other dishes. The type of mezze served depends on the region, although some, like stuffed grape leaves, hummus, and boereks are made throughout Turkey.

dairy

Milk is used in the preparation of numerous puddings and halvas (a popular dessert). In the city of Kahramanmaraş (also called by its older name, Maraş) goat's milk is used to make the world-famous Maraş ice cream.

Yogurt has been used in Turkey for over 4,500 years, and is often considered Turkey's culinary gift to the world. It plays an important role in Turkish cuisine and is an integral part of everyday life; it is used in everything from sauces to soups, mezze and salads (such as *cacık*), desserts, and drinks. Yogurt is most commonly made using sheep's milk in Turkey, but it can also be made from cow's milk or goat's milk.

Goat, sheep, and cow cheeses are also popular. They are frequently mild white cheeses that are served plain, herbed, or salted. Cheese often accompanies breakfast, and is also used to fill boereks or syrupy desserts. Popular varieties include *hellim* (*halloumi*), crumbly feta-type cheeses, ricotta, dry cottage cheeses, Gruyere-type cheese, and varieties similar to pecorino Romana. Some of these are: *Kaşar* cheese (a kind of pecorino), string cheese (known as *dil Peyniri*), *Çerkez* cheese (similar to mozzarella, *kelle* or basket cheese (a soft, buttery, white cheese), and *tulum* (a crumbly cheese prepared in sheepskin bags).

soups

As an important part of Turkish cuisine, Turkish soups run the gamut from light and delicate to hearty and substantial. Soup has always been both an inexpensive and nourishing source of sustenance and one that can be put together with almost any ingredients, which is perhaps why it was adopted by mosque soup kitchens and the Janissaries alike. The Janissaries (an elite corps in the service of the Ottoman Empire formed around 1365) eventually gained great power, and

Top: Turkish ceramic pottery © *Swisshippo*; bottom: Turkish tiles © *Ender Cilgin*

prized their soup cauldron above all other possessions. On the front of their caps they had a jeweled, gilded-silver ornament that usually was the repository for a spoon. Versatility and a rich heritage have made soups commonplace in Turkish home cooking.

Soups in Turkey are generally based on meat or chicken stock and are served at the start of the meal. If the soup is thin and delicate it is more likely to be used as a first course at a formal dinner. Soups that are more filling can be a meal in themselves, served with a salad and hearty bread. Lentils, peas, rice, tomatoes, potatoes, small meatballs, vermicelli, semolina, and barley are the chief ingredients of Turkish soups. Yogurt and dried mint are used freely as garnish. Lentil soups are the most common and best-loved variety. *Tarhana* Soup (page 135)—a centuries-old soup made from dried milk—is also very popular.

boereks

A boerek (*börek* in Turkish) is a pie of thinly rolled flaky pastry most commonly stuffed with meat, cheese, spinach, or potatoes. The original Turks were nomads from the grasslands bordering China and Mongolia; it is from this heritage that these delectable pastries are believed to have originated as descendants of the dumplings of Far Eastern cuisine. Boereks may be served in place of a hot main dish, but they are also served for breakfast or as part of a mezze.

salads

Fresh vegetables are abundant in Turkey and are a part of every meal. They are usually served at the start of the meal, often as part of a mezze, rather than after the main course. Unlike salads in other countries, some Turkish salads can be cooked; these are often served with hearty bread as a light lunch. The contents of salads will vary with the seasons since everything is fresh. Purslane, dandelion, and spinach roots are favorites.

meat dishes

The most popular meat in Turkey is lamb, but many dishes call for beef and veal. Pork is usually imported and used mainly by minority communities. The majority of recipes call for ground meat; though cubed meat is used in kebabs. Many recipes combine meat with vegetables or fruit, stretching the meat further. Some examples are Apricot Stew with Lamb (page 277) and Quince Stew with Lamb (page 311).

kebabs

Kebabs developed as an ideal food for an army on the move; they could be prepared whenever the soldiers had a chance to stop and prepare a fire. Grilling meat over wood is one of the oldest cooking methods known to man and one used by the early Turks as they roamed the steppes. The court cooks of Topkapi Palace (the primary residence of the Ottoman Sultans) recognized the unique flavor that meat and fish adopt when cooked over fragrant wood, and they elevated this method to one of refined elegance. In an old Ottoman recipe from Marmara, chicken kebabs are flavored with onion juice and cinnamon to create a marvelous, easy dish.

koftas

Koftas (*kofte*) are made from finely minced meat mixed with spices, onions, and various other ingredients. They come in diverse shapes and sizes and they are named according to the cooking method, ingredients, or shape. They can be formed into balls, ovals, or lemon shapes and then grilled, fried, boiled, or baked. Some have provocative names such as Ladies' Thighs.

poultry dishes

One of the best-known chicken dishes is Circassian Chicken (a dish of shredded chicken in a walnut paste, see page 90 for the recipe). It is served both as a mezze and a main course. Varieties of chicken kebab and other chicken dishes are common, as well as the use of chicken stock in soups.

The Turkish word for turkey is *hindi*, which means India fowl. It is a favorite poultry, and is usually stuffed with a special kind of pilaf. Goose and duck are not commonly used in Turkish cooking, though quail is. These are usually roasted or grilled.

fish dishes

Turkey has over 5,000 miles of shoreline and fish and seafood are abundant. The seas around Turkey provide some of the best seafood in the world. Lobsters, squid, mussels, shrimp, swordfish, bluefish, bonito, grouper, monkfish, sea bass, red mullet, mackerel, anchovies, and sardines are found in the coastal waters along the shores of the Black Sea, the Sea of Marmara, the Aegean, the Mediterranean, and the Bosporus (which is thought to provide the most delicious seafood). Common dishes include: Sardines Baked in Clay (page 150), grilled squid, and Broiled Branzino (page 92).

vegetable dishes

Vegetables are a favored staple of everyday Turkish cuisine and an integral part of most Turkish recipes. The vegetables used depend on the seasons and regions in which they are grown. Vegetables are often considered meals in themselves, and are usually accompanied by rice or bulgur and served cold or at room temperature. Favorites include eggplants, bell peppers, tomatoes, okra, squash, green beans, spinach, leeks, artichokes, celery, and cucumbers.

The Ottomans became experts in enhancing the natural flavors of foods. Using culinary embellishments, they were able to turn a simple ingredient into an exquisite morsel. This is most evident in the variety of stuffed vegetable dishes that originated during this period. Vegetables were stuffed with rice, meat, or other varieties of vegetable. Probably the best-known example of this art is *Imam Bayıldı*, or The Imam Fainted, a stuffed eggplant dish that was so good the imam is said to have fainted when he first tasted it. Other examples include Cabbage Rolls Stuffed with Chestnuts, Fresh Okra with Chickpeas, and Sautéed Swiss Chard. These dishes are still an important part of traditional Turkish cuisine.

pilafs and breads

Rice has always been a staple in the Turkish diet, probably from the time when the Ottoman armies used rice as sustenance during their march. With pilafs, the Turks developed a most sophisticated way of cooking the grain. Many of the pilafs popular in Turkey today retain the name of the sultan under whose reign they were introduced. Bulgur—cooked, dried, and partly debranned cracked wheat—is also a popular ingredient for pilafs in Turkey and throughout the Middle East. Bulgur is also frequently used in soups, *dolma* (stuffed vegetable dishes), meat dishes, and salads. Shelled and green (freekeh) wheat are also popular.

Bread is served with almost every meal in Turkey. The preparation of the thin, round, flat, village bread of the eastern Mediterranean is an art that must be learned from an early age. Stuffed flatbread (*gözleme*) and flatbread with toppings (*pide*) are popular light meals. Cornbreads, in varying degrees of dryness, are also common, especially in the Black Sea region. The type of bread served differs in popularity according to region.

desserts

The Ottoman Empire was famous for its sweets and pastries. Turkish delight and baklava are just two. Turkish sweets are rich in butter and sugar, and are often soaked in thick sugar syrup. Desserts can be fried in oil, milk-based (like *Aşure* or Noah's Milk Pudding), fruit-based (such as compotes), or in a class of *helva* (a variety of dessert). Turkish delight (*lokum*) is prepared with flour, sugar, and butter or oil. Cookies and sweets are often served with coffee or tea rather than after a main meal.

drinks

For centuries, coffee has played a secondary but essential role in Turkish cuisine and culture. It has its own terminology, expressions, and customs. Other drinks include Turkish tea and yogurt drinks. If you prefer an alcoholic drink, try *raki*, which is made of anise, and is sometimes referred to as "lion's drink" because you must be as strong as a lion to drink it!

the delights of turkish cuisine

Almost every food culture comprises food elements that are valued for their nutritious and decorative qualities, and recognizes that eating small amounts of many different foods is healthier than eating large amounts of just one. Traditional Turkish dishes utilize a variety of vegetables, legumes, meat, poultry, fish, grains, fresh fruits, herbs, and milk-based foods such as cheese and of course, yogurt. The variety is endless; eggplant alone can be prepared in over 40 different ways. Zeynel Abidin Uzun—proprietor of Kazan Restaurant in McLean, Virginia—told me "a chef is not really a chef until he can prepare at least 60 eggplant dishes." He also told me that it is "not enough for a dish to taste good or look nice, it must also be balanced so it is easy to digest and doesn't leave you feeling uncomfortable or bad. For instance, because eggplant is acidic, it does well when prepared with yogurt or oregano to balance it. A cuisine is beautiful because things go together. As a diner, you don't want to be someone's experiment!"

Turkish cuisine has been built on a legacy of creativity and experimentation. Since it requires very little special equipment, it is generally quite easy to prepare. As Nur told me when we were writing our first book, *A Taste of Turkish Cuisine*, "In Turkey we talk about individuals with tasty hands. This implies that they have wonderful recipes and are excellent cooks." Someone with "tasty hands" cooks from instinct, from experience or touch, rather than with recipes or measurement. We hope you will find that you have tasty hands or that you will acquire them by learning more about Turkish cooking and preparing the wonderful recipes Turkey has given us. Remember that the Turks are well known for their generous hospitality and love of wonderful food and you will follow their example in combining the three most important things in life: food, family, and friends.

helpful hints and tips:
a quick guide to turkish cooking

Turkish food requires very little fancy equipment, and most ingredients are available in supermarkets, Middle Eastern markets, and health food stores. If you have trouble finding any of the ingredients, consult the shopping guide on page 325.

Throughout this book, flour refers to all-purpose flour; freshly ground pepper is black pepper; eggs are large; and potatoes are golden potatoes. We use olive oil and canola oil (canola oil because it is readily available, healthful, has a high burning temperature, and because it takes on the taste of the foods made with it). If you prefer other oils, try them with our recipes and see how they work! In recipes that call for stock or broth, use whichever you have on hand, and adjust seasoning accordingly (broth may have higher sodium levels than stock).

The range of unfamiliar ingredients is very small. If you cannot find Aleppo pepper, substitute 3 parts paprika to one part red pepper flakes or cayenne, but if preferred, just paprika will do. Be sure to use the glossary if you come across other unfamiliar ingredients.

Try to find phyllo leaves in the suggested size or sizes. Be careful because some of the brands cut the leaves in half (these are often packaged separately in the box), and this smaller size is not suitable for most of our recipes. Vegetables and fruits are best in season, but some recipes call specifically for dried fruits.

Cooking with Pasta:
If you are going to mix pasta with a sauce do not rinse it in cold water because you want the starch from the pasta to bind with the sauce. Rinse pasta if it is going to be used in a salad because rinsing keeps it from sticking together.

Dry Roasting Nuts:
Place nuts in a non-stick skillet or pan and heat over medium heat for 5 to 7 minutes, shaking the pan from time to time so the nuts don't burn.

A Quick Legume Tutorial:
Lentils and beans are among the healthiest foods available, but many cooks don't really understand or know how to work with them. So here are a few hints and tips:

Hints:
Adding epazote (an herb also known as wormseed) to your beans during the last half hour of cooking they are less likely to give you gas. Soaking your legumes overnight will have a similar effect and the more you rinse the less gas you will have!

Cooking with Dried Legumes:

All dried legumes (except black-eyed peas and split peas) should be soaked before use. Use the quick soak method if you are in a hurry; otherwise, soak overnight. Dried chickpeas should be soaked in salted cold water overnight (1 heaped teaspoon of salt for 1 cup of chickpeas). It is not necessary to soak black-eyed peas but soaking for 2 hours before use reduces the cooking time.

Quick Soak:

For each pound of dried beans, bring 8 cups of water to a boil in a 4- to 5-quart pan over high heat. Add rinsed beans; boil for 10 minutes. Remove from heat; cover, let stand for 1 hour. Drain and discard the water, then rinse well in cold water.

Soaking Overnight:

For each pound of beans, pour 8 cups of water into a large bowl. Add rinsed beans, let soak at room temperature until the next day. Drain, discard water, and rinse well.

Cooking Times:

Cooking times vary depending on the type of legumes and the length of time they have been stored. The older the legume, the longer it takes to cook, so it is not advisable to combine newly purchased legumes with those already on your shelf.

For each pound of dried legumes (unsoaked weight) pour 8 cups of cold water into a 3 to 4-quart pan. Add legumes (soaked if necessary) and bring to a boil over high heat. Then reduce heat, cover, and simmer until tender to the bite. If needed, add water to keep the legumes moist. Start tasting when the minimum recommended time is up; when they are done, legumes should be tender but not mushy. (For black beans, this is usually 1 1/2 hours to 2 hours.)

black sea

mezze and salads

Cornmeal and Cheese 6
Fried Eggplants with Cornmeal 7
Green Lentil and Fine Bulgur Salad 8
Leeks and Eggs 9
Pasta with Two Cheeses and Walnuts 10
Vegetable Salad 12
Firdevs's Homemade Cottage Cheese 13

soups

Bean Soup with Noodles and Greens 14
Corn Soup 15
Kale or Collard Green Soup 16
Pumpkin, Collard Green, and White Bean Soup 17
Spinach Soup 18

pilafs, boereks, and bread

Best Rice Pilaf 19
Bulgur with Green Beans 20
Cornbread 21
Rice with Cranberry or Red Kidney Beans 22
Rice with Mushrooms 24
Spinach and Egg Boerek 25
Walnut Bread 26

meat and chicken

Chicken with Shelled Wheat 27
Cornmeal Koftas 28
Lamb Shanks with Orzo 29
Pearl Onion Stew 30
Stuffed Collard Greens 31
Stuffed Onions 32

fish

Anchovies with Cornmeal 34

Trout Baked in Terracotta 35

Anchovies with Rice 36

vegetables

Collard Greens with Bulgur and Cranberry Beans 38

Fresh Cranberry Beans in Olive Oil 39

Mashed White Beans with Cornmeal and Sautéed Onions 41

Sautéed Swiss Chard 42

Zucchini with Bulgur 43

desserts and sweets

Apple Halves with Walnuts 44

Buttered Sweet Plums 44

Bourma 46

Cornmeal Halva with Hazelnuts 47

Custard-Filled Phyllo Pastries 48

Sweet Lips 51

The Black Sea region is protected by high mountains that lie parallel to the coastline, and rivers cascade through the mountains. Along the coastline lie many beautiful fishing towns and villages. In the spring, wild flowers cover the hills. Black Sea cuisine features the anchovy, and also collard greens, corn, Swiss chard, dried white and cranberry beans, green flat beans, tea, and hazelnuts that grow in the region.

Cornbread is the basic bread here, most famously, a distinctive variety made by the indigenous Laz people. Cornmeal frequently serves as a substitute for flour in baking and cooking; here, halva and baklava are prepared with cornmeal instead of flour. Away from the coast and closer to Central Anatolia, wheat products are more common.

Naturally, the Black Sea coast is famous for its seafood, especially anchovies, or *hamsi*. Anchovies are considered to be the "prince of fish," and Turkish cuisine features many different ways of preparing them. They can be coated with cornmeal and fried, baked, or used in pilafs and boereks. They are so beloved here that they are even used in desserts like *Hamsi Tatlısı*, a sweet pastry made from anchovies, flour, eggs, and fruit preserves. Anchovies are salted and stored in cans to be used when fresh ones are not available. Many poems, anecdotes, and songs have been inspired by this little fish. Fishing is a major industry in the Black Sea region, especially in the port city of Samsun. Samsun is famous for turbot, which is available there throughout the winter months.

But the Black Sea region has more to offer the culinary inquisitor than seafood. It is known for both its high quality local produce and culinary innovation. In the west, the province of Bolu has produced many chefs for five-star hotels and restaurants throughout the country. A famous cooking school in the Bolu town of Mengen hosts an annual cookery festival. During the reign of the Ottoman Empire, the palace kitchen employed many chefs from Bolu.

South of Samsun, the region's Central Asian heritage is most evident in the province of Amasya and specialty dishes include stuffed vine leaves, and varieties of *kofte*. The city of Kastamonu is famous for its rice and beautiful wooden architecture. The province of Sinop produces excellent quince and chestnuts.

In the center of the region, Tokat is scattered with vineyards, whose delicious grapes are used for making wine and molasses. Grape molasses is valued for its ability to provide energy, and is often served during the coldest days of winter. Pickles, especially those made from flat green beans, are also very popular here, and are usually served sautéed in butter.

The high plateaus in the area have an abundance of grass for grazing cows. Milk and milk products, including specialty cheeses such as ricotta, cottage cheese, *Kaşar* cheese (a kind of pecorino), string cheese (known as *dil Peyniri*), and *Çerkez* cheese (similar to mozzarella), are popular in this region.

Black Sea hazelnuts are considered to be among the finest in the world. They are exported to many countries and hazelnut oil is frequently used in cooking. The coastal provinces of Giresun and Ordu are the centers of hazelnut production in Turkey, and hazelnuts have made their way into the local culture. Ordu is a beautiful port situated at the foot of the Forest Hills, and the home of an annual Golden Hazelnut Festival. The Port of Giresun has long handled the local produce.

The nearby city of Trabzon is famous for its butter, as well as varieties of pide (a pizza-like pastry) and thick-crusted wheat breads. To the east, the city of Rize, built on a mountain slope, is covered with tea bushes, giving the appearance of a green pillow. Other important cities in the region are Düzce, Bilecik, Bolu, Zonguldak, Bartin, Karabük, Kastamonu, Sinop, Samsun, Amasya, Çorum, Tokat, Gümüşhane, Artvin, and Bayburt.

Tea bushes © Erdal Bayhan

cornmeal and cheese

Mısır Kuymağı
Trabzon

This dish is most commonly served straight from the skillet in small quantities and eaten with a dessert spoon. The combination of cheese, cornmeal, and butter is rich and delicious. It is a wonderful accompaniment to any stew in the place of rice.

Serves 4 to 6

2 cups water
3 tablespoons butter, divided
Sea salt
¾ cup cornmeal
1 cup mozzarella cheese, cut into ½-inch squares

In a medium-size skillet (a nice one that can be brought to the table) combine the water, 2 tablespoons butter, and salt and bring to a boil. Slowly add the cornmeal, stirring constantly, and lower the heat to simmer. Stirring constantly, cook until the mixture thickens, about 10 minutes. Add the cheese and continue stirring until it melts, about 4 to 5 more minutes. Add the remaining tablespoon of butter, mix well, and serve immediately.

fried eggplants with cornmeal
Mısır Unlu Patlıcan Tava
Trabzon

This vegetarian recipe does double duty since it can be a light lunch or an appetizer. In this recipe, eggplants are dipped in cornmeal twice (like sea bass), until they become thick. Nicknamed "poor man's sea bass," eggplants are often used as a meat substitute because they add heartiness to a dish.

Eggplants were being used in China as far back as the 5th century. Italian eggplants are smaller, curved, plump, firm eggplants with purple skin; while in the United States we mainly use big, deep purple eggplants. This recipe is from Nur's friend Gönül Dinlenç, who is from Trabzon.

Serves 4

4 (4- to 5-inch) eggplants
4 cups water
Sea salt
Canola oil for frying
3 large eggs, beaten well
1 cup cornmeal plus more if needed

Wash the eggplants. Leaving an inch of peel on the top and bottom, peel off 1/2-inch strips of skin, lengthwise, at 1/2-inch intervals, making a striped effect. Repeat until all eggplants have been striped.

Starting just below the 1-inch uncut space at the top of the eggplants, make four, evenly spaced, lengthwise cuts, forming four equal-size pieces that are connected at the top but separate at the bottom. (Be careful not to cut the eggplants into individual pieces.)

Place the eggplants in a colander and generously sprinkle with salt. Let stand 30 minutes, rinse and drain well.

In a large pan, heat 4 cups of water with 1 teaspoon of salt. Add the eggplants and boil over medium heat for 7 to 10 minutes or until cooked through. Drain well and pat dry with paper towels.

In a medium skillet, heat enough oil to reach a depth of half an inch.

Place beaten eggs in a pie pan and dip eggplants in the eggs, turning to coat well. Place the cornmeal on another plate, and dip eggplant into cornmeal. Gently press on the eggplants so the four pieces fan out, still connected at the top. Repeat dipping first into eggs, then cornmeal, again pressing lightly to maintain fan shape.

Fry eggplants until golden brown. Cover a plate or cookie sheet with layers of paper towel for draining the eggplants after frying. Arrange eggplants on a platter and serve with yogurt.

green lentil and fine bulgur salad

Bat

Tokat

This salad is usually served for lunch or as a vegetarian main meal. Bulgur is a form of wheat available in different textures from fine to course. It can be purchased in health food stores and Middle Eastern markets. Keep in mind that the lentils need to be soaked before using. If desired, they can be soaked the night before.

Serves 4 to 6

4 cups water
1 cup dried green lentils, soaked in water to cover for 3 to 4 hours, drained
½ teaspoon sea salt
⅔ cup fine bulgur
2 tablespoons tomato paste
¾ cup walnuts, coarsely chopped in a food processor
5 to 6 scallions, white and most of the green, finely sliced crosswise
1 green bell pepper, stems, seeds, and ribs removed, finely diced
2 medium tomatoes, finely diced
½ tablespoon dried basil
½ teaspoon Aleppo pepper
Freshly squeezed juice of 1 lemon
3 tablespoons finely chopped Italian flat-leaf parsley
3 tablespoons finely chopped fresh dill
Freshly ground pepper

Bring 4 cups of water to a boil in a medium-size pan. Add lentils and salt. Reduce heat to simmer, and cook, covered, for 30 to 35 minutes, or until tender.

Remove from heat and stir in the bulgur, mixing well. Place the lid on the pan and let the mixture cool. Stir in the tomato paste and walnuts, and mix well with a wooden spoon. Add the scallions, diced green pepper, tomatoes, dried basil, Aleppo pepper, lemon juice, parsley, and dill. Salt and pepper to taste. Mix well.

Serve in a shallow serving dish.

leeks and eggs

Pırasa Mıhlaması
Central Black Sea

Mıhlama—a technique for cooking leeks, mushrooms, spinach, Swiss chard, potatoes, and even ground beef with eggs—is very popular all over the Black Sea region. This vegetarian dish is usually served for lunch, and makes an impressive yet inexpensive dish for entertaining.

Serves 2

2 tablespoons butter
2 tablespoons canola oil
1 carrot, peeled and coarsely grated
1 onion, finely chopped
1 pound leeks, outer leaves removed, washed, cut crosswise into ¼-inch thick slices
2 large eggs
Sea salt
Freshly ground pepper

In a medium-size skillet, heat the butter and oil over medium heat. Sauté the carrots and onions, stirring, for 5 minutes. Add leeks and continue to cook for another 7 to 10 minutes, or until leeks are soft.

Using a wooden spoon, move vegetables aside in two spots, making 2 holes, and break an egg into each hole. Cover the skillet and cook until the egg white is done and the yolks are still soft. Sprinkle with salt and pepper to taste and serve hot with cornbread.

Variation: If you want to substitute ground beef, use 1 chopped onion; 2 cubanelle peppers or green bell pepper, finely chopped; 2 chopped tomatoes; salt; pepper; and 1/2 pound ground beef. Sauté everything in oil until cooked. Break eggs into the holes and cook until whites are firm.

9

pasta with two cheeses and walnuts
Peynirli Cevizli Eriştesi
Safranbolu

I discovered this lovely, easy dish in Safranbolu. Since I always keep these ingredients on hand, it is perfect for unexpected company or a quick dinner. In Turkey, this is made with thin matchstick-size strips or twists of homemade pasta. If you cannot find this type of pasta, use matchstick size pieces of fettuccini or in a pinch, penne. If needed, pasta can be heated in a 350°F oven for 5 minutes after everything is mixed together.

Serves 6 to 8 as an appetizer, 4 to 6 as a main course

1½ pounds pasta
2 to 3 tablespoons unsalted butter or extra-virgin olive oil
1 cup (or more) freshly drained and crumbled feta cheese
About ¼ cup grated Parmesan, plus more for serving
1 cup (or more) roughly chopped walnuts
A bunch of fresh flat-leaf parsley, stems removed, and roughly chopped
¼ teaspoon red pepper flakes, optional

Prepare pasta according to package directions. Drain well and place in a large serving bowl (ovenproof if you plan on heating it). Stir in butter or oil.

In a medium-size bowl, combine the cheeses, nuts, parsley, and pepper flakes (if using). Toss pasta with the cheese mixture. Heat if desired. Serve with a bowl of additional Parmesan.

vegetable salad

Sebze Salatası
Amasra

This vegetarian salad is made with cooked vegetables in a light vinegar-based dressing. Potatoes and eggs make the dish a complete meal, but it is also a good accompaniment to any grilled food.

Serves 4 to 6

2 medium potatoes, boiled with skin on, cooled
2 medium carrots, peeled and boiled until just tender (but still crisp)
4 large eggs, hard-boiled, divided
1 cup frozen peas, cooked according to package directions
1 bunch scallions (about 4 to 5), white and most of the green, thinly sliced crosswise
½ bunch of Italian flat-leaf parsley, finely chopped

Dressing:
2 tablespoons hot water
¼ cup white vinegar
½ cup olive oil
Sea salt
Freshly ground pepper

Remove skin from cooked, cooled, potatoes and dice along with carrots into 1/4-inch pieces. Place in a salad bowl. Dice 2 hard-boiled eggs into 1/4-inch pieces (saving the rest for the dressing) and add to the salad, mixing well. Add peas, scallions, and parsley and mix well.

In a blender, combine the two reserved hard-boiled egg yolks (add the whites to the salad bowl) with the hot water and blend well. Add vinegar and blend. Slowly add the olive oil, while the machine is running. Season with salt and pepper to taste. Pour dressing over the vegetables, toss well, and serve.

firdevs's homemade cottage cheese

Çökelek Peyniri
Rize

Firdevs is from the East Black Sea region. She loves this fresh, white cheese, but it is hard to find in Washington, DC, where she now lives. She asked her family for the recipe and shared it with us. This dry cottage cheese is fresh, tasty, and light. Use it for breakfast, on salads, and as a filling for ravioli.

Makes about 2 cups

1 gallon (16 cups) whole milk
⅔ cup white vinegar
Salt, if desired

Place milk in a 5- to 6-quart steel pot (it must be steel). Cover and let it sit on the kitchen counter for 14 to 15 hours (or more) until it thickens to the consistency of loose yogurt.

Place pot over high heat and cook just until your little finger can't take the heat. Turn off the heat and pour in the vinegar; do not stir. Cover and let sit for 30 minutes.

Return to the heat and boil the milk for about 15 minutes until it comes to a hard boil. While milk is boiling, line the colander with cheesecloth and place over a large bowl or pot. Remove milk from the heat and pour into the colander. You can use a yogurt bag if you have one. Let drain for 10 to 12 hours. Add salt if desired.

bean soup with noodles and greens
Fasulye Çorbası
Artvin

Because it is rich, nourishing, and excellent for a winter lunch, this soup is a meal in itself. If the soup gets too thick, add more stock.

Serves 4 to 5

6 to 7 cups chicken stock
½ cup small white beans, soaked overnight in cold water, drained
¾ cup angel hair pasta, broken into matchstick-size pieces
1 cup baby spinach leaves, washed and drained (optional)
Sea salt
Freshly ground pepper
2 tablespoons butter
1 large onion, finely chopped
1 tablespoon tomato paste
1 teaspoon Aleppo pepper

14

Bring 6 cups of stock to a boil in a 2-quart pot. Add drained beans and simmer on low heat, partially covered, for 45 minutes, until done.

Add pasta and spinach (if using), and salt and pepper to taste. Mix well and cook for 10 to 15 more minutes.

Meanwhile, in a small skillet, melt the butter and sauté the onions until golden brown. Add tomato paste and Aleppo pepper to onions and mix well. Stir onion mixture into the soup and cook for 5 more minutes.

corn soup

Mısır Çorbası
East Black Sea

This simple, hearty soup made from corn, milk, cheese, and bread, is a great way to use fresh, canned, or frozen corn, and stale bread. The recipe was given to Nur by a dear friend from the Eastern Black Sea region. Nur loves it with grated cheddar sprinkled on top.

Serves 6

3 tablespoons butter, divided
1 cup yellow or white cornmeal
6 cups chicken or vegetable stock
Sea salt
Freshly ground pepper
1½ cups milk
1½ cups fresh, frozen, or canned whole corn kernels (if using canned, drain)
3 stale pieces white bread, toasted, cut into ¼-inch squares
1 teaspoon Aleppo pepper
3 to 4 tablespoons grated cheese (optional)

Melt 2 tablespoons butter in a medium-size soup pot, over medium heat. Reduce heat to low, add the cornmeal, and sauté for 4 to 5 minutes, stirring constantly.

Add the stock, sea salt, and freshly ground black pepper to taste. Cook for a minute or two and slowly add the milk and corn kernels, if fresh or frozen. (If using canned corn, add corn 5 minutes before the soup is finished.) Cook, uncovered, for 15 to 20 minutes, stirring occasionally.

Meanwhile, melt 1 tablespoon butter in a small skillet and sauté the croutons until golden brown on both sides. Stir in the Aleppo pepper. Mix well.

Pour soup into a serving bowl and arrange the croutons on top. If desired, sprinkle grated cheese on top.

kale or collard green soup

Kara Lahana Çorbası
Rize

This vegetable soup uses kale as its base, along with carrot, zucchini, onion, green pepper, string beans, and potatoes. Kale, sometimes called borecole, is a form of cabbage. It is dark green and resembles its relative, wild cabbage, but the central leaves do not form a head. It is a healthy and nutritious food, an excellent source of vitamins K, C, A, and manganese. This is a great vegetarian dish.

Serves 6 to 8

1 bunch kale or collard greens, washed, drained, and coarsely chopped
1 peeled carrot, coarsely chopped
1 peeled zucchini, coarsely chopped
1 large onion, coarsely chopped
1 large green pepper, coarsely chopped
10 string beans, ends removed and chopped
2 medium potatoes, peeled and coarsely chopped
Salt
Freshly ground pepper
9 to 10 cups chicken or vegetable stock, or water, divided
¼ cup flour
¼ cup yellow cornmeal
1 tablespoon butter

In a 3-quart pot, combine all the vegetables, salt and pepper to taste, and 8 cups of stock or water, and bring to a boil. Lower heat to simmer and cook, covered, until the vegetables are done, about 45 to 50 minutes. Place the vegetables in a blender, purée, and return to the pot.

In a small pan, combine the flour and yellow cornmeal and dry sauté over low heat for about 5 to 6 minutes, stirring constantly (there is no butter or oil). Remove from heat and cool.

Whisk a cup of water into the flour mixture and return to low heat, whisking constantly until it thickens.

Add the thickened flour mixture to the puréed vegetables; bring to a boil, and cook, stirring, for another minute or two so the flavors can blend. Add the butter and correct seasoning if needed. Serve hot.

pumpkin, collard green, and white bean soup
Balkabaklı Çorbası
Trabzon

Colorful, tasty, and healthy, this soup made from beans, collard greens, and pumpkin is perfect for fall and winter. In the Black Sea region, it is made with oven-dried, cracked corn. Because this is not available in the United States, either rice or bulgur can be substituted. Serve with a slab of warm bread.

Serves 8

9 to 10 cups chicken stock
6 ounces dried, small white beans (preferably navy beans), soaked overnight, drained
Sea salt
¼ cup medium-grain white rice or bulgur
10 ounces frozen, chopped collard greens, defrosted and drained
14 ounces pumpkin, peeled, diced into ½-inch squares
Dried chili pepper (optional)
1 tablespoon yellow cornmeal
2 tablespoons butter
Freshly ground pepper
A few flakes of Aleppo pepper

Bring 9 cups of chicken stock to a boil in a 3-quart pot, over medium heat. Add the beans and reduce heat to simmer. Cover and cook until the beans are done, 30 to 35 minutes. Stir in salt, rice, collard greens, pumpkin, and chili pepper (if using). Mix well and cook for 15 to 20 minutes, or until the vegetables are tender (but not falling apart). If the soup seems too thick, add the remaining cup of stock.

In a small bowl, whisk the cornmeal with 1/4 cup of soup. Pour this mixture into the soup, whisking constantly. Add the butter and season with freshly ground pepper to taste and the Aleppo pepper, mixing well.

spinach soup

Ispanak Çorbası
Samsun

This easy-to-make vegetarian soup can be prepared with frozen spinach and pantry staples. Vegetable soups enable us to enjoy cooked vegetables that have retained their nutrients; the cooking liquid is not discarded so the soup is rich in flavor and has the added bonus of vitamins and minerals.

For something different, substitute nettles for the spinach if you can find them in the farmers' market. Nettles are very common in the Black Sea region and have many uses: in soups, as a purée, salad, or even in some lamb stews. Remember to wear rubber gloves when working with nettles so you don't hurt your hands. Remove the stems and wash nettles several times. Blanch them in salted water once or twice; the sting disappears when the nettles are cooked.

Serves 4 to 5

2 tablespoons butter
1 medium onion, finely chopped
2 tablespoons flour
10 ounces frozen spinach, defrosted and finely chopped
1½ tablespoons uncooked medium-grain rice
4 to 5 cups chicken or vegetable stock
Sea salt
Freshly ground pepper
½ cup plain yogurt
1 large egg yolk

Heat butter in a medium soup pot over medium heat. Add onion and sauté for 5 minutes. Whisk in flour and sauté for a few more minutes. Add the spinach, rice, stock, and salt and pepper to taste. Cover and cook over medium heat for 20 to 25 minutes until the rice is cooked. Using an immersion or a regular blender, purée the soup.

In a small bowl, whisk together the yogurt and egg yolk, and slowly add 1/2 cup of the hot soup. Whisking constantly, pour the yogurt mixture back into the soup, and continue to cook, stirring constantly, until soup thickens, 3 to 4 minutes. Serve with cornbread.

best rice pilaf

Ala Pilav
Kastamonu

Kastamonu is a well-known western Black Sea city famous for its cuisine, including many rice dishes that are unknown in other parts of Turkey. The best quality rice grows in the nearby town of Tosya, and Siyez is well known for its delicious, coarse brown bulgur. This once-forgotten pilaf of older generations is named for the best quality rice, bulgur, and lentils that enrich the dish.

Serves 4 to 6

1½ cups water
Sea salt
½ cup dried green lentils, soaked 3 to 4 hours in cold water, drained
¼ cup (½ stick) butter
¾ cup uncooked extra-long-grain rice, soaked in salted warm water for 30 minutes, drained
½ cup coarse bulgur, unwashed
2½ cups hot chicken stock
Freshly ground pepper

Place water in a small pot with salt and bring to a boil. Add the drained lentils and cook covered, over medium-low heat, for about 15 to 20 minutes or until the lentils are cooked but not split. Check them to avoid overcooking. Drain the lentils and set aside.

In a medium pan, heat the butter, stir in the drained rice, and sauté for 4 to 5 minutes, stirring constantly. Add the bulgur and lentils and mix well. Stir in the hot stock and season with salt and pepper to taste. Cook, covered, over medium-low heat for about 15 to 20 minutes or until all the liquid has been absorbed and holes appear on the surface. Remove from the heat.

Remove the lid from the pan, cover the pan with a double layer of paper towels or a kitchen towel and replace the cover. Let stand for 10 minutes. Mix well with a wooden spoon and serve with any vegetable or meat dish.

bulgur with green beans

Taze Fasulyeli Bulgur Pilavı
Artvin

This pilaf, traditionally made during the winter months, combines dried green beans, onions, tomatoes, and bulgur. In Turkey, many vegetables, such as eggplant, tomatoes, and squash, are dried for winter use, then later rehydrated and stuffed, or used in recipes. Nur tried this pilaf with fresh beans and found it to be delicious. She serves it with salad and yogurt as a tasty vegetarian lunch or as a side dish for main courses.

Serves 4 to 6

1½ pounds fresh, green, flat beans
3 tablespoons butter
¼ cup canola oil
2 onions, finely chopped
2 tomatoes, peeled and finely chopped
1 tablespoon tomato paste
Sea salt
Freshly ground pepper
1 cup water
3 cups hot chicken stock
½ teaspoon Aleppo pepper
1½ cups coarse bulgur, uncooked
3 tablespoons finely chopped Italian flat-leaf parsley

Trim the ends of the beans and cut them crosswise into 1-inch pieces. Wash well and drain.

Heat the butter and oil in a medium pan. Add the onions and sauté for 5 to 6 minutes. Stir in the beans and continue cooking for another 5 to 6 minutes. Stir in the tomatoes, tomato paste, and salt and pepper to taste, along with one cup of water. Simmer covered for 15 to 20 minutes, until beans are tender but not overcooked. At this point there should be no liquid left in the pan. If there is, turn the heat higher and let the liquid evaporate or be absorbed.

Add the hot chicken stock, bring to a boil, and add the Aleppo pepper and bulgur, mixing well. Lower the heat and simmer, covered, for 15 to 20 minutes until all the liquid has been absorbed and holes appear on the surface.

Remove the lid, cover the top of the pan with a kitchen towel or a double layer of paper towels, replace the lid, and let stand for 10 minutes. Gently stir with a wooden spoon and transfer to a serving dish. Sprinkle with parsley and serve.

cornbread

Mısır Ekmeği
Central and East Black Sea

This recipe uses yeast and has to rise, unlike American cornbread recipes, which use baking powder. This is a typical Black Sea semi-dry cornbread. Some people in the region prefer even drier ones; different textures of bread are paired with different dishes. Drier breads tend to be served with soups and stews, while the softer, moister breads serve as accompaniments for dry items like cheese. Nur always heats this dish before serving. Sometimes it is crumbled into soups and stews.

Makes about 8 pieces

2½ cups cornmeal
1 tablespoon sugar
¼ ounce active dry yeast
1 teaspoon sea salt
1 cup milk, warmed
1 large egg
3 tablespoon margarine, room temperature
Cooking spray for greasing the pan
2 tablespoons canola oil

In a medium-size bowl, combine cornmeal, sugar, yeast, and salt, mixing well. Add the warm milk, cover, and let rest at room temperature for about 30 minutes. Add egg and margarine; knead for 2 to 3 minutes.

Grease an 8 x 6 x 2-inch bread pan and place dough in it. Wet your hands and press the dough evenly into the baking pan. Cover with a clean dish towel and let the dough rest at room temperature for 40 to 60 minutes, or until it doubles in volume. Preheat oven to 375°F. Brush the top of the dough with canola oil and bake for 40 to 45 minutes, or until done.

rice with cranberry or red kidney beans
Barbunyalı Pilav
Kastamonu

The best quality rice is grown around Kastamonu, so naturally its people are very creative with rice dishes. In summer, fresh vegetables—including mushrooms, eggplant, zucchini, and green beans—are used in place of dried beans. Turkish families used to have different kinds of rice as a side dish every day. Now pilafs are used as a lower calorie alternative. Half a cup of soaked, cooked green lentils can be added to this dish, making it even richer; or you can omit the cranberry beans and substitute a 15.5-ounce can (1 1/2 cups) chickpeas that have been washed and drained. This is another nice vegetarian dish.

Serves 6 to 8

5 tablespoons butter
2 cups uncooked extra-long-grain rice, soaked in warm water for 30 minutes
Sea salt
Freshly ground pepper
15.5-ounce can (1½ cups) cranberry beans or red kidney beans, washed and drained
4 cups hot vegetable or chicken stock

Heat butter in a 2-quart pot and add the rice. Sauté, stirring, for a few minutes and season with salt and pepper to taste. Stir in drained beans and hot stock. Cook, covered, over medium heat for 15 to 20 minutes or until all the liquid is absorbed and holes appear on the surface.

Remove pot from the heat, uncover the pot and place a kitchen towel over the top of the pot. Replace the lid and let stand for 10 minutes. Mix well with a wooden spoon and serve as a side dish with any meat, poultry, or vegetable.

rice with mushrooms
Mantarlı Pilav
Kastamonu

This is a rich, tasty side dish for special occasions. In the original recipe, the mushrooms are boiled with a little lemon juice, drained, and added to the rice. Nur tried it that way, but found the flavor and taste to be much better in this version, in which she sautés the mushrooms and then adds the rice. In the western Black Sea area, many different kinds of mushrooms grow in the forests, especially after rain when they start coming up under the trees. With their meaty flavor, the villagers call mushrooms "peasants' meat."

Local people know the different kinds of mushrooms very well and whole families go out to pick them. Mushrooms are available for most of the year, except for the winter months. A wide variety of Black Sea dishes are made using mushrooms.

Serves 6

3 tablespoons butter
¼ cup olive oil
1 pound any mixture of 3 or 4 kinds of your favorite mushrooms, cleaned and sliced
2 cups uncooked extra-long-grain rice, soaked in warm water for 30 minutes and drained
Sea salt
Freshly ground pepper
4 cups hot chicken stock
2 tablespoons finely chopped fresh dill

Heat the butter and oil in a medium pan and sauté the mushrooms on high heat for 5 to 10 minutes. Stir in the rice, salt and pepper, and hot chicken stock. Cook, covered, over medium-low heat until all the liquid has been absorbed and holes appear on the surface.

Remove from heat, remove the lid from the pan, and cover the top of the pan with a kitchen towel. Replace the lid and let stand 10 to 15 minutes. Stir gently with a wooden spoon, place on a serving dish, and sprinkle with chopped dill.

24

spinach and egg boerek

Lemis
Gümüşhane

These filled boereks can be served with yogurt and a salad as a nice vegetarian lunch or on their own as an appetizer. Boereks are sheets of thinly rolled pastry—often a paper-thin variety called *yufka*—that are layered or filled with a variety of fillings. They can be baked, broiled, or cooked on a griddle. It is said that no Turkish girl should marry before mastering the art of making these pastries.

Serves 2 as a main course, or 4 as an appetizer

Dough:
1⅓ cups flour
1 teaspoon sea salt
½ to ¾ cup water

Filling:
2 tablespoons butter, melted
2 medium onions, finely chopped
1½ pounds baby spinach leaves, washed and drained well
Sea salt
Freshly ground pepper
2 large eggs, lightly beaten

1 to 2 tablespoons butter, melted

Place the flour and salt in a large bowl and mix well. Slowly start adding the water, mixing and kneading well to make a smooth dough. Divide the dough into 4 egg-size pieces, roll them into balls, and place them on a plate. Cover, and let stand for 30 minutes.

In a large skillet, heat the butter and sauté the onions until translucent, about 5 minutes. Add spinach and sauté for another 5 minutes, mixing well. Season with salt and pepper to taste, then add beaten eggs. Cook, stirring, until mixture resembles scrambled eggs. Remove from heat and cool.

On a lightly floured surface, roll out one of the balls of dough into a 10-inch round. Divide spinach mixture into fourths. Place one-fourth of the filling on the right side of the rolled dough (imagine a straight line dividing the circle of dough in half), spreading it all over the right half. Fold the left side of the circle over the filling (making a half moon or "D" shape) and gently press with your fingertips or fork tines to seal the edges together tightly. Repeat until all the dough and filling has been used.

Heat a large nonstick pan and cook each boerek for 3 to 4 minutes on each side until golden brown (in a larger skillet you can probably cook two at a time). Brush with melted butter and place on a serving platter. Serve hot.

walnut bread

Cevizli Çörek
West Black Sea

This is a nice, quick bread to serve at teatime or breakfast with cheese or jam. It is made using Turkish walnuts.

Serves 6

2 cups flour, sifted, plus ¼ to ½ cup extra for rolling and flouring
2 large eggs, divided
⅔ cup warm milk
¼ cup sugar
¼-ounce envelope active dry yeast
1½ teaspoons sea salt
1 to 2 tablespoons water
Canola oil, for oiling bowl
¾ cup coarsely chopped walnuts
Cooking spray, for greasing the pan

Place the flour in a medium bowl with one whole egg, one egg white (save the second yolk for the glaze), milk, sugar, yeast, and salt. Mix well and work into a soft dough. You may need to add 1 to 2 tablespoons of water if dough is too hard; it should be a little bit sticky. Place in a lightly oiled bowl, cover with a kitchen towel, and let rise for 30 minutes in a warm place.

Generously flour a working surface and place the dough in the center. Flour your hands and pat the dough to work it into a rectangular shape. Using a floured rolling pin, roll the dough into a rectangle about 14 inches in length and 6 inches in width. Sprinkle the walnuts all over the dough. Fold the dough from the outer edges towards the center, covering the nuts and rounding the edges as you go.

Grease a 13-inch round cake pan and place the round dough in the center, cover with a kitchen towel, and let rise for 30 minutes in a warm place.

Preheat oven to 375°F. Brush the top with the remaining egg yolk and bake 30 to 35 minutes until golden brown.

chicken with shelled wheat

Keşkek

Kastamonu

This very special dish is often served at weddings. It is made with wheat, a symbol of prosperity and fertility, and chicken legs. It is tasty, inexpensive, and great for a crowd. Nur's helper Hüsniye (who has worked with her for the past 27 years) shared this recipe with us. She prepared a wedding feast for her son with the help of friends and relatives. This was the highlight of the feast! It takes some extra time to prepare but it's worth it. You can substitute lamb for the chicken if desired. It is hot, hearty, and a great winter dish.

Serves 4 to 6 as a main course

1½ cups shelled wheat, soaked overnight in 4 cups of water
1 medium onion, sliced
2 tomatoes, peeled, seeded, and diced
1 teaspoon salt
2 whole chicken legs with thighs
6 cups water

Topping:
6 tablespoons butter
2 teaspoons Aleppo pepper

Drain wheat well. Place the sliced onions in a 5-quart pot. Cover the onions with the tomatoes. Place drained wheat and a teaspoon of salt over tomatoes and cover with chicken.

Pour 6 cups water over the chicken and bring to a boil. Reduce to medium heat and as scum begins to form, skim it off (about 10 minutes). Cover, reduce heat to simmer and cook; do not stir. Occasionally, carefully lift the pot and shake it a few times from side to side.

After 90 minutes, remove chicken from pot, but let remaining ingredients keep cooking. Let chicken cool until you can handle it; with a fork, shred chicken from bones. Discard skin and bones and return chicken to the pot. Cover partially and simmer for another 30 minutes.

Remove cover and begin to stir and beat with the back of a wooden spoon until the chicken disappears into the wheat and forms a cooked oatmeal-like consistency, about 10 to 15 minutes. Arrange chicken and wheat on a serving platter.

Melt butter in a small skillet. When it starts sizzling, turn off heat and stir in Aleppo pepper, mixing well. Pour over chicken and wheat.

cornmeal koftas

Trabzon Köftesi
Trabzon

Simply called Trabzon koftas in Turkey, these meatballs are made with beef or ground veal and cornmeal seasoned with thyme. They make a great appetizer to have on hand for guests, since the meatballs can be frozen for up to a month. Serve hot as a first course with a vegetable salad.

Serves 4 to 5. Makes 25 to 30 meatballs.

4 to 5 tablespoons canola oil, plus extra for oiling your hands
1 pound ground beef or veal
1 cup cornmeal, divided
½ tablespoon dried thyme
Sea salt
Freshly ground pepper
1 tablespoon butter

Oil your hands lightly. In a bowl, combine the beef, 1/2 cup cornmeal, thyme, salt, and pepper, working the ingredients together into a smooth paste with your hands. Pinch off pieces of the mixture and roll into walnut-size meatballs.

Place the remaining 1/2 cup of cornmeal into a shallow plate and roll the meatballs around, coating them on all sides. Remove meatballs from cornmeal and set aside.

In a medium-size skillet, heat the butter and oil. Fry the meatballs until golden brown on all sides, about 3 minutes per side, shaking the pan often to prevent sticking. Drain well on paper towels.

lamb shanks with orzo

Şehriyeli İncik
Amasra

The original recipe for this dish keeps the lamb on the bones, but Nur prefers to remove the bones, making it easier to eat. The marrow, which slowly oozes from the lamb bones while this dish is cooking, is considered to be a delicacy throughout Turkey and much of the Mediterranean and Middle East. Orzo is a pasta shaped like grains of rice. It is popular in soups and stews. Serve with a vegetable dish.

Serves 4 as a main course

3 tablespoons butter, divided
1 tablespoon canola oil
4 lamb shanks
6 cups boiling water
1 onion, peeled, cut into quarters
Sea salt
Freshly ground black pepper
5 scallions, sliced
2 medium tomatoes, peeled, finely diced
1½ cups orzo
½ teaspoon dried thyme

Heat 1 tablespoon of butter and the oil in a large pot. Sear the lamb shanks, turning to cook on all sides. Continue cooking until the outer meat has changed color.

Stir in the water, onion, and salt and pepper to taste. Bring to a boil, reduce heat to medium, cover and cook for 70 to 80 minutes. Remove the lamb shanks, place on a plate, and set aside. Measure the cooking liquid and set aside 3 cups to cook the orzo.

In a large skillet, heat 2 tablespoons of butter and add the scallions. Sauté for a minute and add the tomatoes. Sauté for 3 to 4 minutes more. Stir in the orzo, add 3 cups of hot stock and the thyme; mix well. Taste for salt and pepper and correct seasoning if needed. Cover and cook over medium heat, stirring occasionally, for 20 minutes.

Meanwhile bone the lamb shanks, removing the meat carefully. Uncover the pot and place the pieces of meat on top of the orzo. Cover, and continue cooking until the orzo is done. Remove from heat and let stand, covered, for 10 minutes.

pearl onion stew

Arpacık Soğan Yahnisi
Zonguldak

This stew of small meatballs simmered with vegetables is full of bold, assertive flavors. Perfect for when you want a familiar, homey-tasting classic with a twist. It is also a way to make a smaller amount of meat stretch further. This healthful dish is typical of the Mediterranean use of meat and can be made ahead.

Serves 4 to 6

1 pound ground beef
1 onion, grated
Sea salt
Freshly ground pepper
2 tablespoons butter
1 pound pearl onions
2 green cubanelle peppers, stems, seeds, and ribs removed, chopped
3 medium tomatoes, peeled, finely chopped
1¼ cups water
1 tablespoon tomato paste
2 tablespoons white vinegar
½ teaspoon Aleppo pepper

Place beef, grated onion, and salt and pepper to taste in a bowl and mix well. Make walnut-size meatballs and set aside.

In a heavy skillet, heat the butter. Add the onions and meatballs, and sauté over medium heat, shaking with the handle of the skillet, about 7 to 8 minutes. Stir in cubanelle peppers, tomatoes, and continue cooking for a few more minutes. Add water, tomato paste, and vinegar. Cook over medium-low heat for 20 to 25 minutes. Sprinkle with Aleppo pepper. Serve with Best Rice Pilaf (page 19).

stuffed collard greens

Kara Lahana Dolması
Rize

This *dolmas* (stuffed vegetables) recipe is unusual in that it uses collard greens instead of grape or cabbage leaves.

Serves 5 to 6. Makes about 45 *dolmas*.

1¼ cups water, divided, plus more if needed
1 bunch (about 15) collard greens, washed and drained
4 tablespoons medium-grain rice, rinsed
10 ounces ground beef
½ tablespoon dried mint
Sea salt
Freshly ground pepper
½ bunch Italian flat-leaf parsley, chopped
2 tablespoons olive oil
1½ tablespoons tomato paste
2 tablespoons butter, melted

Bring a large pot of water with a teaspoon of salt to a boil. Lower heat to medium and blanch the collard greens for 4 to 5 minutes, in 3 to 4 batches. Place in a colander to drain and set aside to cool.

Lay the greens on a work surface. Cut the top 3 1/2 inches off each leaf and set aside. Carefully cut around the ribs so that they can easily be removed. Set the ribs aside for later use. Repeat until each leaf has been ribbed and cut into three pieces. Arrange the pieces on a plate, discarding any broken or ripped pieces.

In a medium-size bowl, combine the rice, ground beef, mint, salt and pepper to taste, 4 tablespoons water, and oil and mix well. Let stand for 10 minutes.

Lay the leaves on a work surface and place two heaped teaspoons of filling on each leaf. Fold the sides of each leaf over the filling and, starting from the bottom, roll the leaf into a cigar shape. Repeat until all the leaves have been rolled.

Line the bottom of a medium-size pan with the reserved collard green ribs. Arrange a snug layer of *dolmas* on top of the ribs. When one layer is finished, start another layer on top of the first until they are all stacked.

Heat one cup of water, add tomato paste and butter, mix well and pour over the stacked *dolmas*. Place a plate over the *dolmas* to weigh them down during cooking. Cover the pot and cook over medium heat for about 35 to 40 minutes. Check the cooking liquid periodically and add more water if needed.

Place on a serving platter and serve with plain yogurt and warm cornbread.

stuffed onions

Soğan Dolması
West Black Sea

Onions are one of nature's most perfect containers. The filling is made from beef flavored with sweet spices, and the pomegranate topping gives this dish a sweet-and-sour taste. Pomegranate molasses is available at Middle Eastern markets and specialty food stores.

Serves 6 as a main course

5 to 6 large yellow onions, unpeeled, plus 1 onion, peeled and finely chopped
1¼ pounds ground beef
½ cup uncooked long-grain white rice, rinsed well
1 teaspoon of an equal mixture of cinnamon, allspice, and cloves
2 cloves garlic, finely chopped
Sea salt
Freshly ground pepper
2 tablespoons tomato paste
2 tablespoons finely chopped flat-leaf parsley
3 tablespoons canola oil, divided, plus more for coating saucepan
1¾ cups water
1 tablespoon butter
½ tablespoon pomegranate molasses or freshly squeezed lemon juice

Peel the yellow onions and cut off the roots. Slit the onion in half, from top to bottom, stopping at the center (don't cut all the way through). Boil onions in a large pot of water over medium heat until softened, about 8 to 10 minutes. Drain well and cool.

In a medium-size bowl, combine chopped onion, ground beef, rice, cinnamon, allspice, cloves, garlic, salt and pepper to taste, tomato paste, parsley, and 2 tablespoons canola oil. Stir in 1/2 cup water and mix well. Let mixture stand for 5 to 10 minutes.

Carefully and gently, separate the onion layers. Cut the bigger outer layers in half. Take out the very centers of the onions (these will not be stuffed) and set aside.

Place 1 tablespoon of meat mixture on a layer of onion and roll up firmly. Repeat this step until all filling has been used.

Coat a heavy saucepan with oil. Cover with sliced onion centers; this will prevent the stuffed onions from sticking to the pan during cooking. Place the onion rolls in the pan, seam-side down and touching each other. Layer the rolls until they are all in the pan.

In a small pan, combine 1 tablespoon butter and the remaining 1 tablespoon of oil, the pomegranate molasses, and 1 1/4 cups of water. Bring to a boil and pour mixture over the onion rolls.

Place a plate over the rolls to weigh them down during cooking. Cover the pan and cook over medium-low heat, about 30 to 45 minutes. After 30 minutes, check to see if the onions are tender. Serve with a salad and yogurt.

anchovies with cornmeal

Mısır Unlu Hamsi Tava
Throughout the Black Sea

The inhabitants of the Black Sea region have enjoyed the combination of anchovies and cornmeal for centuries. Corn came to Turkey from the New World in the 16th century. It quickly became popular throughout not only Turkey, but Italy (where it is known as *granturco,* or Turkish grain) and Romania as well. In the Black Sea area, anchovies are typically paired with pantry items like rice and corn because these are available during the winter season. In Turkey, a pan with a special lid is used to flip the fish. We use a flat dinner plate.

Serves 3–4

1 pound fresh anchovies, cleaned★
About ¾ cup fine yellow cornmeal
½ teaspoon sea salt
Canola spray for greasing

Lightly grease a 10-inch skillet. Place the cornmeal and salt on a plate or bowl and dip the anchovies in the mixture, coating them on all sides. Place a vertical row of dipped anchovies, laid side-to-side, down the center of the skillet. Start another row to the left of the first, angling the fish toward the bottom of the pan, so that they are diagonal to the first row. Start another row to the right of the first row, and angle the fish so that they mirror the second row. Continue adding rows, following the pattern of the second and third rows, until the pan has been filled; then fill in any spaces with the remaining anchovies.

Cook fish for 3 to 4 minutes, then cover pan with a plate and flip the fish over. (The anchovies will stick together as they cook.) Slide the anchovies back in the pan and cook for another 3 to 4 minutes on the other side. Serve hot.

★ *Cleaning anchovies:* Using your fingers, snap the heads and tails off the anchovies. Run your index finger down the middle of their undersides, removing the bone and cleaning out the inside. Rinse the anchovies and drain well.

trout baked in terracotta

Kiremitte Alabalık
Trabzon

This is a tasty and light main course made with trout fillets, pepper, tomato, and garlic, and prepared in a clay baking pan. In the Black Sea region, clay dishes for cooking fish come in all sorts of sizes and shapes: round, oval, and rectangular. Clay-pot cooking is one of the healthiest of cooking methods because it requires hardly any fat and the food retains its flavor, thereby enhancing the whole dish. Clay pots seal in the flavor and don't need to be checked on during cooking.

The acidity of the tomatoes adds a bright, piquant flavor to this recipe. Tomatoes are also a great source of vitamins A and C. If you do not want to struggle with fish bones, any kind of filleted fish would be fine to use.

Serves 2

4 trout fillets, or 2 whole fish
3 tablespoons butter, melted, divided
1 large onion, peeled, cut in half, and thinly sliced
½ teaspoon Aleppo pepper
Sea salt
Freshly ground pepper
2 green cubanelle peppers or 1 green bell pepper, stems, seeds, and ribs removed, sliced into ½-inch-thick strips
3 tomatoes, peeled and cut into ½-inch-thick slices
6 garlic cloves, peeled and kept whole
2 tablespoons finely chopped fresh Italian flat-leaf parsley

Preheat oven to 375°F. Wash the fish under running water. Pat dry with a paper towel.

Coat a clay baking dish or other ovenproof baking dish with 2 tablespoons of melted butter. Spread the onions slices around the bottom, and season with Aleppo pepper and salt and pepper, to taste. Add half of the sliced peppers, half of the tomatoes, and all of the garlic cloves.

Place the fish on top and brush with the remaining tablespoon of butter. Add the rest of the peppers and tomatoes, and the finely chopped parsley. Cook for 20 to 25 minutes and serve immediately.

Variation: Substitute the trout with 1 pound of anchovies. Prepare anchovies as described on the previous page. Grease a 10-inch round baking dish with 1 tablespoon butter. Arrange the anchovies in the pan as described in the last recipe. Pour the sautéed vegetables (as above) on top of the anchovies, spreading them evenly.

Bake 20 to 25 minutes at 375°F. Sprinkle with 2 tablespoons of chopped parsley and serve hot.

anchovies with rice

Hamsili Pilav
Samsun

This wonderful recipe combines rice, pine nuts, currants, and spices. It comes from Nur's mother-in-law's early days of marriage in Samsun. She made it for the family every winter during anchovy season. It works best with fresh anchovies. Nur prefers to use Turkish baldo rice in this recipe, but if you prefer to use long-grain white rice, cook it with the ratio of 2 cups water for every 1 cup of rice.

Serves 6 to 8

Butter for greasing
1 cup Turkish baldo rice

4 tablespoons butter, divided
2 medium onions, finely chopped
2 tablespoons pine nuts
2 tablespoons currants, soaked in
     warm water for an hour
Sea salt
Pepper

¼ teaspoon ground cinnamon
¼ teaspoon ground allspice
1 cup water
½ bunch Italian flat-leaf parsley,
     finely chopped
½ bunch fresh dill, finely chopped
5 scallions, whites and part of the greens,
     sliced
1 tablespoon butter
2¼ pounds anchovies, cleaned (page 34)
2 lemons, cut into slices for garnish

Preheat oven to 350°F. Butter an 11 x 7-inch Pyrex baking pan. Soak rice in salted water for 25 minutes, rinse well, and drain.

In a pot, melt 3 tablespoons butter; add onion and sauté for 5 minutes over medium heat. Add drained rice and pine nuts. Mix well and continue to sauté, stirring, for 3 to 4 more minutes. Add currants, salt, pepper, cinnamon, allspice, and 1 cup water. Mix well, then bring to a boil. Reduce heat, cover and simmer for 10 to 15 minutes or until water has been absorbed. Turn off heat, uncover, place a kitchen towel over the rice, and let stand for 10 minutes. When cool, add parsley, dill, and scallions. Mix well and set aside.

Open the anchovies up so they lay flat, and place them in the prepared baking dish skin-side down. Overlap anchovies, so that one half reaches the middle of the next fish.

Cover the entire bottom of the dish and part way up the sides with overlapping anchovies. Carefully spoon the rice over them. Gently press down on rice with your hand or a spatula. Then cover the rice with the remaining anchovies, this time skin-side up, continuing to overlap them.

Brush the top with melted butter and bake for 20 to 25 minutes. If desired, turn upside down onto a large rectangular serving platter and decorate with lemon slices. Serve with a mixed green salad. This dish can also be served directly from the baking dish.

collard greens with bulgur and cranberry beans

Kara Lahana Yığması
Trabzon

Serve this hearty combination of collard greens and beans with warm cornbread as a vegetarian lunch.

Serves 4 or 6 as a lunch main course

3 cups water, divided
½ teaspoon salt
1 bunch collard greens
2 tablespoons butter
2 tablespoons extra-virgin olive oil
1 large onion, finely chopped
3 large tomatoes, peeled and coarsely chopped
1 teaspoon sugar
Sea salt
Freshly ground pepper
¼ cup coarse bulgur
½ cup canned cranberry beans or small white beans, drained
¼ teaspoon Aleppo pepper

In a medium-size pan, heat 2 cups of water and 1/2 teaspoon salt. Wash collard greens and remove the thick center rib of the collard greens by folding the leaf in half and slicing off the rib from the bottom half, leaving the tender top half of the rib. Chop the greens coarsely. Add the greens to the pan and cook, stirring, over medium heat, for 7 to 8 minutes; drain well.

In another medium-size pan, heat the butter and oil, and sauté the onion for 5 to 6 minutes. Stir in the tomatoes, sugar, salt and pepper, mixing well, and continue to cook for another 2 minutes.

Add the collard greens, bulgur, and 1 cup of warm water, mixing well. Cook, covered, over medium-low heat for 25 to 30 minutes; then add the beans. Mix well and cook for 7 to 8 minutes. Sprinkle with Aleppo pepper and serve.

fresh cranberry beans in olive oil

Zeytinyağlı Barbunya
Throughout the Black Sea

Cranberry beans are brown with wine-colored splotches (the color fades when cooked) and a sweet flavor reminiscent of chestnuts. In the United States, berlotti is the most common variety of cranberry bean, and fresh cranberry beans are available in the summer. To shell the beans, just press on the inside curve of the pod, split open, and pop them out. This appetizer should be served at room temperature. When served with a green salad and warm country bread, it can be a vegetarian main course for four.

Serves 4 to 6

6 cups water, divided, plus more if needed
Sea salt
2 pounds unshelled fresh cranberry beans (to make about ¾ to 1 pound shelled beans)
½ cup extra-virgin olive oil
1 large onion, finely chopped
6 to 7 cloves garlic, peeled, cut in half lengthwise
1 medium carrot, peeled and diced into ½-inch cubes
1 large golden potato, peeled and diced into ½-inch cubes
2 large tomatoes, peeled and finely chopped
½ teaspoon Aleppo pepper (or to taste)
1 teaspoon sugar
1½ cups warm water, plus more if needed
2 tablespoons finely chopped Italian flat-leaf parsley

Place 4 cups of water in a medium pot with 1/2 teaspoon salt and bring to a boil.

Add shelled beans, lower heat to medium, and cook for 10 to 15 minutes. Remove pan from the heat and drain beans in a colander.

In a 2–quart pan, heat the oil and sauté the onion and garlic until translucent, about 4 to 5 minutes. Stir in the carrot, potato, and tomatoes, mix well and continue to cook for another 3 to 4 minutes, then season with salt to taste. Stir in Aleppo pepper and sugar; mix well and taste for seasoning. Adjust if necessary. Stir in water. When mixture has heated, add the drained beans and cook, covered, over medium heat for 35 to 40 minutes, checking the cooking liquid periodically; you may need to add another 1/4 to 1/2 cup water. Remove from heat and sprinkle with parsley.

mashed white beans with cornmeal and sautéed onions

Mısır Unlu Fasulye Ezmesi
Rize

White lima beans are mashed with cornmeal, butter, and onions to make this dish. It is a great vegetarian side dish to serve with meat, poultry, or fish.

Serves 4

3½ cups water
½ pound dried white lima beans, soaked overnight in water, drained
Sea salt
¼ cup cornmeal
3 tablespoons butter or ¼ cup extra-virgin olive oil
1 large onion, cut in half and thinly sliced into half-moon-shaped pieces
½ teaspoon Aleppo pepper

In a medium pan, bring 3 1/2 cups of water to a boil. Add the beans and salt to taste and cook, covered, over medium heat, 45 minutes. There should be 1 1/2 cups cooking liquid left. Reserve liquid.

Using a potato masher, coarsely mash the beans with 1 1/2 cups of the cooking liquid and stir in the cornmeal. Cook over medium-low heat for 25 to 30 minutes, stirring constantly. Taste for salt and adjust seasoning. Remove from heat and set aside.

Heat the butter or olive oil in a medium skillet over medium heat; add onions and sauté for 5 minutes. Reduce heat and continue cooking for 12 to 15 minutes more. Sprinkle with Aleppo pepper and stir onion mixture into puréed beans. Serve warm.

41

Fresh cranberry beans in olive oil

sautéed swiss chard

Pazı Kavurma
East Black Sea

Swiss chard is sometimes confused with spinach. When purchasing Swiss chard, look for dark green leaves, bright white, yellow, or red stems, and make sure there is no bruising. If the leaves are too large, the stems may be tough. The leaves can be used like spinach: cooked or served raw in salads. The stems are used in soups or stews, or they can be braised and used in other dishes. To remove the center rib before cooking, fold the leaf in half, and slice off the rib. This dish can be served with a green salad and cornbread as vegetarian main course, or as a side dish for meat or poultry. The Aleppo pepper or crushed red pepper flakes give this dish a little kick.

Serves 10 as a side dish, or 6 as a main course

2 bunches Swiss chard, thick stems removed, finely chopped
2 tablespoons butter
2 tablespoons extra-virgin olive oil
2 medium onions, finely chopped
¾ cup canned cranberry beans, drained
Sea salt
¼ teaspoon Aleppo pepper or crushed red pepper flakes

Place the Swiss chard in a large bowl filled with water. Press the pieces underwater with your hands a few times. Let them soak for a few minutes, then drain well. Repeat this process several times until there is no sand left on the bottom of the bowl.

Heat the butter and oil in a large skillet and sauté the onions, stirring, for 5 to 6 minutes, or until translucent. Add the Swiss chard, mix well, and cook, stirring, until it wilts, about 2 to 3 minutes. Continue to cook over medium heat for 8 to 10 minutes.

Stir in the beans, salt, and Aleppo pepper or red pepper flakes. Cook for another 7 to 8 minutes.

Variation: Substitute the beans with 1/2 tablespoon tomato paste and 2 tablespoons coarse bulgur. Follow the first part of recipe as above, but cook chard for 2 extra minutes. Then stir in tomato paste, bulgur, and 1/4 cup hot water, mixing well. Season with salt and pepper to taste, and cook, covered, for another 10 to 15 minutes. Sprinkle with Aleppo pepper.

zucchini with bulgur

Kabaklı Bulgur Pilavı
West Black Sea

This tasty, filling, summer dish—made with a combination of zucchini, bulgur, cubanelle peppers, and tomatoes—is great for outdoor entertaining. It can be served as a vegetarian main course, appetizer, or light lunch.

Serves 6 to 8

5 medium zucchini
⅓ cup extra-virgin olive oil
2 medium onions, finely chopped
4 to 5 cloves garlic, finely chopped
2 green cubanelle peppers, stems, seeds, and ribs removed, coarsely chopped
1 cup canned, diced tomatoes, drained
2 teaspoons tomato paste
Sea Salt
Freshly ground pepper
½ cup coarse bulgur
1½ cups warm water

Garnish:
1 tablespoon chopped fresh Italian flat-leaf parsley
1 tablespoon chopped fresh dill
1 tablespoon chopped fresh mint

Garlic Sauce:
2 cups plain yogurt
2 to 3 cloves garlic, minced
Sea salt to taste

Wash the zucchinis and scrape the outer peel, making a striped design. Cut the zucchinis lengthwise into 4 pieces. Cut each piece, crosswise, into pieces about 1 1/2- to 2-inches long.

In a small saucepan, heat the oil over medium heat and sauté the onions, garlic, and peppers for 5 to 6 minutes, stirring constantly. Add the tomatoes and tomato paste, season with salt and pepper to taste, mix well and cook, stirring, for 5 more minutes. Remove from the heat and set aside.

In a large skillet, arrange half of the zucchini, skin-side down. Pour half of the sauce over the pieces, and then top with the remaining zucchini, also skin-side down. Sprinkle the bulgur so that it covers the top and add 1 1/2 cups of warm water. Bring to a boil. Reduce heat to simmer, and cook, covered, over medium-low heat, for 20 minutes. Remove pan from heat and let sit for 30 minutes so the bulgur can absorb all the liquid.

In a small bowl, combine the yogurt, garlic, and salt; mix well. Arrange the zucchini on a serving platter. Sprinkle with parsley, dill, and mint and serve with the garlicky yogurt sauce.

apple halves with walnuts

Elma Gallesi
Amasya

This homey dish of baked apples is great in winter because apples are always available. Nur uses Gala apples in this recipe. Hazelnuts can be substituted for the walnuts. Serve with cream or cookies.

Serves 6

3 whole apples, peeled
2 tablespoons butter
½ cinnamon stick
5 to 6 cloves
½ cup sugar
¾ cup water
6 tablespoons coarsely chopped walnuts

Cut peeled apples in half and core them. Melt the butter in a heavy skillet. Sauté the apples, cut side down, over medium-low heat for 3 to 4 minutes. Add the cinnamon stick and cloves. Reduce heat and cook for 8 to 10 minutes, until apples are lightly browned on both sides. Add the sugar, 3/4 cup water, and cook for 20 to 30 minutes over low heat, until they are tender. Remove from heat and let cool. Arrange apples on a shallow serving dish and decorate the centers with the chopped walnuts.

44

buttered sweet plums

Erik Gallesi
Amasya

This dish is a variation of Apple Halves with Walnuts. It can also be served with cream or cookies.

Serves 4

1½ tablespoons butter
9 ounces (about 20) dried plums
¼ cup sugar (or more to taste, depending on the sweetness of the plums)
½ cup water
2 to 3 tablespoons blanched, sliced almonds

Heat the butter in a nonstick saucepan; add the plums and sauté for 3 to 4 minutes. Add the sugar and 1/2 cup water; mix well and simmer for 10 minutes. Remove from heat and let cool. Arrange on a serving plate and sprinkle with almonds. Serve at room temperature.

bourma

Burma Tatlısı
Trabzon and Rize

These pinwheel-shaped rolls of phyllo—stuffed with nuts and covered in syrup—are a real Turkish delight! This recipe uses a long, 1/2-inch-thick rolling stick called an *oklava*. These are available in Middle Eastern or Turkish markets, but I use a dowel from a hardware store! The syrup can be made weeks ahead and refrigerated until you are ready to use it.

Serves 8

Syrup:
1 cup sugar
1 cup water
1 teaspoon freshly squeezed lemon juice

7 (13–14 x 18-inch) sheets phyllo, at room temperature
1 cup finely chopped walnuts or hazelnuts
¼ cup butter (½ stick) melted
3 to 4 tablespoons coarsely chopped pistachio nuts

To Prepare the Syrup:
Combine the sugar and 1 cup water in a small pan. Cook, stirring, over medium heat until the sugar has dissolved. Cook for another 10 to 15 minutes over low heat, and stir in the lemon juice. Cook for another 2 to 3 minutes, stirring once or twice. Remove from heat and let cool, then refrigerate.

Butter a 10-inch round baking dish. Place the stack of phyllo on a work surface and cover with a very lightly dampened cloth so the phyllo doesn't dry out as you work. Lay a sheet of phyllo on your work surface and sprinkle with 2 tablespoons of finely chopped walnuts or hazelnuts. Place your *oklava* on the longer edge of the sheet. Carefully fold the edge over the stick and gently roll up the phyllo until the whole sheet is rolled around the stick. Using your fingers, gradually push the rolled sheet toward the center, from both ends, so it looks wrinkled. Carefully and gently remove the stick. Pinch or press to seal each end of the dough.

Carefully roll the first wrinkled log into a pinwheel (I wind mine around my index finger). Place the pinwheel in the center of the baking dish. Repeat the process with the remaining phyllo, adding and pinching each wrinkled log to the previous one to expand the pinwheel, until the baking dish is full and you have one large coil of pastry.

Preheat oven to 350°F. Melt the butter and pour it over the top of the pastry, making sure the surface is well buttered. Bake for 35 to 40 minutes or until golden-brown. Remove from the oven and ladle the cold syrup over the top. Set aside until the syrup has been absorbed. Cool and sprinkle with chopped pistachio nuts.

cornmeal halva with hazelnuts

Mısır Unu Helvası
Giresun

This is a unique dessert for your next dinner party. Halva is a sweet dessert, often made of flour or semolina, butter, sugar, milk, and nuts. In the Black Sea region, however, it is made with locally produced cornmeal and hazelnuts. Halva is one of the oldest Turkish sweets and signifies good fortune. It is also traditionally prepared by a bereaved family to be served to friends and family after a funeral. Hazelnuts can be purchased already skinned at Middle Eastern markets.

Serves 8

Syrup:
2 cups sugar
2 cups water

2 cups yellow cornmeal
9 tablespoons butter, melted
1 cup ground, skinned, roasted hazelnuts
½ cup heavy cream
2 to 3 tablespoons coarsely chopped hazelnuts (for decoration)
Oil or cooking spray for greasing

To Prepare the Syrup:
Bring the sugar and water to a boil in a small saucepan. Reduce heat and simmer for 3 to 4 minutes. Remove from heat and set aside to cool.

In a nonstick, 10- to 12-inch skillet, dry sauté the cornmeal over medium-low heat for 3 to 4 minutes, stirring constantly. Add melted butter and cook for 10 to 12 minutes, stirring constantly. Stir in the ground hazelnuts and mix well. Still stirring, slowly ladle in the cold syrup, mixing well. Cook for another 6 to 7 minutes or until all the liquid has been absorbed and the halva has thickened. Remove from the heat.

Spray a round, 5 1/2-inch bowl or dish with oil. Pour in halva and press lightly with the back of a wooden spoon. Then turn upside down onto a round serving platter and serve with cream. Garnish with coarsely chopped hazelnuts.

custard-filled phyllo pastries

Laz Böreği
Trabzon

In Turkish, this sweet pastry is called *Laz Böreği* because of its origins in the large Laz community of the Black Sea region. Nur's family loves this dessert. Syrupy phyllo and custard makes it just the thing for any sweet tooth. Nur's late mother-in-law learned this recipe from her friends and neighbors in the Black Sea city of Samsun. She made the paper-thin phyllo layers from scratch—a very time-consuming process—so this dessert was only prepared on special occasions.

Today, store-bought phyllo dough works just as well, and Nur's family says it is as good as grandma's! This recipe is definitely worth trying. The syrup can be made weeks ahead and stored in the refrigerator. The whole recipe can be made the day before serving and refrigerated.

Serves 8

16 (13–14 x 18-inch) sheets phyllo, at room temperature
2 sticks butter, melted

Syrup:
1½ cups sugar
1½ cups water
½ tablespoon freshly squeezed lemon juice

Filling:
3 cups cold milk
3 heaped tablespoons cornstarch
1 to 2 tablespoons flour
5 tablespoons sugar
2 large egg yolks
1 teaspoon vanilla

To Prepare the Syrup:
Place the sugar and water in a 1-quart pot and bring to a boil. Lower heat to simmer, and cook, stirring, for another 9 to 10 minutes. Stir in the lemon juice and cook for another minute or two. Remove from heat, set aside to cool, and then refrigerate.

To Prepare the Filling:
Place the milk in a medium saucepan along with the cornstarch, flour, and sugar, and mix well. Cook over medium heat, whisking constantly, until the mixture bubbles. Lower heat to simmer and continue whisking for another 4 to 5 minutes. Remove from the heat, place a little of the filling in a small bowl, and quickly whisk in the egg yolks, one at a time, mixing well. Return egg yolk mixture

to pan, whisking quickly and constantly, so the mixture does not curdle. Whisk in the vanilla. Remove from heat and let the mixture cool at room temperature.

Butter an 11 x 7 x 2-inch baking pan. Cut a stack of 8 phyllo sheets in half across the shorter width, to make 16 sheets of phyllo. Cover with a very lightly dampened cloth so they don't dry out as you work.

Preheat oven to 375°F. Place a sheet of phyllo in the bottom of the baking pan and brush with butter before adding the next sheet. Repeat this step until you have used all 16 sheets. Spread the cold custard on the top sheet.

Cut the remaining 8 sheets of phyllo in half and layer on top of the custard, brushing each sheet with butter before adding the next. When all the sheets have been used, use a sharp knife to gently cut the top layers into 8 equal pieces, leaving the bottom layers intact for now, to hold the custard.

Brush the top with any leftover butter and bake for about 40 to 45 minutes until the top part is golden brown. Remove from the oven and slowly ladle the cold syrup all over the top until it has been absorbed. Set aside for at least six hours before serving. Refrigerate and serve cold.

sweet lips
Dilber Dudağı
East Black Sea

These hazelnut-filled, lip-shaped sweets are known as Ladies' Lips in Turkey. Because Turkish cooks always use fresh, local ingredients, they use hazelnuts from the Black Sea region, but you can substitute walnuts if desired.

Serves 8 to 10. Makes 43 sweets.

Syrup:
1 cup sugar
1 cup water
1 teaspoon freshly squeezed lemon juice

Butter for greasing pan
15 (13–14 x 18-inch) sheets phyllo, at room temperature
1½ cups, plus 2 tablespoons finely chopped, skinned hazelnuts
¼ cup butter (½ stick)

To Prepare the Syrup:
Place the sugar and water in a small pan, and cook, stirring, over medium heat until the sugar has dissolved. Continue to cook, stirring, over medium-low heat for 10 to 15 minutes. Stir in the lemon juice and cook for another 3 to 4 minutes. Remove from heat and set aside to cool.

Butter a 10-inch round baking dish. On a clean surface (preferably marble), layer 15 sheets of phyllo dough, one on top of another and then cover with a slightly damp towel to prevent the dough from drying out.

Fold back about 3 inches of the damp cloth and use a 2-inch round cookie cutter to cut one round of 15 layers from the stack. Place a teaspoon of finely chopped hazelnuts on the round and fold in half, over the filling, to form a "D" shape. Gently press the edges with your fingertips and place on the prepared baking dish with the top of the "D" against the outer edge of the pan.

Repeat this process. When placing the "lips" on the baking dish, the straight edge of one should overlap slightly with the rounded edge of the one next to it. You will be making two rows of pastries; the outer row will contain about 28 pastries and the second row will contain about 15. Place the last round of pastry in the center of the pan, without filling it. This decorative touch gives the dessert a nice appearance.

Melt the butter and brush over the pastries, making sure all the pastries are well coated. Bake for 40 minutes or until golden brown. Remove from the oven and pour (room temperature) syrup over all of the pastries. Cover with aluminum foil and set aside. Before serving, sprinkle with chopped hazelnuts.

Custard-filled phyllo pastries (Laz Böreği)

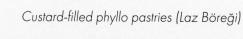

marmara

meat and chicken

fish

vegetables

desserts and sweets

The Marmara region is the culinary center of Turkey. What was historically Thrace now includes land spread across Bulgaria, Greece, and Turkey. Eastern Thrace lies entirely in the Marmara region, which is the door that opens into Europe. The region's—and the country's—most important city, İstanbul, lies on the Bosporus, the waterway that forms the boundary between Europe and Asia. İstanbul's culture and cuisine have been enriched by its proximity to Europe and its Greek, Jewish, and Armenian minorities, among others.

İstanbul's strategic position isperhaps the reason for its historic importance. It has been the capital of three successive empires: Roman, Byzantine, and Ottoman. During the reign of Fatih Sultan Mehmet 11, known as The Conqueror of İstanbul, Topkapi Palace became the center of the culinary arts in Turkey. Hundreds of chefs from different parts of the large empire dedicated themselves to creating the best recipes for the Sultans. Each specialized in a different type of dish. During this period, culinary activity developed and formed a sophisticated cuisine, shaping the contemporary Turkish diet.

The Thrace region is well known for its rich variety of cheeses. Valued by a succession of empires, white cheese has become a staple of Turkish cuisine, often served for breakfast with a variety of olives, breads, and homemade preserves. Turkish cheeses vary in flavor and texture; young cheeses are less salty than aged cheeses, which also have a stronger taste. Nowhere is the rich heritage of cheese-making more evident than in the Edirne province, which is famous for the production of high quality white cheeses made from sheep or cow's milk. Here, *Kaşar* cheese (a kind of pecorino Romano) is produced from sheep's milk. On the westernmost part of Turkey, close to the Greek and Bulgarian borders the city of Edirne is famous for its beautiful Islamic architecture. It was for some years the capital of the Ottomans, and in the 18th century, it was one of the seven largest cities in Europe. The people of Edirne can trace their origins back to the rule of the Macedonians.

West of İstanbul, the city of Tekirdağ is located on the northeastern coast of the Sea of Mamara and flanked by the mountain Tekirdağ for which it is named. It is the capital of the Tekirdağ province, and an important commercial harbor with beautiful sandy beaches. Sunflower fields and vineyards cover the surrounding countryside and the high quality white grapes of Tekirdağ are a boon to the wineries found there. The nearby cities of Şarköy and Murefte are home to annual wine festivals and tastings, which feature wine from the Tekirdağ province. Sunflower oil is produced from the sunflowers grown in this region. Tekirdağ is also well known for its high quality *raki*, a favorite alcoholic drink of Turks. Much like the Greek ouzo or the Arab aarak, *raki* has an anisette flavor and turns white when mixed with water. Kofta (meatballs), cheese halva, cherries, and fish dishes are also well-known local specialties of Tekirdağ and the surrounding towns.

North of Tekirdağ the city of Kırklareli is the capital of the Kırklareli province, which neighbors Bulgaria, and lies on the coast of the Black Sea. Thanks to its rich cultural sites, sandy beaches, and numerous fresh fish restaurants, the city of Kırklareli is a charming place to visit. Numerous varieties of fresh fish are local specialties. Starting in September when the waters of the Black Sea start to get cold, the fish migrate to the warmer Marmara Sea. Bonito, mackerel, bluefish, and grey mullet begin to appear in the markets, one after the other.

Edirne bridge © Sumandic

On the southeastern shore of the Marmara, overlooking the slopes of the Uludağ Mountains, the city of Bursa is Turkey's fourth largest city, and the capital of the Bursa province. It is a bustling center of industry and culture; Bursa was the first capital of the Ottomans and many original Ottoman buildings remain. Sometimes called "Green Bursa," the city is covered with parks and gardens overlooking the plain. This fertile region produces a variety of fruits, vegetables, and high quality lamb. The famous *döner* kebab originated in Bursa, and it tastes different there because the lamb is pasture-fed. The city is the center of the silk trade in Turkey, and of fruit and vegetable farming including: peaches, figs, okra, eggplants, artichokes, and chestnuts. Specialty dishes of the region often include chestnuts—which are cooked in lamb stews, with rice or bulgur, or peeled and cooked in syrup—a treat called glazed chestnuts.

The city of İzmit lies north of Bursa on the easternmost part of the Marmara. It is a prosperous industrial city and the center of the Kocaeli province. Local specialties include a famous sweet called *pişmaniye* made with thousands of thin layers of drawn sugar.

People from the Eastern Black Sea, and those of Caucasian and Bosnian origin settled in the cities of Düzce and Adapazarı, on the eastern border of the Marmara Region. These peoples' influence dominate the cuisine of the area, with such dishes as Circassian Chicken (page 90), corn-cake, dumplings stuffed with cheese, turnover boereks, and Circassian cheese or *Cerkes Peynir* (a type of mozzarella). The region is also known for its high-quality yellow potatoes, which are used in many different dishes.

On the southwestern shore of the Sea of Marmara, the provinces of Balıkesir and Çanakkale border the Marmara and Aegean regions, and have coastlines along both seas. Like the İstanbul province, Çanakkale has territory in both Europe and Asia. The cuisine is representative of this significant location.

cheesy fried eggplants

Kızarmış Peynirli Patlıcan
İstanbul

Nur was named after her aunt, Nuriye, who made this vegetarian dish and always loved to eat fried, cheesy eggplant on a fresh, thick slice of bread.

Makes 9 sandwiches

2 Japanese eggplants, each 8 ounces and about 12 inches long
Sea salt
6 ounces white cheese (such as feta), crumbled
4 tablespoons finely chopped Italian flat-leaf parsley
2 large eggs, separated and divided
Freshly ground pepper
¾ cup canola oil for frying
¾ cup dry Italian-seasoned breadcrumbs

Cut the stems off each eggplant. Peel off 1/2-inch strips of skin at 1/2-inch intervals, creating a striped effect. Repeat until all the eggplants are striped. Cut each eggplant crosswise into about 18 1/2-inch-thick slices. Sprinkle both sides with salt, place in a colander, and set aside for at least 30 minutes. Rinse eggplant slices well and pat dry with paper towels.

In a bowl, mix the white cheese and parsley with a fork, add 1 egg yolk, and mix well. Taste for salt (the salt from the cheese may be enough) and season with salt and pepper to taste.

Take a slice of eggplant, place 2 heaped teaspoons of the cheese mixture on top, and cover with another slice of eggplant, making a sandwich. Repeat this process until you have used all of the eggplant slices.

Heat oil in a large skillet. Place breadcrumbs in a shallow bowl or pan. Beat the remaining eggs in a shallow bowl. Dip the eggplant sandwich in egg and then dredge in the breadcrumbs. Fry sandwiches in hot oil until golden brown on both sides. Don't crowd the pan; if necessary, fry in batches. Drain well on paper towels before serving.

59

hot pepper sauce
Acıka
Adapazarı

This seasoned pepper purée was the first thing Nur learned from Sabiha Çevik, who taught her a number of Circassian dishes. She always keeps a jar in the refrigerator so it was ready to use in different recipes. When using this sauce, don't add salt until the end of the cooking time or it may end up too salty.

Makes about 1½ to 1¾ cups

2 tablespoons mild Aleppo pepper (or to taste)
1 tablespoon hot Aleppo pepper
½ cup cold water
12-ounce can or jar roasted red peppers (about 5), rinsed and drained, seeds
    removed, chopped
1½ teaspoons dried basil
1½ teaspoons ground coriander
10 cloves garlic
5 teaspoons sea salt
olive oil

Soak the mild and hot Aleppo pepper in the water and let the pepper absorb the water.

In a bowl, combine the chopped red peppers, the soaked Aleppo pepper, basil, coriander, garlic, and salt. Mix well and purée in a food processor until smooth.

Place the sauce in a clean jar and top with 1/4-inch olive oil. Keep refrigerated.

It will keep for quite a long time because it is heavily salted. After every use, make sure there is enough oil on the top to prevent discoloring.

ottoman-style onions and eggs
Soğlanlı Yumurta
İstanbul

Usually served after a soup course, this dish of caramelized onions and eggs scented with cinnamon was a favorite of the Sultans during Ramadan. You need patience to prepare this vegetarian dish but the result is extraordinary and worth the effort. In Turkey, if you can make this perfectly, you are considered a good cook!

Serves 4

4 tablespoons butter
1 pound (4 to 5 medium) onions, cut in half and thinly sliced
½ cup water
1 tablespoon white vinegar
1 teaspoon sugar
4 large eggs
Sea salt
Freshly ground pepper
Cinnamon, to taste

Heat the butter in a 12-inch skillet; add onions, and sauté over very low heat for 35 to 45 minutes until they are golden brown (caramelized). Success lies in your patience, as you must stir frequently. Stir in 1/2 cup water and vinegar, turn the heat to high, and boil for a few minutes. Sprinkle sugar over the mixture and mix well.

Using a wooden spoon, make 4 spaces among the onions and break an egg into each space. Sprinkle with salt and pepper to taste and cinnamon if using and cook until the whites are completely done and yolks are still soft. Serve immediately as an appetizer with warm bread.

poached eggs with garlicky yogurt
Çılbır
Tekirdağ

This simple vegetarian dish is made from eggs, yogurt, and garlic. It is best to serve it with warm, fresh country bread so you can mop your plate when you finish the eggs.

Serves 6

2½ cups water
Sea salt
1 teaspoon white vinegar
6 large eggs
3 cups plain yogurt, at room temperature
3 to 4 cloves garlic, minced
2 tablespoons butter
1 teaspoon paprika

In a medium pan, bring lightly salted water to a boil. Add vinegar and mix well.

Break an egg into a ramekin and slide the egg into the water. Reduce the heat and simmer for a few minutes until the white is set and the yolk is still soft. Carefully remove the egg from the pot using a slotted spoon and drain. Cook remaining eggs in the same way. Arrange eggs on a shallow oval dish or serving plate.

Whisk together yogurt, garlic, and salt in a bowl. Pour over the eggs. Melt the butter, mix with the paprika, and drizzle some over the garlicky yogurt and serve.

rice patties
Pirinç Köftesi
İstanbul, Thrace region

These crispy vegetarian koftas are an excellent snack to serve with drinks, and a great way to use leftover rice as long as it is not too buttery. You can also shape the rice into larger cakes (the size of burgers or croquettes).

Makes 18 to 20 small patties

2 tablespoons butter
1 large onion, finely chopped
1 cup uncooked Turkish baldo or long-grain rice
2 cups warm vegetable or chicken stock
Sea salt
Freshly ground pepper
1 cup grated mild cheddar cheese
1 large egg, lightly beaten
1 cup dry Italian-seasoned breadcrumbs
Canola oil for frying

In a medium-size sauté pan, heat the butter and sauté the onion, stirring, for 5 minutes. Stir in the rice and cook for a few more minutes. Add the stock and season with salt and pepper. Cook over medium-low heat, covered, until all the liquid has evaporated and holes appear on the surface, about 25 minutes. Remove from heat and let stand for 10 minutes. Remove lid and let cool.

Transfer the rice to a bowl and stir in the grated cheese and beaten egg. Check seasoning and adjust salt and pepper if needed.

Place the seasoned breadcrumbs on a shallow plate or pie pan. Mix the rice well with a wooden spoon. Pull off a walnut-size piece of the rice mixture and make a small ball with your hands. Flatten the ball of rice with your fingertips. Repeat this process until you have made about 18 to 20 patties.

Heat the oil in a large frying pan. Coat both sides of the patties with breadcrumbs and fry in batches until golden brown; do not crowd the pan. Serve hot.

garden salad

Bahçe Salatası
The Marmara coastline

This salad uses a dressing made with lemon juice, not vinegar, for a fresh, light acidity. It is simple and quick to prepare.

Serves 6 to 8

Salad:
2 bunches baby arugula
1 Spanish onion, peeled, sliced in rings
1 cup diced ricotta salata, or any feta-type white cheese
About 15 cherry tomatoes, halved

Dressing:
Freshly squeezed juice of 1 lemon
3 cloves garlic, minced
1 teaspoon Dijon mustard
4 to 5 tablespoons extra-virgin olive oil
Sea salt
Freshly ground pepper

Wash arugula leaves and remove any stems. Dry and arrange the arugula in a salad bowl. Add the onion rings, cheese, and tomatoes.

In a bowl, whisk together the lemon juice, garlic, mustard, olive oil, and salt and pepper to taste. Pour the dressing over the salad and toss well.

white radish salad

Turp Salatası
İstanbul

The combination of carrots, Japanese radishes, scallions, parsley, and olives make this a unique salad. Radishes are Asian in origin. Japanese, or daikon radishes, are crisp, mild, cucumber-shaped radishes with juicy white flesh. They are hotter than red radishes but milder than black ones. This variety is used in a lot of Japanese and Chinese cooking. If possible, do not get overly large ones.

Serves 6 to 8

Salad:
2 medium carrots, peeled, coarsely grated
1½ pounds Japanese radishes, peeled and coarsely grated
1 bunch scallions, whites and some greens, cut into ½-inch lengths
3 tablespoons finely chopped fresh Italian flat-leaf parsley
7 to 8 black olives for garnish

Dressing:
Freshly squeezed juice of 1 lemon
4 to 5 tablespoons extra-virgin olive oil
1 teaspoon white vinegar
Sea salt

Place the grated carrots in the center of a shallow platter. Arrange the grated radishes around the carrots. Sprinkle scallions and parsley on top and garnish with olives.

In a small bowl, whisk together the lemon juice, olive oil, vinegar, and salt to taste. Drizzle over the salad and serve.

russian salad

Rus Salatası
İstanbul

This recipe is a combination of boiled potatoes, carrots, cornichons, peas, and hard-boiled eggs. It was brought to Turkey by White Russians fleeing Russia after the 1917 revolution, and has been adopted into Turkish cuisine. Russian Salad is ideal for a buffet, and traditionally Nur serves it on New Year's Eve. A great accompaniment to roasted turkey, this salad is best if prepared the day before, covered, and refrigerated.

Serves 6

2 medium golden potatoes, boiled
2 medium carrots, peeled and boiled
1 cup small pickled cornichons
1 cup cooked peas
4 hard-boiled eggs, divided
Sea salt
2½ teaspoons Dijon mustard
1½ to 2 cups mayonnaise
7 to 8 black olives for garnish

Dice the potatoes, carrots, and pickled cornichons into 1/4-inch cubes. Place in a large bowl and add the peas. Finely chop two eggs and add to the mixture. Add salt to taste, mustard, and mayonnaise. Mix well and check the seasoning; if needed, add more mayonnaise.

Arrange on a serving platter. Garnish with the olives and the remaining eggs, cut into quarters.

chickpea soup

Nohut Çorbası
İstanbul

This is a very old, healthful, often forgotten recipe from the Ottoman Empire.

Serves 6

1 cup dried chickpeas, soaked overnight in 3 cups lightly salted water
3 cups chicken stock
1 teaspoon salt
Freshly ground pepper
½ teaspoon cinnamon
1 teaspoon cumin
3 tablespoons butter, divided
1 tablespoon canola oil
3 slices of white bread, crusts removed, and diced into ¼-inch cubes
1 teaspoon paprika
1 whole lemon, cut into 6 wedges

Place the chickpeas and the soaking water in a 2-quart pan, and bring to a boil. Lower the heat and simmer, covered, 45 to 50 minutes. Remove from heat and let cool.

In batches, transfer the chickpeas and their cooking liquid to a food processor and purée until smooth (or use an immersion blender). Return mixture to the pan.

Add the chicken stock and season with salt and pepper to taste. Cook, covered, over medium heat, about 20 minutes. Remove from heat, add cinnamon and cumin, and mix well.

Meanwhile, in a medium frying pan, heat 2 tablespoons butter and the oil and sauté bread cubes until golden brown, about 3 to 4 minutes. Remove the croutons with a slotted spoon and drain on a double layer of paper towels.

Heat 1 tablespoon butter in a small skillet and stir in the paprika. Remove from the heat and mix well.

Place soup in individual soup bowls, top with croutons, and drizzle the paprika mixture over the top.

Serve hot with lemon wedges.

ottoman-style lentil soup

Osmanlı Mercimek Çorbası
İstanbul

This is a very old recipe that dates back to the Ottoman Empire. It is perfect for cold winter nights.

Serves 8

3 tablespoons butter, divided
2 onions, finely chopped
1 carrot, peeled and finely diced
2 green cubanelle peppers, stem, seeds, and ribs removed, finely diced
3 cloves garlic, finely chopped
1 small, dry, red chili pepper (optional)
2 heaped tablespoons flour
8 cups hot chicken stock plus more if needed
1¼ cups red lentils, washed and drained
2 tablespoons medium-grain rice, washed and drained
Sea salt
Freshly ground pepper
1 cup milk
2 tablespoons olive oil
3 slices white bread, crusts removed, diced into ¼-inch cubes
1 teaspoon paprika for garnish

In a 3-quart pot, heat 2 tablespoons butter and sauté the onions for 4 to 5 minutes, stirring constantly. Add carrot, cubanelle peppers, garlic, and red chili. Mix well and cook for an additional 5 minutes. Stir in flour, mix well, and add the hot chicken stock. Mix well and stir in lentils and rice. Bring to a boil and season with salt and pepper to taste. Reduce heat to simmer, and cook, covered, 35 to 40 minutes. Remove from heat and remove the red chili pepper.

Using an immersion blender or food processor, purée the soup. Add the milk, taste, and adjust seasoning if needed. Return to the pan and cook, uncovered, over medium heat for 5 minutes. If the soup is too thick, add more chicken stock.

In a medium frying pan, heat the oil and the remaining butter. Sauté the bread cubes until golden brown. Remove from pan with a slotted spoon and drain well on paper towels. Place soup in a tureen and top with croutons and paprika. Serve hot.

pumpkin soup

Balkabağı Çorbası
Edirne

This puréed soup is made with onions, pumpkin, rice, and milk. The term "pumpkin" is used to iden-tify nearly all hard-skinned squash. What the term refers to changes from region to region and from country to country.

Serves 6

3 tablespoons butter
2 large onions, finely chopped
2 pounds pumpkin or butternut squash, peeled, cut into 1-inch cubes
½ cup medium-grain rice, washed and drained
6 cups chicken stock
1 teaspoon cumin
Sea salt
Freshly ground pepper
A pinch freshly grated nutmeg
1½ cups milk

Topping:
2 tablespoons heavy cream
1½ tablespoons finely chopped Italian flat-leaf parsley

Melt the butter in a 3-quart pot. Add the onions and sauté, stirring, until translucent, 5 to 6 minutes. Add the pumpkin cubes, rice, chicken stock, cumin, and salt and pepper to taste; bring to a boil. Reduce heat to low and simmer, covered, for 45 to 55 minutes, stirring occasionally.

Transfer soup in batches to a food processor and process until smooth (or use an immersion blender). Return soup to the pot, add a pinch of nutmeg and the milk, mix well, and cook for another 5 to 6 minutes over medium heat.

Transfer the soup to a soup tureen, pour the cream in the center, and garnish with the finely chopped parsley. Serve hot.

semolina soup

İrmik Çorbası
İstanbul

This hearty soup is made with chicken broth, semolina, and milk, and is topped with croutons seasoned with Aleppo pepper.

Serves 6

6 to 7 cups chicken stock
½ cup semolina
1 cup milk
2 large egg yolks
Sea salt
Freshly ground pepper
2 tablespoons canola oil
2 tablespoons butter, divided
3 slices white bread, crusts removed, diced into ¼-inch cubes
½ teaspoon Aleppo pepper

In a 2-quart pot, bring 6 cups of chicken stock to a boil. Lower heat to medium and whisking constantly, slowly add semolina. Cook, uncovered, for 10 minutes, stirring most of the time.

In a small bowl, mix together the milk and egg yolks. Slowly pour into the semolina soup, whisking rapidly. When soup starts bubbling, remove from heat (this will take 5 to 6 minutes). At this point, if your soup is too thick, stir in more stock. Season with salt and pepper to taste.

In a medium frying pan, heat the oil and 1 tablespoon butter; sauté the bread cubes until golden brown. Remove from pan with a slotted spoon and place on paper towels to drain. In a small skillet, heat 1 tablespoon butter and stir in the Aleppo pepper. Remove from heat and drizzle over the croutons.

Transfer soup to a tureen and top with croutons. Serve hot.

wheat, lamb, and chickpea soup

Kuzu Etli Nohutlu Buğday Çorbası
İstanbul

This is an 18th-century Ottoman recipe made from shelled wheat, lamb shanks, onions, and chickpeas. Poached fish, such as sea bass (cut into bite-size pieces), can be used instead of lamb—but add it just before serving.

Serves 6

1 cup shelled wheat, soaked in water to cover overnight
10 cups water, divided
2 lamb shanks, washed and drained
1 onions, kept whole, plus 3 onions, finely chopped
5 to 6 peppercorns
1 bay leaf
4 tablespoons butter
½ cup canned chickpeas, washed, drained, skins removed
1 tablespoon flour
2 large egg yolks
Freshly squeezed juice of 1 lemon
1 teaspoon cinnamon
Freshly ground pepper

Drain the wheat. In a 2-quart pot cook the wheat in 6 cups of water over low heat, covered, until very tender, about 60 to 70 minutes. Remove from heat and let cool until warm to the touch. Using a wooden spoon, push the wheat through a fine mesh colander and set aside.

Place the lamb, whole onion, peppercorns, bay leaf, and 4 cups of water in a 2-quart pot. Bring to a boil. Reduce heat to simmer, cover, and cook for 1 1/2 hours. Skim off any foam or scum. Remove lamb from the pot and place on a plate to cool. Pour the stock through a colander and set aside. Shred the lamb into bite-size pieces, discarding the bones and any fat.

In a 3-quart pot, heat butter and add the diced onions. Sauté for 6 to 7 minutes, stirring; add 5 to 6 cups of reserved stock and the wheat. Simmer, covered, for 15 to 20 minutes. Add lamb pieces and chickpeas, and mix well.

Place a ladleful of soup in a bowl and let it cool for a few minutes. Whisking constantly, add the flour, egg yolks, and lemon juice. Very slowly, pour this mixture into the soup, whisking constantly. Simmer for 1 to 2 more minutes. Sprinkle with cinnamon and freshly ground pepper. Serve hot.

pilafs, boereks, and pastas

bosnian leek boerek

Pırasa Böreği

Thrace region

Best eaten warm, this dish is an excellent main course and can be served with any kind of salad; or use it as a first course at a dinner party. Leeks are a cold-weather vegetable that can be used in a variety of cooked dishes from soups to risotto. Make sure to rinse them well and clean all the grit from between the layers. If you don't like the strong onion taste of this dish, you can substitute more leeks for the onion.

Serves 6 to 8

3 tablespoons canola oil
1 tablespoon plus 1 teaspoon butter
1 large onion, peeled and finely chopped
2 pounds leeks, hairy roots and damaged leaves removed, washed, drained,
    thinly sliced crosswise
Sea salt
Freshly ground pepper
1 cup coarsely grated cheddar cheese
3 large eggs, beaten
4 tablespoons canola oil
2 cups whole milk
½ cup plain yogurt
4 tablespoons butter, melted
1 teaspoon butter, for greasing
24 (13 or 14 inch x 18-inch, or 12 x17-inch) sheets phyllo, at room temperature
2 tablespoons sesame seeds

In a 10-inch skillet, heat the oil and 1 tablespoon butter, and sauté the onion for 3 to 4 minutes. Add the leeks and continue sautéing for another 6 to 7 minutes, mixing well. Season with salt and pepper to taste. Remove from heat and let cool. When mixture is cool, stir in cheese and mix well.

In a bowl, combine the eggs, oil, milk, yogurt, and melted butter; whisk well. Preheat oven to 350°F. Generously grease a 9 x13-inch baking pan with 1 teaspoon butter.

Lay the phyllo leaves on a work surface and cover with a slightly dampened kitchen towel to prevent them from drying out. Place a sheet of phyllo in the baking dish and brush with the egg mixture.

Cover with another sheet of phyllo and brush with the egg mixture. Continue layering and brushing until 12 sheets of phyllo have been used. Do not brush the 12th sheet. Spread the leek mixture evenly over the top sheet of phyllo. Place another 12 layers of phyllo on top of the leek filling, brushing each with the egg mixture. Brush the top sheet with the remaining mixture and sprinkle with sesame seeds. Cut the boerek into 2-inch squares and bake for 40 to 50 minutes or until golden brown on top.

bulgur pilaf with chestnuts
Kestaneli Bulgur Pilavı
Bursa

This simple pilaf becomes elegant with the addition of chestnuts, dried fruit, allspice, and cumin. Chestnuts are full of fiber and low in fat. They are used in a wide variety of Marmara dishes as a paste, puréed, or roasted. This pilaf can also be made with rice; just use 2 cups of extra-long-grain white rice instead of the bulgur.

Serves 6 to 8

4 tablespoons butter
1 tablespoon canola oil
3 medium onions, finely chopped
2 cups coarse bulgur
4 cups chicken stock
2 tablespoons dried sultanas or dried currants, soaked in water to cover for an hour
1 teaspoon allspice
1 teaspoon cumin
Sea salt
5.28-ounce package roasted, shelled chestnuts

In a medium-size pan, heat the butter and oil and sauté the onions for 5 to 6 minutes. Add the coarse bulgur and chicken stock, mix well, and bring to a boil. Stir in the sultanas or currants, allspice, cumin, salt, and chestnuts. Reduce heat to simmer, cover, and cook until all the liquid has been absorbed and holes start to form on the surface.

Remove from heat , remove lid, place a double layer of paper towel over the bulgur, cover, and let sit for 10 to 15 minutes. Mix well and serve with any main course.

75

chickpea ravioli

Nohutlu Mantı
Bursa

Called *mantı* in Turkish, these vegetarian dumplings are similar to ravioli and served in a rich yogurt sauce. They are believed to have originated in China but varieties of *mantı* have been eaten in Turkey for over 600 years. (There are also versions that use meat.) The key is to make sure you roll the dough very thin. You will need an *oklava* (a long, thin rolling pin available in Turkish markets) or 1/2-inch dowel from the hardware store.

Serves 8 to 10

Dough:
1 cup water
1 large egg
1½ teaspoons salt
3 cups flour plus a little more for kneading, divided

2 (15.5-ounce) cans (3 cups) chickpeas, drained
6 cups water
1 teaspoon plus 1 tablespoon sea salt, divided
1 teaspoon canola oil
6 cloves garlic, crushed or minced
3 cups plain yogurt
3 tablespoons butter
2 teaspoons dried mint
1 teaspoon Aleppo pepper

In a large bowl, whisk together the water, egg, and salt. Add 2 cups of flour, whisking, then, using your hands, try to form it into a ball of dough. Slowly add another 1/2 cup of flour, mix well, and try again. Add another 1/2 cup of flour and mix until the dough forms a ball.

Begin kneading the dough in the bowl, then transfer to a lightly floured surface, add 1 to 2 tablespoons of flour, and knead until dough forms a smooth, elastic ball. Divide dough into two balls; cover with a dishtowel.

Lightly flour a work surface and, using a rolling pin, roll out one of the balls of dough. When dough is about 1/16-inch thick, lay your *oklava* along one edge and begin rolling up the dough, flouring lightly each time you roll the dough around the *oklava* (so it doesn't stick). When dough is completely rolled around the *oklava*, place your hands in the middle and roll it back and forth a few times. Unroll the dough, place the *oklava* on a different part, and repeat the process until the dough is paper-thin and the circle is around 19 inches in diameter. Cut the dough into 1-inch squares. Repeat this process with the remaining dough.

Lightly flour a baking sheet. Roll each chickpea between your palms to remove the outer skin. Place a chickpea in the center of each square of dough. Bring the corners together over the chickpea and pinch to seal, making a parcel. Place the parcels on the baking sheet as you work.

In a 4-quart pot, bring 6 cups of water to a boil with 1 tablespoon of salt and 1 teaspoon canola oil. Add the ravioli and cook, covered, on high, stirring occasionally, for about 6 minutes or until done.

While cooking, mix together the crushed garlic and yogurt in a bowl. Melt butter in a small skillet; when it sizzles, turn off the heat and add mint and Aleppo pepper, stirring until mixed. Pour over the yogurt sauce.

Drain ravioli and place in a serving bowl. Stir in yogurt sauce and serve hot.

Hint: The secret to preparing good dough is to roll the dough in different directions, not just in one direction.

eggplant boerek

Patlıcanlı Börek
İstanbul

This recipe originates from the Sephardic Jews who settled in İstanbul when they were expelled from Spain in the 15th century. It is from Nur's friend Eliza Asa. Unlike individually wrapped boereks, this one is baked like lasagna and cut into pieces for serving. It is an excellent main course for vegetarians, and a good make-ahead dish for a large group. Serve with a salad.

Serves 6

Dough:
½ cup warm water
¾ cup canola oil
¼ cup melted butter
1 teaspoon white vinegar
1½ teaspoons sea salt
3½ cups plus 2 tablespoons flour
1 large egg yolk, beaten

Filling:
2 large eggplants, (about 1½ pounds total)
5 tablespoons any feta-type white cheese
1 cup plus 3 tablespoons grated cheddar cheese
Sea salt
Freshly ground pepper

Wash eggplants. Pierce the skin of the eggplants all around with the top of a small sharp knife. Cook over an open flame, turning occasionally, until the skin is charred and the flesh has softened. Set aside to cool for a few minutes. Hold each eggplant by the stem and remove the skin, peeling from top to bottom with a knife. Discard the stems. Finely chop the eggplants, place them in a fine sieve, and let drain for a few hours.

In a large bowl, combine the water, oil, butter, vinegar, and salt and mix well. Gradually add the flour until a ball of dough has formed. Knead well.

Place drained eggplant in a bowl and mix in white cheese and 1 cup of cheddar cheese; season with salt and pepper to taste.

Preheat oven to 350°F. Divide dough in half. Grease a 10 x 7 x 2-inch, rectangular baking dish. On a lightly floured surface, roll one of the pieces of dough to fit the baking dish. Place the dough in the baking dish and cover with the eggplant filling. Roll out the remaining ball of dough and cover the filling. Brush the top of the dough with the egg yolk and sprinkle with the remaining 3 tablespoons of grated cheddar cheese.

Bake for 30 to 35 minutes, remove from oven, and cut into 12 square pieces. Serve warm.

rice with chicken, almonds, and saffron

İstanbul Pilavı
İstanbul

In Turkey, this luxurious dish is known as İstanbul Pilaf. Saffron is the most expensive spice available and it is best stored in the refrigerator. The dish is tastiest with Turkish saffron.

Serves 6

1 pound (about 2) chicken breasts, cut into ½-inch cubes
Sea salt
Freshly ground pepper
⅓ cup plus 2 tablespoons canola oil, divided
½ cup blanched almonds
2 cups extra-long-grain white rice, soaked in warm, lightly salted water for 20 minutes
4 tablespoons butter
¼ teaspoon saffron threads, soaked in ⅓ cup warm water (or 1 teaspoon powdered turmeric)
4 cups chicken stock
3 tablespoons finely chopped fresh dill

Season chicken cubes with salt and pepper to taste. In a medium-size skillet, heat 2 tablespoons of oil and sauté the chicken cubes on all sides until golden brown. Remove from pan and set aside.

In a small skillet, heat 1/3 cup oil; add the blanched almonds and fry for 3 to 5 minutes, stirring constantly, until light brown or pink. Remove nuts with a slotted spoon and drain well on a double layer of paper towel to remove all excess oil.

Drain the rice. In a large skillet, heat the butter and sauté the rice for a few minutes, stir in the soaked saffron with its soaking water, and the chicken stock. Mix well and season with salt and pepper to taste. Add the cooked chicken cubes and bring mixture to a boil. Reduce heat to medium-low, cover, and simmer for 20 minutes until all the liquid has been absorbed and holes appear on the surface. Remove from heat, place a double layer of paper towel over the rice, and cover the pan. Let stand for 10 minutes then mix well.

Arrange nuts on the bottom of a 12-inch round shallow dish, then spoon the rice over the nuts, pressing it down gently with the back of a wooden spoon. Turn upside down on a round serving platter. Sprinkle with fresh dill and serve as a main course.

rice with lamb and dried apricots

Kabuni Pilav
İstanbul

This unique tasting, 15th-century Ottoman pilaf is fit for a sultan. In it, rice is flavored with a combination of lamb, cinnamon, dried apricots, and chickpeas. Serve with a salad.

Serves 6 to 8

1 pound leg of lamb, cut into ½-inch cubes
1 cup water plus more if needed, divided
1 cinnamon stick
1 cup water plus more if needed, divided
2 medium onions, finely chopped, divided
2 teaspoons cumin, divided
6 tablespoons butter, divided
Freshly ground pepper
Sea salt
15 dried apricots, soaked 4 to 5 minutes in water to cover, drained well
2 cups extra-long-grain white rice, soaked in lightly salted warm water for
    20 minutes, drained well
1 cup canned chickpeas, washed and drained
4 cups hot beef or chicken stock

In a medium-size pan, combine the lamb, 1/4 cup of water, and the cinnamon stick. Cover and cook over medium heat until the lamb releases its juices, about 10 minutes. Add 1 chopped onion, 1 teaspoon cumin, 1 tablespoon butter, and freshly ground pepper and cook over medium-low heat, covered, until the lamb reabsorbs all the liquid. At this point check to see if the lamb is tender enough. If not, add 1/3 cup of hot water and continue to cook until tender. Season with salt to taste, cover, remove from heat, and set aside.

In a medium-size skillet, heat 2 tablespoons butter and sauté the apricots, stirring, for 3 to 4 minutes. Add 1/2 cup water and cook until the apricots are soft and all the liquid has been absorbed, about 10 minutes. Remove from heat and set aside.

In a large skillet, heat 3 tablespoons butter, add 1 chopped onion and sauté for 5 to 6 minutes. Add the drained rice, mix well, and continue cooking for 3 to 4 minutes, stirring constantly. Stir in the cooked lamb, the drained chickpeas, and the stock, and mix well. Season with salt and pepper and the remaining teaspoon of cumin. Cover, bring to a boil, reduce heat to simmer, and cook for 20 to 25 minutes until all the liquid has been absorbed and holes appear on the surface.

Remove from heat, arrange cooked apricots on the rice, cover with a double layer of paper towel, and cover pan with the lid. Let sit for 20 to 25 minutes. Mix well with a slotted spoon, being careful not to break up the apricots. Arrange on a serving platter.

turkish polenta
Kaçamak
Tekirdağ

Polenta, served from Italy to Romania and beyond, is a basic accompaniment to many dishes. It can be served warm and soft, sometimes enriched with garlic, butter, or cheese. Sometimes it is cut into slices that are baked, fried, or grilled. When it was difficult to find flour during World War II, this was a meal in itself. This recipe comes from Nur's mother and brings back her memories of that difficult time. Serve with a salad.

Serves 6

3 cups water
1½ cups yellow cornmeal
2 tablespoons extra-virgin olive oil
Sea salt
2 tablespoons butter
½ teaspoon Aleppo pepper

Combine water, cornmeal, and olive oil in a pan and cook over medium-low heat, stirring constantly to prevent any lumps from forming. The polenta is done when it is well blended, holes have started to appear on the surface, and the sides can be easily pulled away from the pan. Remove from heat and season with salt to taste. Scoop the mixture into a serving dish with a medium-size ice cream scoop.

Melt the butter in a small skillet and remove from heat when it sizzles. Immediately stir in the Aleppo pepper and mix well. Pour over polenta and serve hot with any main course.

meat and chicken

inegöl kofta

İnegöl Köftesi
İnegöl, Bursa

İnegöl is a town in the province of Bursa famous for its kofta. Varieties of kofta are often named according to their region, shape, the cooking method, or their ingredients. To make kofta, shells of finely minced meat combined with spices, onions, and other ingredients are filled and shaped, then grilled, fried, broiled, or baked. They are usually lemon shaped.

Nur's brother took her to Bursa on their way to Yalova, where their mother had a summerhouse. They visited a kofta restaurant called Haci Aziz, which has been there since 1934, passing down from father to son. The owners kindly gave Nur this recipe and told her that the quality of the meat and the ratio of veal to lamb are very important in this dish. In the plateaus of Bursa, veal and lamb are fed in pastures where thyme grows wild, giving this meat a delicate thyme flavor.

The preparation for this dish begins the night before so the flavors can blend. It is always served with white bean salad and onion relish. French fries are also a good accompaniment.

Serves 6. Makes 38 to 40 koftas.

1 pound ground veal
½ pound ground lamb
3 to 4 slices stale white bread, crumbled in a food processor
1 teaspoon sea salt
¼ teaspoon freshly ground pepper
½ teaspoon baking soda
3 to 4 tablespoons olive oil, divided
1 large onion, finely grated
1 tablespoon water

In a large bowl, combine veal, lamb, breadcrumbs, salt and pepper, baking soda, and 1 tablespoon olive oil. Mix well, cover, and refrigerate overnight.

Remove meat mixture from refrigerator; add grated onion and 1 tablespoon water. Knead and mix well with your hands.

Place remaining 2 to 3 tablespoons of oil on a small plate and wet your hands with the oil; this helps shape the koftas and they cook in the oil that the meat absorbs. Take a piece of the mixture and make a 2-inch long, 1-inch wide koftas (an oval that looks more or less like your thumb). Repeat until all the meat mixture has been used.

Heat a heavy nonstick pan. Without crowding the pan, cook koftas in batches for 4 to 5 minutes on each side. Each serving is about 6 koftas.

lamb cooked in clay

Dağar Kebabı
Balıkesir

This dish is named for the clay casserole dish (called *dağar* in Balıkesir) in which it is usually made. You can use one of the clay pots that are sold in gourmet shops. This dish—made with lamb, onions, garlic, potatoes, peppers, and tomatoes—is usually served hot with rice and crusty bread to dip into the tasty juices.

Serves 6

2 pounds boneless leg of lamb, cut into 2-inch cubes
1 teaspoon cumin
Sea salt
Freshly ground pepper
8 to 10 pearl onions, peeled and kept whole
10 cloves garlic, peeled and kept whole
10 ounces (about 3 medium) golden potatoes, peeled and quartered
2 to 3 green cubanelle peppers or 1 green bell pepper, stems and seeds removed, coarsely chopped
3 large tomatoes, peeled and coarsely chopped
3 tablespoons butter, melted
½ cup water
5½ ounce package shelled and roasted chestnuts

Preheat oven to 400°F. In a large bowl, season lamb lightly with cumin and salt and pepper to taste. Mix well and add pearl onions, garlic, potatoes, green peppers, tomatoes, and butter. Mix well again, using your hands and making sure all the meat and vegetables are coated with the butter and spices.

Place mixture in a 10-inch round or oval clay pot and add 1/2 cup of water. Cover with a double layer of aluminum foil and cook 30 minutes, then lower the temperature to 375°F and continue cooking for another 1 1/2 hours.

Remove from the oven, remove foil, and stir in the chestnuts. Replace the foil and cook for another 20 minutes.

spring lamb liver stew

Ciğer Yahnisi
Thrace

In this tasty dish, lamb's liver is paired with tomato paste, cinnamon, scallions, broth, and red wine vinegar. It was the favorite springtime dish of Nur's maternal grandfather, Halil Kivanç. Serve with crusty bread.

Serves 4 as a lunch main course

1½ pounds lamb's liver, fine skin removed, and cut into 1-inch cubes
2 tablespoons butter
1 tablespoon olive oil
3 medium onions, halved and thinly sliced
2 teaspoons tomato paste
Sea salt
Freshly ground black pepper
½ teaspoon cinnamon
5 to 6 scallions, white and most of the green, sliced crosswise
2 tablespoons red wine vinegar
1 bay leaf
1 cup hot beef or chicken stock, or water
2 tablespoons finely chopped Italian flat-leaf parsley

Rinse the liver cubes and drain well. Set aside. Heat the butter and oil in a skillet; add onions and sauté until golden brown, about 6 to 7 minutes. Add liver and continue stirring until the color changes. Add tomato paste, salt and pepper to taste, cinnamon, scallions, vinegar, and bay leaf.

Mix well and add 1 cup hot stock, or water. Bring to a boil, reduce heat to simmer and cook, covered, until tender, about 20 to 25 minutes. Remove the bay leaf. Arrange on a serving platter and sprinkle with parsley.

ottoman army stew

Kul Aşı
İstanbul

This stew is made from lamb simmered with tomato, garlic, cinnamon, and cloves. It is a very old Ottoman dish used by the Janissaries, the first Ottoman standing army. The Janissaries were an elite corps in the service of the Ottoman Empire from around 1365. The cauldron in which one-pot meals were cooked was their most highly valued item—and if one was lost, the officer could be dismissed or strangled to death. The Ottomans combined cinnamon with lamb, giving the dish a unique flavor. This recipe was given to Nur by her friend Fatoş Üner.

Serves 5 to 6 as a main course

4 tablespoons butter
1 large onion, finely chopped
2 pounds boneless leg of lamb, cut in 1-inch squares
10 cloves garlic, halved
2 large tomatoes, peeled and grated
3 tablespoons white vinegar
½ teaspoon freshly ground pepper
1 teaspoon ground cinnamon
½ teaspoon ground cloves
½ teaspoon Aleppo pepper
Sea salt
1½ to 2 cups beef stock

Melt butter in a 2-quart pan over medium heat and sauté the onions until golden brown, about 8 to 9 minutes. Add lamb and garlic, and cook for another 3 to 4 minutes. Stir in grated tomatoes, vinegar, pepper, cinnamon, cloves, Aleppo pepper, sea salt to taste, and beef stock.

Mix well and cook, covered, over low heat for about 40 to 45 minutes. Check to see if lamb is tender. If not, cook for another 5 to 10 minutes, adding more stock to the stew if necessary. Serve with rice or warm, crusty bread.

chicken kebabs

Tarçınlı Tavuk Kebabı
İstanbul

This authentic 18th-century Ottoman dish has remained virtually unchanged for 300 years, and is still very popular. It is quick, easy, and fabulous! Once, when I had unexpected company I used skinned, boned chicken thighs since that was all I had in my freezer; it was terrific. Now I keep frozen packages of chicken thighs on hand to make this dish. To prepare onion juice, finely grate one or two large onions and press the pieces through a fine sieve using the back of a wooden spoon.

Serves 4 to 5

2 chicken breasts and 2 chicken legs with thighs, boned and cut into 1½-inch cubes
  (or 4 to 5 boned, skinned chicken thighs cut into 1½-inch cubes)
¼ cup onion juice
1 teaspoon salt
1 teaspoon freshly ground pepper
1 teaspoon cinnamon
4 tablespoons butter, melted

Place the chicken cubes in a shallow dish and pour onion juice over them. Season with cinnamon and salt and pepper, to taste. Mix well, cover, and refrigerate for at least an hour. Remove from the refrigerator one hour before cooking and set aside at room temperature.

Thread the chicken onto skewers with 4 to 5 pieces of chicken per skewer. Repeat until each skewer has been threaded. Heat grill or broiler, brush chicken with melted butter, and cook for about 10 to 12 minutes, turning to brush with butter. Cook on all sides. Brush with melted butter again and serve hot.

circassian chicken

Çerkez Tavuğu
Adapazarı

This chicken salad is made with shredded chicken that is bound together with a walnut paste. Versions of this dish are also found in Russia and Peru. This excellent, authentic recipe is from Sabiha Çevik, and is different from the version Nur and I make—the hot pepper sauce makes all the difference.

I first had this dish at a luncheon at Nur's residence in Washington, DC, about seven years ago and it has become one of my favorite party dishes; I love serving it at barbeques! Since there is no dairy in the salad, it keeps well. At first, taking the time to shred the chicken into thin strips was a pain, but it makes such a difference to the finished product.

It is always better to prepare this dish a day in advance, allowing the flavors to blend together. Traditionally, it is served with Turkish Polenta (page 83).

Serves 8 to 10

1 (3- to 3½-pound) whole chicken, washed and drained
1 medium onion, quartered
1 small carrot, peeled and washed
10 black peppercorns
1 bay leaf
Sea salt
7 cups water
3½ cups walnuts
6 to 7 teaspoons hot pepper sauce (or to taste), divided (page 61)
4 to 5 pieces stale white bread, crusts removed
3 to 4 cloves garlic, coarsely chopped
4 cups chicken stock

Place chicken in a 3-quart pot; add the onion, carrot, black peppercorns, and the bay leaf and season with salt. Add the water and bring to a boil. Remove any scum with a slotted spoon, lower the heat to simmer, and cook, covered, for about 50 to 55 minutes until the chicken is very tender.

Remove the chicken and let cool. Discard fat, skin, and bones, and shred chicken into very thin, 2-inch-long pieces (I use a fork); set aside. Strain the warm stock and save it for later use.

Divide walnuts into 3 batches. Place one batch in the food processor, add 2 teaspoons of hot pepper sauce, and process until fine. Transfer to a large bowl. Process the remaining walnuts in two batches, each with 2 teaspoons of hot sauce. Transfer mixture to the bowl.

Carefully hold the side of the bowl with one hand and knead the mixture with the other. After 4 to 5 minutes, you will start to see the oil seep out of the walnuts. Take 3 to 4 tablespoons of the oil and place in a small cup to use later as a garnish. Wash your hands well.

Add the stale bread, garlic, another teaspoon of hot pepper sauce, and the warm, reserved chicken stock. Mix well and let stand for 10 minutes so the bread can absorb the stock. Taste and adjust salt if needed.

Place the shredded chicken in a large bowl. In batches of 3 to 4 ladlefuls, process the walnut mixture until fine. Pour over chicken and check salt. Mix well, cover, and refrigerate overnight.

Arrange chicken on a serving platter and drizzle the walnut oil in swirls over the top. Serve cold.

Variation: As a great vegetarian alternative, substitute 2 pounds of shelled, boiled cranberry beans or 2 pounds green flat beans, boiled in salted water and drained. Toss with the sauce and serve cold.

broiled branzino

Izgara Levrek
İstanbul and all coastal regions of Marmara

Branzino, or European sea bass (in Turkish, *levrek balığı*), has a silvery skin like striped bass, but without the stripes, and it has a firm, white, mild-flavored flesh. Branzino is now farm-raised. It is one of the most prized of all Mediterranean fish and makes great eating.

Serves 4

4 whole branzino (about ¾ pound each), washed and drained
Sea salt
Freshly ground pepper
Canola oil for brushing
Lemon wedges

Season the fish, inside and out, with salt and pepper to taste. Cut two or three diagonal slashes in the skin on both sides of each fish. Brush lightly with oil and broil for 7 to 8 minutes on each side, until cooked. Serve with lemon wedges and a green salad.

fried mussels or squid with tarator sauce

Tarator Soslu Kızarmış Midye Kalamar
Throughout Marmara

Tarator sauce is made from thick slices of white bread, garlic, salt, ground walnuts, olive oil, and lemon juice. It is also delicious with fried vegetables.

Serves 6 to 8

Batter:
1 cup flour
⅔ cup beer
Sea salt
2 large whole eggs, separated

Tarator Sauce:
1 cup stale white breadcrumbs (made in the food processor or blender from stale bread)
¼ cup whole milk or water, or a mixture of both
⅔ cup extra-virgin olive oil
⅔ cup walnuts
2 tablespoons white vinegar or 2 tablespoons freshly squeezed lemon juice
¼ teaspoon Aleppo pepper
Sea salt
Freshly ground pepper

2 pounds (about 60 to 62) farm-raised mussels or 2 pounds squid
1½ cups water
1 cup canola oil for frying

To Prepare the Batter:
Sift flour into a medium-size bowl and whisk in beer and salt. Add 2 egg yolks and whisk until well blended. Cover and let rest in the refrigerator for about an hour. Remove from refrigerator and bring to room temperature.

In a small bowl, whisk the egg whites with a pinch of salt until they form a peak. Slowly and gently fold the egg whites into the batter using a rubber spatula.

To Prepare the Sauce:
Place breadcrumbs in a bowl and pour in the milk, mixing well. Let stand for 5 to 6 minutes; then stir in the oil, mixing well.

Place walnuts in a food processor and process until fine. Add the soaked bread, milk, and oil, and pulse a few minutes. Add vinegar, Aleppo pepper, and season with salt and pepper to taste. The mixture should be smooth. Set aside.

To Prepare the Mussels:

Scrub the mussels with a wire brush under running water, discarding any damaged or open mussels that do not close when tapped with a knife. Soak in water for 20 minutes. Carefully cut off the beards.

Place 1 1/2 cups of water in a 2-quart pot, bring to a boil, add mussels, and cook for 3 to 4 minutes until wide open. Drain well and set aside. Discard any unopened mussels. When cool enough to handle, remove the meat and discard the shells.

Heat the oil in a 10-inch frying pan. Dip the mussels in the batter and fry for 2 to 3 minutes on each side until golden brown. Drain well on paper towel.

To Prepare the Squid:

Clean the squid; holding a squid at its base (avoid putting pressure on the ink sack in the middle of the body), remove and discard the quill (the transparent spine of the squid) by running your finger along the inside of the squid. Pull the head and tentacles off the body to remove the innards and ink sack, being careful not to puncture the ink sack!

Cut the heads off the squid below the eyes, discard, and reserve the tentacles. Cut the bodies into 1/4-inch-thick rings. Repeat with the rest of the squid.

Dip the squid into the batter and fry 2 to 3 minutes until golden brown. Do not crowd the pan. Drain well on paper towel.

Serve warm as an appetizer with tarator sauce, warm bread, and lemon wedges.

fish patties
Balık Köftesi
İstanbul

In this recipe, fish are steamed on lettuce leaves then mixed with grated potato, breadcrumbs, eggs, currants, and pine nuts, and formed into patties. Steaming the fish instead of boiling or poaching it yields a much more flavorful dish. Leftover grilled or baked fish can also be used.

Serves 4. Makes 14 or 15 patties.

1½ cups water
2 to 3 lettuce leaves
1 pound sea bass, halibut, or any white fish fillets (to make 2 cups fish flakes)
Sea salt
Freshly ground pepper
1 medium onion, finely grated
2 medium golden potatoes, boiled with skin on, cooled, peeled and grated
3 slices stale white bread, crusts removed and crumbled
2 large eggs, lightly beaten
4 tablespoons chopped Italian flat-leaf parsley
2 tablespoons currants, washed, soaked in water, and drained (optional)
2 tablespoons pine nuts (optional)
1 cup dried breadcrumbs
1½ cups canola oil for frying

Place a medium-size steamer rack in a pan with 1 1/2 cups simmering water. Place lettuce leaves on the rack and cover with fish fillets. Season fish with salt and pepper to taste. Cover and steam until fish flakes easily when tested with a fork, about 8 to 10 minutes. Remove fish, and when it cools, crumble or flake it and set aside.

In a bowl, combine the grated onion, grated potato, crumbled stale bread, eggs, parsley, currants and pine nuts (if using), and the crumbled fish. Mix well, knead mixture with your hands, and form into 14 to 15 oval fish patties. Cover and refrigerate for an hour or two before frying.

Place breadcrumbs in a shallow dish or pan and roll the patties in crumbs to cover both sides. Heat the oil in a large skillet, and when hot, add the patties. Do not crowd the pan. In batches, cook the patties for 2 to 3 minutes on each side until golden brown. Serve with a salad and a vegetable dish.

fried sardines in sauce

Soslu Kızarmış Sardalya
Tekirdağ

This recipe uses "real" whole sardines, served with a sauce of red wine vinegar, raisins, currants, and pine nuts. Don't even think of using those oily little fish squeezed into a can! Buy them fresh. This dish was a favorite of Nur's mother. It should be made the day before serving, and is eaten cold.

Serves 4

4 tablespoons olive oil
2 medium onions, cut in half, thinly sliced
2 tablespoons red wine vinegar
1 tablespoon golden raisins, soaked in a cup of warm water for 30 minutes
1 tablespoon dried black currants, soaked in a cup of warm water for 30 minutes
1 tablespoon pine nuts
1 teaspoon sugar
Pinch of sea salt
½ cup canola oil for frying
⅔ cup flour
Freshly ground pepper
1½ pounds sardines, each about 6-inches long, heads removed, cleaned, and gutted

Heat olive oil in a skillet over medium heat and sauté onions, stirring, for 5 minutes. Lower heat and continue to cook, stirring, for 12 to 13 more minutes. Add vinegar, raisins, currants, pine nuts, sugar, and salt to taste. Mix well, and cook for another 2 to 3 minutes. Set aside.

Preheat oven to 350°F. In another large skillet, heat canola oil. Mix flour, salt and pepper to taste, and place on a plate or in a pie pan. Dip fish in the mixture, coating on all sides. Fry for 2 to 3 minutes on each side.

Place fish in an ovenproof baking dish, pour sauce on top, and bake for 5 minutes. Let cool, cover, refrigerate, and serve cold the next day.

cabbage rolls with chestnuts

Kestaneli Lahana Dolması
Bursa

The unusual combination of ingredients makes this an excellent vegetarian main course, buffet dish, or first course. The addition of pine nuts, currants, cinnamon, allspice, mint, and dill really enhance the flavor. This dish always tastes best if it is made a day in advance. Serve cold with lemon wedges.

Serves 8 to 10

1½ cups uncooked medium-grain
    white rice
Sea salt
1¼ cups extra-virgin olive oil, divided
2½ pounds onions, finely chopped
5 tablespoons pine nuts
3 tablespoons dried currants
1 tablespoon sugar
10½ cups water, divided
1 teaspoon cinnamon

1 teaspoon allspice
1 tablespoon dried mint
½ bunch Italian flat-leaf parsley, washed,
    drained, stems and leaves finely chopped
½ bunch fresh dill, washed, drained, stems
    and leaves finely chopped
2 (2½-pound) cabbages
2 (5.28-ounce) packages shelled and
    roasted chestnuts, halved

99

Soak the rice in warm salted water for 20 minutes. Drain well and set aside. In a large saucepan, heat 1 cup oil. Add the onions and pine nuts and sauté, stirring, 12 to 15 minutes. Add the drained cooked rice, mix well, and cook for 3 to 4 minutes. Add salt to taste, currants, sugar, and 1 cup warm water. Cover and simmer over medium heat until all the liquid has been absorbed, about 4 to 5 minutes. Remove lid and add cinnamon, allspice, and mint. Mix well and stir in finely chopped parsley and dill. Mix again, remove from heat, and set aside to cool.

Using a sharp knife carefully cut out the core of the cabbage to loosen the leaves. In a 6-quart pot, combine 8 cups of water, 1/2 tablespoon salt, and bring to a boil. Add the cabbage to the boiling water cored-side up; cover, and boil for 3 to 4 minutes. Remove the lid and, using a fork and tong, remove the outer leaves, making sure not to break them. Cover the pot again and repeat, removing more leaves with a tong until you reach the center of the cabbage.

Drain and cool the leaves. Set aside torn or curly leaves for later use. Cut the rest of the leaves vertically in half, discarding the thick veins in the middle. Place the leaves rib-side down on a work surface. Place a tablespoon of rice filling and one chestnut half on one of the cabbage leaves. Fold the sides of the leaf over to cover the filling and roll it from bottom to top (like folding an envelope). Repeat until you have stuffed and rolled all of the leaves. Place the torn or curly leaves in the bottom of a heavy saucepan in a single layer.

Place the rolled cabbage leaves in a single layer in the pan with the loose ends down. When the first layer is done, you can make the second layer on top of the first. Add 1 1/2 cups warm water and 1/4 cup olive oil. Check salt. Cover with a layer of torn or curly leaves. Place a plate upside down on top of the cabbage rolls to weight them down during cooking. Bring to a boil, reduce heat, cover and simmer for 60 to 70 minutes.

Remove from heat. Let cool for at least 4 to 5 hours, and refrigerate. Arrange on a serving platter and serve cold.

eggplant and flat green beans in tomato sauce
Çiğ Kızartma
Çanakkale

Flat green beans are usually available all year round, but peak time is in the summer. Make sure you buy clean, well-shaped, smooth, crisp beans. Cut off the stem ends, but leave the little curved tip if it looks nice. This dish is an excellent vegetarian main course and should be served at room temperature with warm crusty bread.

Serves 4 to 6

1 pound flat green beans
2 medium onions, finely chopped and divided
6 to 7 cloves garlic, sliced, divided
2 to 3 green cubanelle peppers, seeds and ribs removed, coarsely chopped
1 pound ripe tomatoes, peeled and finely chopped, divided
Sea salt
¼ cup water
4 small eggplants (about 1 pound total)
½ cup extra-virgin olive oil

Trim the ends off the beans and cut them in half, wash and drain. In a medium-size pan, combine with half of the chopped onions, half of the garlic, half of the cubanelle peppers, and half of the tomatoes. Sprinkle with a little salt and add 1/4 cup of water. Bring to a boil, lower heat and simmer, covered, for 15 minutes.

While beans are cooking, wash eggplants. Starting an inch below the stem, cut each eggplant into 4 lengthwise slices, leaving the tops intact. Sprinkle with salt and let stand for 30 minutes. Wash well and squeeze gently with your fingertips to remove excess water.

Uncover beans, and add the rest of the tomatoes, layered with the rest of the cubanelle peppers. Arrange eggplants on top with the remaining onions and garlic. Season with salt and add the olive oil. Bring to a boil, cover vegetables with an upside-down plate that fits over them in the pan, and cook over medium-low heat, covered, for 60 to 70 minutes. Check to see if beans are done; if not, continue to cook for another 10 to 15 minutes.

Arrange on a serving dish with eggplant mixture on one side and bean mixture on the other side. Serve each guest a whole eggplant and some beans.

the imam fainted

İmam Bayıldı
İstanbul

The Ottomans were experts in enhancing the natural flavors of foods. This is most evident in this rich vegetarian appetizer. As the story goes, the dish got its name because it was so good the imam fainted when he first tasted it!

Serves 8

8 (6- or 7-inch) Italian or Dutch eggplants
5 teaspoons salt, divided
1 cup vegetable oil, for frying
¾ cup extra-virgin olive oil
4 medium onions, cut into thin semi-circles
8 cloves garlic, finely chopped
3 medium tomatoes, peeled, seeds removed, and finely chopped
2 teaspoon finely chopped Italian flat-leaf parsley
2 teaspoon sugar
1 large tomato, sliced
1 green bell pepper, seeds and ribs removed and cut into ½-inch squares
1 cup water

Wash the eggplants. Remove the leaves from around the stem, leaving the stem on. Leaving 1 1/2-inch borders of peel at the top and bottom of each eggplant, peel off the skin. Using a small, sharp knife make a deep, lengthwise slit in the center of the peeled area (without cutting through the eggplant). Repeat until all the eggplants have been peeled and slit. Sprinkle with 4 teaspoons salt and let it stand for 30 minutes. Rinse with cold water and dry on paper towel.

Heat the vegetable oil in a deep frying pan. Line a jelly roll pan with a double layer of paper towel. Fry the eggplants in batches of 3 or 4 (depending on the size of the pan), until lightly browned on all sides, 4–6 minutes. Roll them frequently for even cooking. Drain on paper towels.

Heat the extra-virgin olive oil in a 2-quart pan, add onions, and sauté for 10 minutes over medium heat. Add garlic and sauté for another 5 minutes, stirring from time to time. Lower the heat slightly, add the chopped tomatoes, and cook for 10 minutes. Turn off the heat and add 1 teaspoon salt, sugar, and parsley. Let cool.

Preheat the oven to 400°F. Lay the cooked eggplants side-by-side, slit-side up in a large Pyrex serving dish, leaving some space between them. Using a spoon, open the slits and stuff with the onion mixture, pressing down to fit as much stuffing as the eggplant will take. Pour 1 cup of water around the eggplants. Garnish each eggplant with a slice of tomato and a green bell pepper square. Cover with aluminum foil and cook for 30 minutes, removing the foil after 20 minutes have passed. Let cool and serve as an appetizer.

giant lima beans in olive oil
Löbye
İstanbul

Sometimes referred to as butter beans or large lima beans, these extra large beans are Peruvian in origin. They have kidney-shaped curves, a creamy texture, and a delicate flavor. Served with a salad, this dish makes a lovely vegetarian main course.

Serves 4

Sea salt
10 ounces dried giant lima beans, soaked overnight, drained
⅔ cup extra-virgin olive oil
5 to 6 garlic cloves, minced
2 medium onions, finely chopped
2 medium carrots, peeled and cut crosswise in ¼-inch-thick pieces
1 teaspoon red pepper paste
1 teaspoon sugar
1½ cups boiling water
2 tablespoons finely chopped Italian flat-leaf parsley
2 lemons, cut into wedges

In a medium-size pan, combine 4 cups of water with 1/2 teaspoon salt. Bring to a boil and add soaked, drained beans and cook, partially covered, for 20 minutes. Drain well and set aside.

In another medium-size pan, heat the olive oil, and sauté the garlic and onions for 7 to 8 minutes. Stir in the carrots and cook for another couple of minutes. Stir in the salt, red pepper paste, sugar, and 1 1/2 cups of boiling water. Add beans, mix and simmer, covered, 20 minutes or until beans are tender.

Arrange on a serving platter and decorate with the parsley and lemon wedges. Serve at room temperature.

Hint: To prevent the skin from slipping off, bring beans to a boil slowly.

103

grape leaves stuffed with lentils and bulgur
Mercimekli Yaprak Dolması
Tekirdağ

In this dish, grape leaves are stuffed with lentils and bulgur and folded into pentagon-shaped parcels before cooking. Nur is the fourth generation to prepare this recipe, and it was her mother's favorite dish. Her grandmother made this dish for family picnics, especially during the Spring Cherry Festival.

Serves 8 to 10. Makes about 60.

7¾ cups water, divided
1-pound jar grape leaves, stems removed
1 cup olive oil, divided
3 medium onions, finely chopped
1 cup dried red lentils, washed and drained
½ cup fine bulgur
Salt
Freshly ground pepper
1 teaspoon sugar
1 tablespoon dried mint
1 teaspoon paprika or Aleppo pepper
4 tablespoons finely chopped Italian flat-leaf parsley
4 scallions, finely chopped

Place 5 cups of water in a 2-quart pot and bring to a boil. Remove from heat. Place 60 grape leaves in the pot and let sit for 2 to 3 minutes. Remove leaves from water and drain well, then rinse in cold water and drain again.

Heat 3/4 cup olive oil in a medium-size pan over medium heat. Add onions and sauté, stirring, until translucent, about 5 minutes. Stir in the lentils and bulgur and mix well. Add 1 1/4 cups water, mix well, and cover. After 2 to 3 minutes reduce heat to low and continue cooking until all the liquid has been absorbed. Remove pan from heat and let stand, covered, for 10 minutes. Remove lid and stir in salt, pepper, sugar, mint, paprika, parsley, and scallions, mixing well. Let mixture cool.

Place grape leaves on a work surface rib-side up, reserving any torn or unused leaves for later use. Place a large tablespoon of the filling on one of the leaves, about one inch from the bottom. Fold the bottom left side over the filling and then the bottom right side over the filling, forming a triangle with the point at the bottom. Fold the upper left side over the filling (across the triangle) and repeat with the right side. Now fold down a little of the top of the grape leaf; then continue to fold down over the filling. You should have a pentagon shape; the stuffed grape leaves will looks like a child's outline of a house with a sloping roof. Turn over and set aside. Repeat until all the leaves have been filled and rolled.

Line the bottom of a medium pan with torn or unused grape leaves, completely covering the bottom. Place stuffed grape leaves in the pan in layers. Add 1 1/2 cups water and the remaining 1/4 cup olive oil to the pan. Sprinkle lightly with salt. Place a plate upside down over the stuffed grape leaves and bring liquid to a boil. Cover pot, reduce heat to simmer, and cook for about 50 to 60 minutes. Remove pan from heat and let rest for 4 to 5 hours before serving. Serve at room temperature.

Hint: If you prefer, you can roll the leaves into cigar-shapes. Place 2 teaspoons of filling along the bottom edge of a leaf, fold the sides over the filling, and roll up the leaf. If leaves are too large, cut them vertically. Do not throw away any damaged or unused leaves.

desserts and sweets

almond squares

Badem Tatlısı
İstanbul

This is a jelled almond dessert, which is cut into squares and served in lemon-flavored sugar syrup. You can buy blanched almonds but it costs less to do it yourself. Just cover the nuts with boiling water and let sit for 3 minutes. Drain well then slip off the skins by squeezing the nuts between your finger and thumb. You can also place them on half of a kitchen towel, cover with the other half, and gently roll them back and forth, and then remove the peel. Make the syrup ahead of time so it can cool. This dish can be made several days ahead and refrigerated in a closed container. Serve with ice cream or whipped cream.

Serves 8 to 10

Syrup:
3 cups sugar
3½ cups water
2 tablespoons freshly squeezed lemon juice
1 tablespoon lemon zest

8 large eggs, separated
⅔ cup sugar
1 cup flour, sifted
3½ cups finely ground almonds
1 teaspoon vanilla
4 tablespoons unsalted butter, melted
¼ teaspoon baking powder
pinch of salt
3½ ounces blanched & slivered almonds

In a medium-size pot, combine the sugar and water and bring to a boil. Reduce heat and simmer for 15 minutes, stirring constantly just until sugar dissolves. Stir in the lemon juice and lemon zest. Continue to cook for another 5 minutes. Remove from heat and set aside to cool for a couple of hours.

Preheat oven to 350°F. Grease and lightly flour a 14 1/2 x 9 1/2 x 2-inch baking pan.

In a mixing bowl, whisk egg yolks and sugar until lemon colored, about 5 minutes. Gradually add the flour, ground almonds, vanilla, butter, and baking powder, mixing well.

In a separate bowl, combine the egg whites with a pinch of salt. Using an electric mixer (with a whip attachment if you have it), beat the mixture on low until it begins to bubble, then turn mixer to high and beat until stiff, but not as glossy as for meringue. Set aside.

Slowly fold the beaten egg whites into the almond mixture. Pour into prepared pan, making sure mixture is spread evenly. Sprinkle top with slivered almonds and bake 30 to 35 minutes, or until a toothpick inserted in the center comes out clean.

Ladle the cold syrup over the top, making sure all of the cake is covered. Let rest for a few hours and cut into 2-inch squares.

quince pâté

Ayva Şekerlemesi
İstanbul

I first learned about quince when Nur taught me how to make quince compote, which is sometimes used to settle the stomach. Quinces look a little like pears and have a tart, delicate flavor. They are used in a number of Turkish stews, desserts, and jams. (When making jam or jelly use the under-ripe green-tinged ones since they are higher in pectin.) When cooked, the fruit turns pink.

Quince is a winter fruit, and it is usually served with Turkish coffee on special occasions, including the winter religious holidays when it is often prepared for guests. This makes a lovely hostess gift and it keeps for months. Quinces are available in Asian markets, specialty stores, and some supermarkets. The recipe can be cut in half if desired.

Serves 10 to 15

4 quinces (about 2 pounds), washed, cut in quarters with skin intact, cored,
    seeds removed and saved
¼ cup water
2½ cups sugar
Freshly squeezed juice of half a lemon, about 1 tablespoon
¾ cup coarsely chopped pistachio nuts or coarsely chopped walnuts (optional)
Cooking spray

Coarsely grate the quinces into a non-stick pot. Put the seeds into a muslin bag, tie the top, and add to the pot with 1/4 cup of water. Cover and cook over low heat for about 50 to 60 minutes, stirring occasionally to prevent sticking. (The peel gives this dish its dark pink color and the seeds make the jelly.) Add the sugar and lemon juice, cover, and cook for about 2 hours, stirring occasionally, until the quinces are well cooked and the mixture is almost the consistency of purée.

Remove the muslin bag and squeeze any juice into the pot, mixing well. Let the mixture cool until warm, then purée in a food processor in batches. Return purée to the non-stick pot and cook for another 20 to 30 minutes until it becomes a thick paste. Remove from heat and let cool for a few minutes.

Spray a 9 x 13 x 2-inch baking dish with oil. Place the quince paste into the prepared dish and press firmly with the back of a wooden spoon or spatula. If desired, cover the top with chopped nuts.

Leave the pâté at room temperature, uncovered, to set for at least 2 1/2 days (it may take 3 days). Spray your knife with oil and cut pâté into 1 1/2-inch squares.

sour cherry bread pudding

Vişneli Ekmek Tatlısı
İstanbul

Cherries first made their way to Turkey from Central Asia. This bread pudding uses sour cherries and has very few other ingredients. You will find yourself sneaking into the refrigerator to eat it day and night! This recipe is ideal for a buffet, or you can halve it for smaller gatherings. Let the bread dry out the night before preparing this pudding. The finished recipe has to be refrigerated overnight. Allow two slices of bread per person and serve with whipped cream.

Serves 8 to 9. Makes 32 to 36 pieces.

16 to 18 slices white sandwich bread
2 to 3 tablespoons butter, softened to room temperature
2 (1 pound, 8-ounce/24-ounce) jars or cans pitted sour cherries
3½ cups sugar
1 cup whipped cream

Remove the crust from the bread and cut each slice in half. Leave bread out overnight to dry out.

Preheat oven to 350°F. Layer the bread on a cookie sheet and spread both sides with butter. Bake bread, turning once, until golden brown, about 10 to 13 minutes. Remove from heat and let cool.

Drain cherries, reserving the liquid. You should have about 2 1/2 cups of cherry liquid. Add enough water to make a total of 4 cups of liquid. Place liquid in a pot, add sugar, and bring to a boil. Reduce heat and simmer, uncovered for 10 minutes, stirring to dissolve sugar.

Add cherries, mix well, and cook for a minute. Remove from heat and set aside. Arrange toasted bread in one layer in a large (15 x 10 x 2-inch) Pyrex baking dish (the bread will expand when cherries and syrup are poured on). Ladle syrup over the bread and spoon cherries around the bread slices. Set aside to cool. Cover and refrigerate overnight.

The next day, turn bread over with a metal spatula. Before serving, arrange bread slices on a serving dish and top each piece of bread with about 5 cherries and a dollop of whipped cream.

Note: Nur uses Marco Polo Bulgarie brand cherries. I sometimes use dark Morello cherries in light syrup. These are sweeter so I cut back the sugar to 2 or 3 cups (or to taste).

108

sultan's pudding with pistachios
Hünkar Muhallebesi
İstanbul

This recipe combines pistachio nuts with milk, mastic, sugar, and vanilla. It is from Elvan Baransel.

Serves 10

10 ounces skinned, unsalted pistachio nuts, coarsely chopped in the food processor
4 cups milk
2 to 3 small pieces of mastic
⅓ cup plus 1 tablespoon sugar
1 teaspoon vanilla
½ cup cornstarch
⅓ cup plus two tablespoons water, divided
1 envelope gelatin
Dash of cinnamon

Lightly spray a 9 x 13 x 2-inch Pyrex baking dish. Line the dish with plastic wrap on the bottom and up the sides. Evenly spread the nuts over the plastic wrap, covering the bottom of the pan. (Use your fingertips to spread them around.) Set aside.

In a 3-quart pot, combine the milk, mastic, sugar, and vanilla and mix well. Cook over medium heat, stirring occasionally, for about 7 to 9 minutes and let the pudding come to a boil.

Mix the cornstarch with 1/3 cup of water. Mix gelatin with 2 tablespoons of hot water. Add the cornstarch mixture to the pot, stirring constantly, and cook until it starts to thicken. Stir in the gelatin, whisking well.

Remove pan from the heat, and using a large ladle, pour the pudding gently over the nuts. Let mixture cool; then refrigerate overnight.

Before serving, turn pudding upside down onto a rectangular serving plate large enough to hold it. Gently remove the baking pan and plastic wrap. Cut into squares and serve with berries.

tulumba dessert
Tulumba Tatlısı
İstanbul

When I first tasted these delicious syrupy sweets, they reminded me of Amish funnel cakes (fried dough). Serve with ice cream and berries.

Serves 8. Makes about 30 to 35 pieces.

Syrup:
4 cups sugar
2 cups water
1 tablespoon freshly squeezed lemon juice

Pastry:
1 cup water
1 tablespoon butter
¼ teaspoon sea salt
1 cup flour
2 tablespoons cornstarch
3 large eggs
4 to 6 cups canola oil, for frying

To Prepare the Syrup:
Place sugar and 2 cups water in a pot and bring to a boil. Reduce heat to simmer and stir in the lemon juice. Cook, uncovered, for 15 minutes, stirring occasionally. Remove from heat, transfer to a large bowl, and let cool for a few hours.

To Prepare the Pastry:
In a 2-quart pan, combine 1 cup water, butter, and salt and bring to a boil, mixing well. Reduce heat to low and slowly add the flour, stirring constantly with a wooden spoon, until you have a smooth, thick dough (that resembles choux pastry), about 5 to 6 minutes. Remove pan from the heat and place the dough on a work surface. Sprinkle the cornstarch over the dough and knead until well blended. Make a hole in the center of the dough, and add one egg, blending well. Repeat with the other two eggs, blending well between each addition until no lumps remain. The result is a soft dough.

In a large frying pan, heat 4 cups of oil to lukewarm (about 110°F); remove from heat. Transfer the dough to a pastry bag with a large star-shaped tip. Return the pan to medium-low heat, and pipe the dough into the frying pan in 1 1/2-inch lengths, eight to ten pieces at a time.

When they start to rise, raise the heat to medium and continue to fry on both sides, turning them until they are golden brown. Gently remove from the oil with a slotted spoon and drain well on paper towels for a minute. Drop them into the cold syrup, stirring well for 3 to 4 minutes.

Remove the pan from the heat to let the oil cool to lukewarm in between each batch. Each time you add a new batch to the syrup, push the newly fried ones to the bottom of the syrup bowl.

Remove to a serving platter and serve with ice cream and berries.

turkish bread pudding
Ekmek Tatlısı
Thrace region

The ingredients for this bread pudding are typical of many other bread pudding recipes, but the lemon-flavored sugar syrup makes it different. Since bread is the "staff of life" in Turkey it is never wasted, even the stale or tired pieces. This is an excellent way to use stale bread. Prepare a day in advance; this pudding is always better served the next day.

Serves 7 to 8

2 cups cold whole milk
7 ounces stale white bread
3 large eggs at room temperature
3 tablespoons butter, melted, cooled to room temperature
2 tablespoons sugar
1 teaspoon vanilla

Syrup:
1 cup water
1½ cups sugar
2 teaspoons freshly squeezed lemon juice

4 tablespoons coarsely chopped pistachio nuts or coconut, to garnish

Pour the cold milk over the stale bread and let the bread absorb it, about 30 minutes. Try to crumble the bread with your hands. (It is easy to crumble once the bread has absorbed the milk.) Transfer to a mixing bowl. Add eggs, butter, sugar, and vanilla and mix with an electric mixer for a minute or two.

Preheat oven to 350°F. Grease a 7 1/2 x 11-inch baking dish. Pour the bread mixture into the prepared baking dish, smooth the top with a rubber spatula, and bake for 60 to 70 minutes or until the top is golden brown. During this time, the middle of the bread pudding may rise up; if it does, just prick it with a toothpick (you may have to do this several times).

To Prepare the Syrup:

Place 1 cup of water in a medium-size pan. Add the sugar and cook over medium heat, uncovered, stirring constantly. When the syrup begins to boil, stir in the lemon juice, mixing well. Reduce heat to simmer and cook, uncovered, for 15 minutes. Remove from heat and set aside. Just before removing the pudding from the oven, heat the syrup again.

Remove pudding from the oven and evenly ladle the hot syrup over the bread pudding, letting it absorb. When the pudding has cooled, cut it into 15 equal pieces and decorate with pistachio nuts or coconut.

Note: To make stale bread, divide a whole loaf into 4 or 5 pieces and remove crusts. Arrange pieces on a baking dish. Set aside, uncovered, for 2 days.

113

aegean

The Aegean shore and magnificent coastline are among the loveliest landscapes in Turkey. The region is located in the west part of the country and is bounded by the Aegean Sea. The main cities in the region are: Kütahya, Afyonkarahisar, Manisa, Izmir, Uşak, Aydın, Denizli, and Muğla.

The mild climate of the Aegean region is suitable for growing many vegetables and fruits, which fill the weekly markets that are set up all along the summer-resort towns and villages of the Aegean shoreline. Villagers sell their high-quality fresh vegetables, fruits, local cheeses, olives, nuts, and handicrafts.

Aegean figs and seedless grapes are of the highest quality, and are known worldwide. Grapes are also grown for red wine production in the province of Denizli.

Olives are a common staple, and a large variety is available in the Aegean region. They are part of everyday life and are often served with breakfast or as a garnish for salads. The coastal city of Urla, which lies in the province of Izmir, is known for its olive oil, which is produced in the region, and many of Urla's olive oil factories trace their history to the beginnings of olive oil production. Olive oil has been used for cooking in Turkey for over 2,000 years. Thanks to this usage (and the healthy qualities of Turkish ingredients), Turkey has a low rate of heart disease. A typical Aegean dish includes vegetables and greens sautéed in olive oil.

The region is also home to a variety of cheeses, which are served with breakfast and used in cooking or to fill boereks and desserts. These include ricotta, *tulum* (which is similar to pecorino Romano and produced in Bergama, in the Izmir province), and *kelle* or basket cheese (a soft, buttery, white cheese).

Seafood commonly takes the place of lamb as the staple meat (though lamb is still used). The most common varieties are: sardines, red mullet, flounder, shrimp, octopus, squid, and mussels (mussels being the most frequently used). Some of the most popular seafood dishes are: Fish in White Sauce (page 152), stuffed squid, shrimp stew, sardines wrapped in grape leaves, stuffed mussels, octopus salad, and salted fish.

Vegetables and greens are also a vital element of local cuisine. These are frequently sautéed in olive oil and served at room temperature, or combined with legumes, rather than meat as is common in the eastern parts of Turkey. As a result, Aegean cuisine is typically very healthful. Greens are such an important staple in the cuisine of the province of Izmir, for example, that their tables are known as "green tables."

Beautiful Izmir, capital of the Aegean region, is the third largest city in Turkey. It has a history that goes back almost 5,000 years and it has been the home of 36 different civilizations. Izmir has been influenced by its Cretan, Bosnian, Albanian, and Sephardic-Jewish populations, and the recipes of these cultures have been adapted into the local cuisine: baby zucchini, fresh black-eyes peas, purslane, dandelion, nettles, beet greens, fennel, shrimp stews, and Stuffed Squid were introduced by the Cretans; several kinds of boerek originated in Bosnia; the Albanians contributed lamb baked in yogurt sauce, Albanian liver, and lamb kebab; and Sephardic Jews brought dishes like spinach and leek patties, zucchini frittata, spinach with white beans, quince pâté, falafel, and a boerek called *boyoz*.

Beach in Kemer © Dareon

Much like the rest of Turkey, legumes (peas, beans and lentils), grains, and lamb dishes feature prominently in Aegean cuisine. This is particularly true in the city of Uşak, which is home to dishes such as: Tarhana Soup, Green lentils with fine bulgur, hot chicken soup, and black-eyed peas pilaf, and Lamb Cooked in Earthenware (page 143).

The use of black-eyed peas in this region is common, especially in the city of Aydın (to the south of Izmir), which also specializes in a dish called *Ekmek Dolması*, Bread Stuffed with Spiced Beef (page 148). To the northeast of Izmir, the Manisa province is known for ground meat patties cooked on a charcoal grill. Other specialties include a variety of eggplant dishes and boereks.

The neighboring provinces of Kütahya and Afyon also have rich local cuisines, and share these dishes: meat sausages with garlic and spices, lentil pies, tahini and walnut boerek, pumpkin jam, *lokum* (Turkish delight) with cream, and bread *kataifi*. Lamb is more commonly used in this area.

artichokes with shelled fava beans

Zeytinyağlı Enginarlı iç Bakla
Izmir

This dish is traditionally prepared on special occasions. When Nur was growing up, her family always knew that important people were coming for dinner if her mother made this dish. Now, Nur serves it as an appetizer for diplomatic dinners.

Sometimes called broad beans, fava beans are large, flat, light beans about 8-inches long. This recipe calls for frozen fava beans, which can be found in Chinese markets. When cooking the delicate-skinned beans, add water gradually to prevent them from falling apart. Artichokes are thistles with an edible flower. When selecting artichokes, choose ones that have tightly packed, crisp leaves with bright coloring.

Serves 6

9¾ cups water, divided
Freshly squeezed juice of 1½ lemons, divided into juice of 1 lemon and juice of
    ½ lemon
1 tablespoon flour
6 fresh artichokes
1 cup extra-virgin olive oil, divided
6 pearl onions, peeled and halved
Sea salt
2½ teaspoons sugar, divided
1 pound shelled, defrosted fava beans
1 large onion, finely chopped
3 tablespoons finely chopped fresh dill

121

Place 3 cups of water in a large bowl with the juice of 1 lemon, the lemon itself, and 1 tablespoon of flour. Mix well and set aside.

Cut the stem off the base of an artichoke. Remove the outer leaves of the artichoke by pulling them down until they snap off. Using a large knife, cut the artichokes in half crosswise, discarding the top half. Remove the leaves from the bottom half, leaving about a 1-inch base attached to the heart. Using a paring knife, trim the dark green leaf stubs from the top and bottom of the heart. Using a teaspoon, remove the hairy choke from the artichoke hearts. Drop the heart into the bowl of water, lemon juice, and flour to prevent discoloring. Repeat using the rest of the artichokes. Discard everything but the hearts.

In a medium-size saucepan, heat 1/2 cup of olive oil. Add pearl onions and sauté for 6 to 7 minutes over medium heat, stirring occasionally. Remove pan from heat. Arrange the artichoke hearts on the bottom of the saucepan, side by side. Spoon the onions evenly over the artichoke

hearts. Sprinkle with 1/4 teaspoon salt and 1 teaspoon sugar. Add 2 cups of hot water and the juice of 1/2 lemon. Place a piece of parchment paper over the entire surface, then cover the pan and cook over medium-low heat for 40 to 45 minutes until the artichokes are tender. If needed, cook for an additional 5 to 10 minutes. Remove from heat and set aside to cool.

Place 4 cups of water in a medium-size saucepan and bring to a boil. Turn off the heat and add the fava beans. Let sit for 5 minutes, remove beans, drain well, and then rinse them in cold water. To remove the skins, make an opening along the top of one side of each bean with the tip of a knife or with your fingertips and gently squeeze beans out from the bottom to the top.

When all beans are skinned, heat 1/2 cup of olive oil in a medium-size pan, add the chopped onions and sauté, stirring, for 6 to 7 minutes on medium heat. Lower the heat and cook for another 3 to 4 minutes. Stir in 1/2 teaspoon salt and 1 1/2 teaspoons sugar. Mix well; add skinned beans and 1/2 cup warm water. Cook, covered, over low heat (the beans are delicate). When all the water has been absorbed, add 1/4 cup of hot water and continue cooking, checking from time to time and shaking the pan from side to side using the handles. When the water has once again been absorbed, test one bean to see if it is tender. If it is not, add a little more water and cook for a few more minutes. Remove from heat and let cool.

Transfer the artichoke hearts and pearl onions to a serving platter. Spoon the beans over and around the hearts and sprinkle with fresh chopped dill.

122

stuffed zucchini flowers

Kabak Çiçeği Dolması
Bodrum and throughout the Western Aegean

Astonish your friends with this fabulous traditional dish, which is a true sweet and succulent delicacy. Preparing the filling a day ahead makes the dish easier to make. In Turkey, Nur gets to the green grocer early in the morning and buys the flowers while they are very fresh and open. In New York, she goes to the farmers' market, and has found that the flowers are twice the size of those available in Turkey. Some of them even have baby zucchinis attached and she cooks these with the flowers. (Large flowers may need two teaspoons of filling.) Be sure to check each flower for bugs and remove any you find.

Serves 6. Makes 20 to 25.

⅓ cup plus 2 tablespoons extra-virgin olive oil
2 medium onions, grated
4 to 5 cloves garlic, finely chopped
2 medium tomatoes, peeled and grated
3 teaspoons sugar

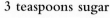

¾ cup uncooked medium-grain rice, soaked for 30 minutes in salted water to cover
7 to 8 scallions, finely chopped
20 to 25 zucchini flowers
½ cup fresh Italian flat-leaf parsley, washed, drained, dried, stems removed and set
    aside, finely chopped
½ cup fresh mint leaves, washed, drained, dried, stems removed and set aside,
    finely chopped
½ cup fresh dill, washed, drained, dried, stems removed and set aside, finely chopped
1¼ cups water
1 lemon, cut into 6 wedges

In a large skillet, heat 1/3 cup of olive oil. When hot, sauté the onions and garlic for 2 to 3 minutes, stirring constantly. Add the tomatoes and continue to cook for another 3 to 4 minutes, mixing well. Add the sugar, rice, and the chopped scallions, mint, parsley, and dill leaves. Mix well and remove pan from the heat. (This can be done a day in advance).

Pick over the flowers and remove any spindly filaments from inside, the stalks, and the leaves. Gently rinse the flowers and turn them upside down to get rid of excess water. Place a teaspoon of rice stuffing in each flower (large flowers may need more). Be careful not to over-stuff or the flowers may split as the rice expands.

As you fill each flower, bring the petals together over the filling; gently twist them together, and tuck the twist under to prevent the flower from opening up.

Line the bottom of a large skillet with the reserved parsley, dill, and mint stems (this prevents the flowers from sticking or burning). Arrange the flowers on top, side-by-side and twist-side down. Sprinkle with a little salt. Drizzle with 2 tablespoons of olive oil and carefully pour in the water. Cut a round piece of parchment paper to fit just inside the skillet and lay over the flowers. Bring the water to a boil for a minute or two and then reduce heat to simmer. Cover, and cook for 25 to 30 minutes.

Remove pan from the heat and let flowers cool for two hours in the skillet. Arrange on a serving platter and decorate with lemon wedges.

black-eyed peas with garlic and lemon

Börülce Teletoru
Muğla and throughout the Southwest Aegean

With their light, smooth texture and subtle savory flavor, black-eyed peas can be identified by their kidney-shape, creamy color, and a black marking that gives them their name. Black-eyes peas are very low in fat and are an excellent source of folic acid. This juicy appetizer can be served hot, warm, or cold.

Serves 4 to 6

¼ cup extra-virgin olive oil
1 large onion, finely chopped
2 tablespoons flour
1 tablespoon tomato paste
3 cups water plus more if needed
1 cup dried black-eyed peas, soaked in water to cover for 2 to 3 hours, drained
Freshly squeezed juice of ½ to 1 lemon, to taste
5 to 6 cloves garlic, finely chopped
Sea salt
2 tablespoons finely chopped Italian flat-leaf parsley

Heat the oil in a 3-quart pot, and sauté the onion, stirring, for 6 to 7 minutes over medium heat. Add flour and cook for another 2 to 3 minutes, then stir in the tomato paste and mix well. Add the water and bring to a boil. Reduce heat to simmer, add black-eye peas, cover, and cook over medium-low heat for 30 to 40 minutes. Stir in the lemon juice, garlic, and salt to taste. Mix well and cook, covered, until soft, 10 to 15 minutes. The liquid that remains gives the dish its juicy texture. (If the black-eyed peas absorb all the water and are still not cooked through, add warm water 1/4 cup at a time and continue cooking until they are tender.) Place in a serving bowl and garnish with chopped parsley.

dandelion salad

Radika Salatası
Izmir

Dandelion greens have long, slender, green leaves with saw tooth edges. They have a subtle bitterness, and taste best when they are young. Boiling them makes them tender and removes some of their bitterness.

Serves 2 to 4

1 bunch dandelion greens, thick stems removed
3 cups water
1 teaspoon sea salt
2 tablespoons freshly squeezed lemon juice
2 garlic cloves, minced
¼ cup extra-virgin olive oil

Wash and drain dandelion greens. Coarsely chop. Place the water and salt in a 2-quart saucepan and bring to a boil. Add the drained dandelion greens and cook over medium heat for 6 to 7 minutes, or until tender. Drain and transfer to a serving platter.

In a bowl, whisk together the lemon juice, garlic, salt to taste, and olive oil.

Pour dressing over the dandelion greens and serve.

125

purslane salad with garlicky yogurt

Yoğurtlu Semizotu Salatası
Bodrum and throughout the Aegean

Purslane is a plant with small green flowers, reddish stems, and a slightly sour, salty taste. The leaves can be cooked as a vegetable or used in salad. This crunchy salad is commonly used as an appetizer all along the coast and served with rustic bread. If you cannot find purslane, baby spinach can be substituted. This dish is excellent for vegetarians.

Serves 4

4 cups purslane leaves with tender stems, cut into 1-inch lengths
1 cup plain yogurt
3 to 4 cloves garlic, mashed
Sea salt
2 to 3 tablespoons extra-virgin olive oil
1 teaspoon mild Aleppo pepper

Wash purslane a few times and drain well; wrap in a double layer of paper towels to dry. Place the purslane in a large bowl.

In a small mixing bowl, combine the yogurt, garlic, and salt to taste. Let mixture stand for 5 or 6 minutes so the flavors can blend. Check salt and adjust if desired. Pour yogurt mixture over the purslane and toss to mix well. In a small bowl, mix the olive oil and the Aleppo pepper, and pour over the salad, mixing gently. Serve immediately.

Variations: This salad can be made with lemon vinaigrette, omitting the yogurt: mix 2 to 3 minced cloves garlic, 2 tablespoons of freshly squeezed lemon juice, 1/3 cup of extra-virgin olive oil, sea salt, and freshly ground pepper to taste. Prepare the purslane as instructed above and toss well with the vinaigrette.

If desired, 2 medium tomatoes cut into 1/2-inch cubes, 4 scallions, thinly sliced crosswise, and 1/2 cup of canned chickpeas, washed and drained, can be added to the salad to make a light, nourishing dish for summer dining.

spinach roots with beets

Pancarlı Ispanak Kökü
Izmir

Bunch spinach is the correct term for spinach root, which is available in Chinese and Middle Eastern groceries. Spinach root is the reddish part of the bottom of the spinach plant. It does not refer to the actual roots that grow underground. There is no substitute for spinach roots, and note that beets always taste better when cooked fresh.

Serves 4

2 pounds spinach with roots (to make 1 pound spinach roots)
5½ cups water, divided
1½ teaspoons sea salt, divided
1 pound (5 to 6) beets, of similar size
⅓ cup freshly squeezed lemon juice
3 to 4 cloves garlic, minced
1 tablespoon extra-virgin olive oil
½ teaspoon sugar
Freshly ground pepper

Prepare the spinach by removing any damaged outer leaves and stems. Remove the leaves and save them to use in other recipes. Gently remove and discard the root ends, leaving the reddish stems intact. Cut the stems and reddish roots into 1-inch lengths; wash and drain well to remove soil or sand. Place 1 1/2 cups of water in a 2-quart pot along with 1/2 teaspoon of salt and bring to a boil. Add spinach stems and roots, lower heat to simmer and cook uncovered for 5 to 6 minutes. Drain well and let cool.

Wash beets and remove stems and root ends. Cut greens away and save them to use in salads.

Heat 4 cups of water in a 2-quart pot with 1/2 teaspoon salt. Add beets, bring to a boil, cover and reduce heat to simmer. Cook on medium-low heat for 40 to 50 minutes until beets are cooked. Test with a toothpick; if it is easy to insert, beets are done. Drain beets and let cool. Slip off the beet skins under running water to prevent purple fingers. Cut beets into round slices.

Prepare dressing in a small bowl: mix lemon juice, garlic, olive oil, sugar, 1/2 teaspoon of salt, and pepper to taste. Arrange the sliced beets in the middle of a round platter and place spinach roots around the beets. Pour the dressing over and serve.

village salad

Köy Salatası
Ayvalık

The villagers of Ayvalık use vegetables from their gardens to make this summer salad. Arugula (also known as rocket) has a peppery flavor, and the leaves resemble those of dandelions.

Serves 6 to 8

1 cup ricotta salata, or other firm white cheese, cut into ½-inch squares
3 large tomatoes (about 1 pound 4 ounces), washed and cut into ¾-inch squares
4 Japanese cucumbers or 1 English cucumber, washed, peeled, halved lengthwise, and sliced
1 medium Spanish onion, cut into rings
1 green bell pepper, washed, seeded, cut into bite-size pieces
1 red bell pepper, washed, seeded, cut into bite-size pieces
½ pound baby arugula, washed and drained
10 pitted black olives

Dressing:
2 tablespoons red wine vinegar
Freshly squeezed juice of ½ lemon
1 teaspoon Dijon mustard
Sea salt
Freshly ground pepper
⅓ cup plus 2 tablespoons extra-virgin olive oil

In a large salad bowl, combine white cheese, tomatoes, cucumbers, Spanish onion, green and red bell peppers, baby arugula, and olives.

In a small bowl, whisk together red wine vinegar, lemon juice, mustard, and salt and pepper to taste. Slowly whisk in olive oil, mixing well. Pour over salad. Toss well and serve as an appetizer or side dish.

zucchini with garlic, yogurt, and walnuts

Cevizli Kabak Ezmesi
Aydın

Light and luscious, zucchini is great for summer entertaining. It is paired with garlic and other ingredients to make this tasty dish. Zucchini are mild and sweet, and come in a variety of colors that range from dark green to yellow to nearly black. Turkish zucchini are short and fat, making them easier to stuff.

Serves 2 to 4

1 pound pale green zucchini
4 tablespoons extra-virgin olive oil, divided
¼ teaspoon sea salt
1 cup plain strained yogurt (page 237)
2 to 3 cloves garlic, minced with ¼ teaspoon salt
½ to ¾ cup ground walnuts
1 tablespoon mayonnaise
3 tablespoons finely chopped fresh dill
½ teaspoon Aleppo pepper

130

Scrape the zucchini from top to bottom on all sides using a vegetable scraper or fork; they should look striped. Trim the ends off the zucchini. Wash and pat dry with paper towel. Grate the zucchini with the coarse side of a grater.

Heat 3 tablespoons olive oil in a medium-size skillet over medium heat. Add grated zucchini and salt and sauté for 8 to 10 minutes or until zucchini is cooked and no liquid is left in the skillet. Remove from heat and let cool. Once cool, stir in the yogurt, garlic, walnuts, and mayonnaise and mix well. Taste and add more salt, if needed. Arrange mixture on a serving platter and top with finely chopped dill.

Mix 1 tablespoon olive oil with the Aleppo pepper and drizzle over the top of the zucchini mixture.

black-eyed pea soup with lamb and noodles

Börülce Çorbası

Izmir

This rich soup is usually served in small portions as an appetizer or it can be served as a meal in itself. The lamb, black-eyed peas, and pasta make it filling. If the soup becomes too thick, thin it by adding more stock. Black-eyed peas are named for the black spot on each pea that looks somewhat like an eye. They may have originated in Asia or North Africa, where they were a staple food for Greeks and Romans. Spanish explorers and African slaves brought them to the southern United States.

Serves 6

2 tablespoons butter
10 ounces boneless leg of lamb, cut into ½-inch cubes
1 large onion, finely chopped
Sea salt
Freshly ground pepper
1 tablespoon tomato paste
5 cups hot chicken stock
1 cup dried black-eyed peas, soaked in cold water to cover 3 to 4 hours, and drained
½ cup angel hair pasta, broken into ½-inch pieces
Dash of cinnamon

131

Heat the butter in a 3-quart pot over medium heat. Add the lamb cubes and sauté until the color changes, 3 to 4 minutes.

Reduce heat to medium-low, cover, and cook for about 10 minutes. Lamb should begin to release its juice. Add the onion, mix well, and cook, 3 to 4 minutes. Season with salt and pepper to taste, and stir in the tomato paste. Mix well.

Add hot chicken stock and bring to a boil. Reduce heat to simmer, cover, and cook for 7 to 8 minutes. Add the peas and continue to cook, covered, 25 to 30 minutes. Check to make sure the peas are cooked and then add the pasta pieces. Mix well and continue to cook, covered, another 7 to 8 minutes.

Remove pot from heat and add cinnamon to the soup, mixing well. Let pot stand, covered, for 30 minutes, so flavors can blend, then serve.

deniz's chicken soup

Arabaşı Çorbası
Uşak, Denizli, and Afyon

This soup, which is a very traditional wedding and New Year's dish, comes from the grandmother of Deniz (Nur's daughter-in-law), who came from Uşak. It is also popular in Western and Central Anatolia. For New Year's Eve, the soup is traditionally prepared with turkey instead of chicken. It is filling, delicious, spicy, and well worth trying. The cooked dough adds a unique taste to the soup while the dried peppers add a kick.

Serves 8

1 whole chicken (about 2½ pounds), washed and drained
1 onion, peeled and quartered
1 bay leaf
1 carrot, peeled and halved
Sea salt
6 black peppercorns
10½ cups water, plus more if needed, divided
4 heaped tablespoons flour
2 tablespoons tomato paste
2 dried hot peppers or 1 teaspoon mild Aleppo pepper (optional)
3 tablespoons freshly squeezed lemon juice
1 tablespoon butter

Dough:
1½ cups chicken stock
1½ cups flour
1½ cups water
Sea salt
Freshly ground pepper

In a 4-quart pot, combine the chicken, onion, bay leaf, carrot, salt to taste, and peppercorns. Add 10 cups of water and bring to a boil. Remove any scum with a strainer or slotted spoon, as it accumulates. Reduce heat to medium-low and cook, covered, 50 to 60 minutes.

To Prepare the Dough:
In a small pan bring 1 1/2 cups chicken stock to a boil. Mix flour and 1 1/2 cups water in a saucepan and season with salt and pepper to taste. Whisk the stock into the mixture and cook over low heat. Continue to cook, stirring constantly, until the mixture thickens. Pour dough into a 9-inch round dish, and set aside to cool for a few hours.

Once cooked, remove the chicken from the pot and set aside to cool. Remove the skin and bones and shred the chicken into bite-size pieces. Strain the stock into a large bowl. You should have 7 cups of stock left (if not, add water).

Place 1/2 cup water and 4 heaped tablespoons of flour in a small bowl. Mix well and set aside.

Place the strained chicken stock, tomato paste, and hot peppers or Aleppo pepper into the pot. Bring to a boil over medium heat, stirring well. Slowly whisk in the flour mixture, mixing well. Cook over low heat until mixture thickens, about 10 to 15 minutes.

Check and adjust seasoning if needed. Stir in the lemon juice, butter, and shredded chicken pieces. Mix well and transfer to a large soup tureen.

To serve, bring cold dough plate to the table along with a serving scoop or spoon. Cut into 1/2-inch squares or spoon into individual soup bowls (3 to 4 pieces per serving).

Pour the hot chicken soup over the dough.

tarhana soup

Tarhana Çorbası
Uşak

Tarhana is a dried, pebble-like pasta created by Central Asian Turks, inspired by the climate and the geography in which they lived. It is one of the rare, centuries-old recipes still popular among the Turkish people. It is usually made in late summer (when tomatoes are in season) and it is laid out on rooftops on linen cloths to dry in the sun. Nur's grandmother used to keep it in cotton bags, as she stored all her grains). Nur makes *tarhana* every two years. This recipe is more than enough for a family of four to use for a year or so.

Tarhana is an essential, especially for Anatolians during Ramadan and the winter months. In wartime—particularly during the cold winter months—armies served it for breakfast because it was easy to carry and highly nutritious. In Turkey, every region has a different way of preparing *tarhana*, using different basic ingredients or additions. Recipes even differ from family to family. This recipe is from Usak, which is famous for the production of traditional *tarhana*. *Tarhana* acts as a thickening agent for simple soups, and it is also delicious fried! If you do not wish to wait weeks as your own dries, it can be found in specialty Turkish, Greek, or Middle Eastern markets.

Tarhana:
2 pounds 3 ounces onions, peeled and coarsely chopped
2 pounds 3 ounces tomatoes, washed and coarsely chopped
2 pounds 3 ounces red bell pepper, skin on, stems and seeds removed, washed, coarsely chopped
5 to 6 green cubanelle peppers, stem and seeds removed, washed, coarsely chopped

3 tablespoons sea salt, divided
14 ounces fine semolina
3½ cups (35.3 ounces) natural full-fat Greek or strained yogurt
   (available in Greek or Mediterranean markets and some supermarkets)
1 bunch fresh dill, washed, drained, dried, finely chopped
1 bunch fresh mint, washed, drained, dried, finely chopped
1 cup dried mint
½ cup red pepper paste (optional)
20 cups flour

Soup (Serves 4):
½ cup *tarhana*
6 cups chicken stock, divided
1 tablespoon tomato-pepper paste (available in Middle Eastern and Turkish markets)
Sea salt
Freshly ground pepper
2 tablespoons butter, divided
2 tablespoons canola oil
4 slices white bread, crusts removed, cut into ¼-inch squares
1 teaspoon Aleppo pepper

To make the tarhana:

Place the onions, tomatoes, red bell peppers, green cubanelle peppers, 1 tablespoon sea salt, in a very large pot and bring to a boil (the mixture will boil because of all the liquid in the vegetables). Reduce heat to medium and cook, covered, for an hour. Remove the pot from the heat, remove the lid, and let mixture cool. Purée with an immersion blender or in batches in a food processor.

Place mixture in a very large bowl and stir in semolina, yogurt, dill, fresh mint, dried mint, 2 tablespoons salt, and red pepper paste (if using). Mix well with a wooden spoon, and slowly stir in the flour (the dough will be a little sticky). Let dough rest in the kitchen for a few hours, then cover and keep in an air-conditioned room for 3 days. The yogurt allows the lactic acid to ferment.

Every day, stir the mixture with a wooden spoon.

On a clean work surface or a kitchen table covered with a clean tablecloth, place a tablespoon of dough and press it with your fingers to flatten. Continue until all the dough has been used.

Let pieces sit overnight and turn them over the next day (if you leave the windows open, especially on a dry day, they will dry faster). *Tarhana* will start changing color as it dries.

Break the pieces into smaller bite-size pieces and let them dry for another 3 to 4 hours.

Force the pieces through a sieve or strainer (don't worry if not all of them go through). To lessen the work, you can dry them completely and then put them in a food processor and process using the steel blade until you have small pieces. Arrange *tarhana* on a couple of deep baking pans and let sit to dry for about 2 weeks, stirring from time to time with a wooden spoon. Store them in airtight jars and keep in a cool place for use throughout the year.

To make the soup:

Soak the *tarhana* in a 2-quart pot with a cup of chicken stock for one hour. Mix well, place on medium-low heat, slowly add the rest of the chicken stock, stirring, and stir in the tomato-pepper paste. Mix well and cook about 10 to 15 minutes, stirring constantly, until the soup thickens and bubbles (the stirring prevents lumps). Season with salt and pepper to taste. (If the soup is too thick, add more chicken stock or water to thin it down.)

Meanwhile, in a frying pan, heat 1 tablespoon butter and 2 tablespoons canola oil and fry the bread cubes until golden brown. Remove from heat and set aside.

Pour the soup into a soup tureen and cover with the cooked bread cubes. In a small frying pan, heat 1 tablespoon butter, and stir in the Aleppo pepper. Mix well and pour over the soup in circles. Serve hot.

135

bulgur pilaf with vegetables

Sebzeli Bulgur Pilavı

Izmir

This is a healthful vegetarian dish. We love the combination of the bulgur and vegetables.

Serves 2 to 4

1 (½-pound) eggplant peeled in stripes, cut into ¾-inch cubes
Sea salt
½ cup extra-virgin olive oil
1 tablespoon butter
1 large onion, finely chopped
1 green bell pepper, seeds, ribs and stem removed, finely chopped
1 (½-pound) zucchini, ends removed, cut into ¾-inch cubes
2 medium tomatoes, finely chopped
Freshly ground pepper
1¾ cups hot water plus more if needed
1 cup coarse, uncooked bulgur

Sprinkle eggplant cubes with salt and set aside for 30 minutes. Rinse well, then drain.

Heat the oil and butter over medium heat in a 3-quart casserole dish; add onion and sauté for 6 to 7 minutes. Add green pepper and sauté for 3 minutes, then stir in zucchini and eggplant. Sauté the vegetables for 4 to 5 minutes. Stir in tomatoes and continue to sauté, 3 to 4 minutes. Season with salt and pepper to taste.

Add hot water, and stir in the bulgur. Reduce heat to low, cover the pot, and simmer until all the liquid is absorbed and holes appear, 15 to 20 minutes. Taste the bulgur; if needed, add a little more water and simmer for a few more minutes.

Remove from heat, remove lid, cover the top of the pan with a kitchen towel or a double layer of paper towels, replace lid and let rest 10 to 15 minutes. Uncover, stir well, and arrange on a serving platter. Serve with yogurt.

137

fried boereks with potato stuffing

Pişi
Izmir

Nur's dear friend, Gülgün Şensoy (who comes from Izmir) gave her this recipe, which was passed down to her from her mother. This dish is the Turkish version of an empanada or knish. It is a delicious teatime or breakfast pastry that will become a favorite with your family and friends. The texture of the dough in this recipe should be soft and malleable, like your ear lobe!

Serves 6 to 8. Makes 16 boereks.

2½ cups canola oil, divided
½ cup plain yogurt
2 large eggs
1 teaspoon baking powder
1 cup grated mild cheddar cheese
1½ teaspoons sea salt
1¾ cups plus 3 tablespoons flour, sifted
3 medium to large golden potatoes, boiled with skins on
½ teaspoon paprika
Sea salt
Freshly ground pepper
¼ cup sesame seeds

In a large bowl, mix 1/2 cup canola oil, yogurt, and eggs, using a whisk. Whisk in baking powder, cheese, and sea salt. Continue to beat the mixture slowly and add the flour a little at a time. Knead well to make a soft dough. Cover and let rest in a warm place until doubled in bulk, 1 to 2 hours.

While the dough is rising, peel the potatoes and finely grate them into a large bowl. Season with paprika and salt and pepper to taste. Set aside.

Divide dough into 16 balls of equal size and place on a lightly floured work surface. Using your fingertips, gently stretch each piece into a 5-inch circle. Spoon a tablespoon of the potato mixture into the center of each circle and fold into a half-moon shape, gently pressing the edges to seal. Spread the sesame seeds onto a plate or pie pan. Brush the tops of the pastries with a little water and dip the tops in the sesame seeds, gently pressing down so they stick.

Heat 2 cups of oil in a deep frying pan and fry the pastries, sesame-seeds-side up, until golden brown. Drain well, sprinkle with sesame seeds, and serve hot.

Breakfast Variations: Leave the dough circles unfolded, omit potato filling, and fry in hot oil until golden brown. Serve with cheese and honey. Another option: brush the surface of the circles of dough with water and sprinkle with sesame seeds, covering the entire surface of the dough. Omit potato filling. Fry until golden brown and serve.

rice with green lentils

Yeşil Mercimekli Pirinç Pilavı
Throughout the Aegean

This healthful, easy dish uses few ingredients, and will complement any meat or poultry dish.

Serves 6 to 8

3 cups water
Sea salt
1 cup dried green lentils, soaked in cold water to cover 3 to 4 hours, drained
¼ cup canola oil
3 tablespoons butter
2 medium onions, finely chopped
Freshly ground pepper
1½ cups uncooked extra-long-grain rice, soaked in warm salted water for 30 minutes, drained
3 cups warm chicken stock

In a medium-size saucepan, bring 3 cups of lightly salted water to a boil. Reduce heat to low, add lentils, cover, and simmer for 20 minutes. Drain well and set aside.

Heat oil and butter in a 3-quart saucepan over low heat; add onions and sauté for about 15 minutes. Season with salt and pepper to taste, stir in the rice, and continue cooking for 3 minutes. Mix in the lentils and warm chicken stock. Bring to a boil, cover, reduce heat to simmer, and cook until all the liquid has been absorbed, about 15 to 20 minutes.

Remove from heat, remove lid and place 2 layers of paper towels or a clean kitchen towel over the rice and replace the lid. Let rest 10 minutes. Gently stir with a wooden spoon and serve with any meat or poultry dish.

green lentil pies

Mercimekli Afyon Böreği
Afyon

These lentil pies are a specialty of the Aegean region. They are called "mouth open" because of the way the filling shows through. The combination of lentils and dough has an unexpected great taste, and is healthful too. This is a wonderful vegetarian dish, although meat can be substituted for the lentils. The dough for these pies must sit overnight, so start this recipe the night before you plan to eat them.

Serves 4 to 5. Makes 10 pies.

1 stick butter, melted
½ cup whole milk
1 teaspoon sea salt
1½ cups plus 2½ tablespoons flour, sifted

Filling:
2½ cups water
Sea salt
½ cup dried green lentils, soaked for 3 to 4 hours in cold water to cover, drained
3 tablespoons canola oil
1 medium onion, finely chopped
Freshly ground pepper
½ teaspoon Aleppo pepper
1 large egg yolk
1 tablespoon water

Mix the melted butter, milk, and salt in a large bowl. Gradually add flour to make a soft dough. Divide the dough into 10 equal balls, and place in a baking dish. Cover with plastic wrap and refrigerate overnight.

Place 2 1/2 cups of water in a pot and bring to a boil. Add a pinch of salt, reduce heat to simmer, and add the lentils. Cook, covered, for 20 minutes (or more if the lentils are not cooked). Drain well.

Heat the oil on low in a frying pan and sauté onion for 15 to 17 minutes. Stir in lentils and sauté for 1 to 2 minutes, mixing well. Remove from heat. Season with Aleppo pepper and salt and pepper to taste. Set aside.

Preheat oven to 350°F. Spray or grease a jellyroll pan. Place the pieces of dough on a lightly floured surface, one at a time. Using your fingertips, gently stretch each piece into a 5 to 6-inch circle. Place 1 1/2 to 2 tablespoons of the lentil filling in the center or each circle, leaving a 1-inch border around the filling. Gently lift the borders, pleating the edges around the filling and leaving the center open.

In a small bowl, mix the egg yolk with 1 tablespoon of water to make an egg wash. Brush the pies with the egg wash.

Arrange the pies on the greased pan and bake until golden brown, about 30 minutes. Serve with tea or as a lunch dish with a salad.

tea bread twists with tahini and molasses

Tahini Çörek

Kütahya

This is a delicious, unusual dish that combines yeast dough with a tahini and grape molasses filling. It is a favorite to serve with eleven o'clock coffee or afternoon tea, when it is common for Turkish ladies to get together.

Makes 18 to 24 pieces

¼-ounce package dry yeast
1 teaspoon sugar
1¼ cup warm water
½ cup warm milk
½ cup canola oil
2 large eggs, divided
½ teaspoon sea salt
2 cups sifted flour plus extra flour for dusting
1 tablespoon poppy seeds

Filling:
½ cup tahini
2 tablespoons canola oil
5 tablespoons grape molasses or
    brown sugar
1 cup coarsely chopped walnuts

Place the dry yeast in a small bowl with sugar and 1 cup warm water. Mix well, cover, and keep in a warm place for 15 to 20 minutes until mixture rises and foam forms on the surface.

Mix the warm milk, oil, 1 egg, salt, and flour in a large bowl. Add the yeast mixture to the bowl, blend well, cover with a kitchen towel, and put in a warm place until it has doubled in bulk, about 35 to 45 minutes.

To Prepare the Filling:

Heat the tahini and oil in a small pot for a few minutes, stirring constantly. Remove from heat and stir in the molasses or sugar, mixing well.

Preheat oven to 350°F. Line a jellyroll pan (about 16 x 11 inches) with parchment paper.

Punch down dough and knead on a lightly floured surface for 5 minutes. Divide dough into 6 equal pieces. Roll each piece out as thinly as you can, or until it is a rectangle about 10 inches long and 8 to 9 inches wide. Brush the surface of each rectangle with the tahini-molasses mixture. Sprinkle the top of each piece with 1/4 cup walnuts and roll into a long log shape. Bend each log into a "U" shape. Connect the ends and twist the two sides together, forming a twist. Tuck the ends under.

Lightly beat one egg. Brush each twist with the egg; then sprinkle with poppy seeds. Place twists on the prepared jelly roll pan and bake for 25 to 30 minutes, until golden brown. Transfer twists to a wire rack for a few minutes; cut each twist diagonally into 3 or 4 pieces. Serve warm with tea.

Variation: You can also shape the "logs" into pinwheel shapes.

lamb cooked in earthenware

Çömlek Kebabı
Uşak

This kebab variety is traditionally made in a *çömlek* (an earthenware pitcher with handles on both sides) and baked in an outdoor wood-burning oven. Any earthenware casserole dish or Dutch oven is suitable for preparing this recipe. Serve with fresh country bread or pita to dip in the delicious juices.

Serves 6 to 8

2 pounds boneless leg of lamb, cut into ¾-inch cubes
1 pound pearl onions, peeled
4 to 5 cloves garlic, halved
2 medium cubanelle peppers, seeds and ribs removed, coarsely chopped
4 large tomatoes, peeled, coarsely chopped
¼ cup olive oil
2 tablespoons butter, melted
Sea salt
Freshly ground pepper
½ teaspoon dried thyme
½ cup lukewarm water
5 medium golden potatoes, peeled and quartered

143

In a large bowl, combine lamb, onions, garlic, peppers, tomatoes, olive oil, melted butter, salt and pepper to taste, thyme, and water. Let stand for 30 minutes.

Place mixture in an earthenware casserole dish or Dutch oven. Bring to a boil over medium heat. Reduce heat to medium-low and cook, covered, about 1 1/2 hours. Uncover, push potatoes cut-side down, into the mixture. Replace the cover and cook for another hour or until the meat and vegetables are tender. Serve with rice and bread.

lamb elbasan with yogurt sauce

Elbasan Tava

Manisa

First introduced to the region by Macedonian settlers, this dish is wholesome and hearty. Lamb is topped with a yogurt sauce and red pepper flakes. For a gourmet presentation, arrange the lamb steaks on individual baking dishes and serve with a salad.

Serves 6

2 tablespoons canola oil
2 tablespoons butter
6 boneless lamb round steaks
    (about 2 pounds in total)
2 medium onions, finely chopped
4 cups hot water
Sea salt
Freshly ground pepper

Sauce:
1½ cups plain strained yogurt (page 237)
⅓ cup flour
1 large egg
2 large egg yolks
½ teaspoon red pepper flakes

In a 4-quart pot, heat oil and butter over medium heat and sauté the meat for 5 to 6 minutes on each side. Add onions and continue cooking for 3 to 4 minutes. Cover the pot and reduce heat to medium-low. Continue to cook until the meat releases its juices, about 15 to 20 minutes. Add 4 cups of hot water and salt and pepper to taste. Cook, covered, for 1 hour and 20 minutes or until tender.

Remove meat from the pot. Place in a baking dish, leaving space between steaks (or use individual baking dishes) and set aside. Preheat oven to 350°F. If there is more than 1 1/4 cups of liquid left in the pot, reduce cooking liquid by boiling until 1 1/4 cups remain. Remove from heat and strain into a bowl. Let cool until you can put your finger comfortably into the liquid.

To Prepare the Sauce:

Whisk strained yogurt, flour, and egg together in a 2-quart pot. Place pot over medium heat, then slowly whisk in the strained cooking liquid. Cook, whisking continuously, until sauce thickens and bubbles begin to show on the surface. Remove from heat and let cool until you can comfortably put your finger in the sauce. Whisk in egg yolks, one at a time, stirring well after each addition.

Pour sauce over lamb steaks, sprinkle with red pepper flakes and bake them until golden brown, about 20 to 25 minutes. Serve immediately with vegetables and rice.

Lamb Cooked in Earthenware

lamb stew with mastic

Sakızlı Kuzu Yahnisi
Izmir

Mastic (also called gum Arabic) is the crystallized resin from the *Pistacia lentiscus* tree. Since ancient times, it has been known for its healing properties. To quote author Diane Kochilas, "It has a wonderful deep aroma and flavor, at once woody, earthy, and musky, like incense." To use mastic in cooking, the rock-hard, somewhat sticky crystals have to be pounded—usually with a little sugar to keep them from sticking to the mortar and pestle or spice grinder. You can find mastic in Middle Eastern, Greek, or Turkish markets. This dish can be easily prepared in advance.

Serves 6 to 8

2 pounds boneless leg of lamb, cut into ¾-inch cubes
¼ cup extra-virgin olive oil or 3 tablespoons butter
1 large onion, finely chopped
2 cloves garlic, finely chopped
1 bay leaf
1 pound pearl onions, peeled
1 cup grated tomatoes, or fresh tomato purée
Sea salt
Freshly ground pepper
2 pieces mastic, ground with ¼ teaspoon sugar
½ cup hot water plus more if needed
1 tablespoon white vinegar
¼ teaspoon cinnamon

Wash lamb cubes and drain. Heat a 5- to 6-quart casserole dish over medium heat and add the lamb cubes without any butter or oil.

Stirring constantly, sauté the lamb in its own juices until it changes color, about 2 to 3 minutes. Reduce heat to medium-low (lamb will continue to release its juices), and continue cooking until the meat reabsorbs all the juices and no liquid is left in the pan. Stir in oil or butter, onion, garlic, bay leaf, and pearl onions. Sauté, stirring constantly, for 5 to 6 minutes. Stir in the tomatoes and season with salt and pepper to taste. Stir in the ground mastic and hot water. Simmer, covered, for 25 to 30 minutes. Add more water as needed.

During the last few minutes, stir in the vinegar and cinnamon, mixing well. Remove from the heat and let sit in the covered pot for 30 minutes before serving, to let the flavors blend.

lamb shanks with romaine lettuce and scallions

Kuzu Kapama
Izmir

Nur and her family eat this dish with a fork and spoon to enjoy the delicious sauce. Lamb shanks are the tenderest part of the lamb. You may discard the bones and any fat before serving. The recipe can be easily doubled.

Serves 2 as a main course

6 cups water
2 lamb shanks with bones (about 2 pounds total)
1 medium onion, peeled and kept whole
1 bay leaf
5 to 6 black peppercorns
4 small gold potatoes, peeled and halved
2 small carrots, peeled and cut into 1-inch long pieces
8 Romaine lettuce leaves
4 scallions, root end removed, cut into 1-inch long pieces
1½ tablespoons freshly squeezed lemon juice
2 teaspoons flour
Lemon wedges (optional)

Place 6 cups of water in a medium-size saucepan and bring to a boil. Add lamb shanks, onion, bay leaf, and peppercorns. Reduce heat to medium-low, cover, and cook for 1 1/2 hours until meat is tender. Add the potatoes and carrots, keeping them separate in the pan.

Place lettuce leaves and scallions over the vegetables. Cover and cook over medium-low heat for another 15 minutes. Remove the lettuce leaves and set aside.

Leaving the liquid in the pan, place the carrots in the center of a serving platter, the lamb shanks around the carrots, and the potatoes around the meat. Cover lamb with the cooked lettuce leaves.

In a small bowl, whisk together 1/4 cup cooking liquid, lemon juice, and flour. Pour into the saucepan with the remaining cooking liquid and cook over high heat, whisking for a few minutes until well blended and bubbling. Remove from heat and pour over the lamb shanks.

Serve in shallow pasta dishes with lemon wedges and lots of cooking liquid.

mini lamb kebabs

Çöp Kebabı
Izmir

This dish shows that fast can still be fresh and good. It was created in Izmir to sell to train passengers; when the train made a short stop, passengers could get off and grab a hot dish, get back on the train, and eat as they continued traveling. It was the beginning of fast food! Soak skewers the night before to save time.

Serves 4 to 6. Makes 12 kebabs.

1 pound boneless leg of lamb, cut into 1-inch cubes
3 tablespoons olive oil
3 cloves garlic, minced
1 tablespoon onion juice (finely grate an onion, press through sieve with back
    of a wooden spoon, save juice)
Freshly ground pepper
Sea salt

In a large bowl, combine the lamb, oil, garlic, onion juice, and pepper to taste. Cover and refrigerate overnight.

An hour before cooking, bring lamb to room temperature. Soak twelve 6-inch-long wooden skewers in water for 30 minutes to prevent them from burning. Thread 5 to 6 lamb cubes on each skewer. Heat a griddle. Over high heat, cook the skewered lamb for 2 to 3 minutes per side; add salt and pepper to taste. Serve with warm bread and a salad.

bread stuffed with spiced beef

Ekmek Dolması
Throughout the Aegean

This unusual dish is served on special occasions, at Sunday meals, or at family get-togethers. It looks complicated, but Nur's whole family loves it, so she makes it frequently. It is amazing what can be done with a simple loaf of bread! Start this recipe at least two days in advance.

Serves 6

10-ounce, round loaf of fresh white or brown bread (the bottom should be about
    6 inches across)
6 tablespoons canola oil

1 pound 2 ounces ground sirloin
1 large onion, finely chopped
1½ teaspoons paprika
Sea salt
Freshly ground pepper
⅓ cup pine nuts
⅓ cup coarsely chopped walnuts
4 tablespoons finely chopped Italian
    flat-leaf parsley
2½ cups chicken or beef stock
2 tablespoons butter

Sauce:
1 cup plain yogurt
2 cloves garlic, minced
½ teaspoon sea salt
2 tablespoons extra-virgin olive oil

Topping:
1 teaspoon Aleppo pepper
1 tablespoon butter

Cut a 3-inch round from the bottom center of the bread using a large cookie cutter or knife. Remove the cut crust and wrap it in plastic wrap to keep it from drying out. Use your fingers to hollow out the inside of the loaf, through the hole (leaving the crust intact). Shred the inside of the loaf into chunks or pieces, and place them on a plate for two days to dry out.

Process the dried chunks in the food processor to make breadcrumbs. Measure and reserve 1 cup of breadcrumbs and store the rest for use in another recipe.

To prepare the sauce, mix yogurt, minced garlic, salt, and olive oil in a bowl. Set aside.

In a medium saucepan, heat the oil over medium heat. Sauté the ground beef for 7 to 8 minutes, stirring occasionally. Add the onion; mix well and continue cooking for another 5 to 6 minutes. Season with paprika and salt and pepper to taste. Remove pan from heat and stir in the pine nuts, walnuts, breadcrumbs, and parsley; mix well. Spoon the beef mixture into the hollowed loaf, pressing gently so all the stuffing fits in. Cover the hole with the reserved round 3-inch piece of crust.

In a 10-inch round 6-inch-high pot, combine the stock and butter and bring to a boil.

Place a 4-inch by 2-inch ramekin upside down in the center of the pot; place the stuffed loaf upside down on top of the ramekin (the bottom with the cut piece is now at the top). Cover the pot and reduce heat to medium. Cook for 25 to 30 minutes, ladling the cooking liquid over the loaf every 4 to 5 minutes. There should be 1/4 cup of cooking liquid left in the pot before you turn off the heat. Turn the stuffed loaf onto a shallow serving dish with the cut piece at the bottom and slowly pour the remaining liquid over the top. Spoon the yogurt sauce over the loaf.

In a small saucepan or skillet, melt the butter and mix in the Aleppo pepper. When the mixture sizzles, pour it over the top. Cut the loaf into 6 equal slices and serve immediately.

sardines baked in clay

Kiremitte Sardalya

Izmir

A heavy clay dish that looks like a pie pan is used to cook this dish. Sardines, which are very popular in the Aegean region, are rich in heart-healthy omega-3 fatty acids, bone-building calcium, vitamin D, and vitamin B12. If possible, use fresh sardines from a fish vendor or specialty market. The addition of bell peppers gives this dish a slightly piquant flavor.

Serves 4

Olive oil or cooking spray to grease the baking dish
4 tomatoes, peeled and finely chopped
4 cloves garlic, finely chopped
5 scallions, root ends removed, sliced crosswise
1 green bell pepper, seeds, stems and ribs removed, finely chopped
1 red bell pepper, seeds, stems and ribs removed, finely chopped
4 tablespoons finely chopped Italian flat-leaf parsley
Sea salt
Freshly ground pepper
12 sardines, each about 6-inches long, cleaned, gutted, heads removed
½ cup extra-virgin olive oil
4 to 6 lemon wedges for garnish

Preheat oven to 375°F. Grease or spray a 10-inch round clay or other baking dish.

In a bowl, mix together the tomatoes, garlic, scallions, green and red bell peppers, parsley, and salt and pepper to taste.

Arrange half of the vegetables in the baking dish. Layer sardines on top, then cover with the rest of the vegetable mixture. Drizzle oil on top. Bake for 20 to 25 minutes until fish is cooked through. Serve with lemon wedges.

fish in white sauce

Sütlü Balık

Izmir

This dish is very flexible; you can select any white fish, such as haddock, sea bass, or lemon sole. As a nice touch for a dinner party, you can bake the fish, mushrooms, and mussels in six individual ovenproof dishes.

Serves 6

1 bay leaf
1 small onion, peeled, halved
1 carrot, peeled, coarsely chopped
3 or 4 sprigs Italian flat-leaf parsley
Sea salt
5 to 6 black peppercorns
2½ cups water
2 pounds white fish fillets
½ tablespoon olive oil
½ pound button mushrooms, wiped clean and halved
18 to 20 mussels, cooked, shelled (optional)

Sauce:
3 tablespoons butter
3 tablespoons flour
2½ cups milk
2 large egg yolks
4 ounces milk cheddar cheese, grated and divided

Place the bay leaf, onion, carrot, parsley sprigs, sea salt to taste, and peppercorns in a large skillet with 2 1/2 cups of water. Bring to a boil, reduce heat, cover, and cook for 5 minutes.

Place fish fillets in the skillet, cover and cook on low heat for 10 minutes. Remove from heat. Remove lid and let fish cool.

Heat oil in a small sauté pan over high heat, and sauté mushrooms for 5 minutes.

Place the fish, mushrooms, and mussels (if using) in a 9 x 13-inch baking dish. Cover and set aside.

Preheat oven to 375°F. Prepare a roux: heat the butter in a saucepan over medium-low heat. Stir in the flour, whisking constantly for 2 to 3 minutes. Be careful not to let the mixture turn dark brown or burn. Gradually add the milk, continuing to whisk constantly. When sauce begins to bubble, remove from heat and let cool until you can comfortably put a finger into it. Stir in egg yolks, one at a time, whisking well after each addition. Mix in half of the grated cheese, and add salt and pepper to taste.

Pour sauce over the fish, mushrooms, and mussels, making sure that everything is well coated. Sprinkle the remaining cheese over the top and bake, uncovered, until golden brown, about 20 to 25 minutes.

monkfish stew

Fener Balığı Yahnisi
Ayvalık

This Mediterranean-style fish stew is made with firm-textured monkfish. According to Aliza Green (*Field Guide to Seafood*) "monkfish are large, deepwater, bottom-dwelling primitive fish." They are also known as "poor man's lobster," and restaurants sometimes substitute them for lobster in salads and bisques. Everyone enjoys the texture and delightfully sweet flavor. Monkfish can be grilled, broiled, sautéed, or used in chowders or stews. This dish has the best flavor when served warm, not hot.

Serves 4

½ cup extra-virgin olive oil
1 large onion, finely chopped
3 cloves garlic, finely chopped
1 teaspoon finely chopped fresh thyme
4 medium tomatoes, peeled and finely chopped
2 cups fish stock
8 small golden potatoes, peeled, halved or quartered
1½ pounds monkfish fillets, cut into 1-inch medallions
Sea salt
Freshly ground pepper
1 tablespoon finely chopped Italian flat-leaf parsley

153

Heat the olive oil in a 3-quart casserole dish; add the onion and sauté for 3 to 4 minutes.

Stir in the garlic and thyme, mixing well, and continue to cook for a minute. Stir in the tomatoes, and cook for another 3 to 4 minutes. Stir in the fish stock and bring to a boil.

Reduce heat to medium-low, cover, and cook for 15 minutes.

Reduce heat to low, add the potatoes, fish, salt and pepper to taste, cover and simmer for 15 to 17 minutes or until potatoes are tender (not mushy).

Remove from heat and let stand, covered, for 30 minutes. Sprinkle with parsley and serve with rice or pasta.

shrimp and squid in lemon vinaigrette

Karidesli Kalamar
Izmir

This is a very simple seafood dish that should be served at room temperature. It is a perfect summer appetizer. Buy cleaned squid from your fish market or specialty store. Be careful not to overcook them or they will be tough and rubbery. To cut down on preparation time you can use precooked shrimp; this will save you the trouble of peeling, cleaning, and cooking.

Serves 6 to 8

2 pounds cleaned squid
1 teaspoon baking soda
1 teaspoon sugar
1 tablespoon freshly squeezed lemon juice
2 tablespoons olive oil

Dressing:
1 teaspoon lemon zest
¼ cup freshly squeezed lemon juice
1 teaspoon Dijon mustard
3 cloves garlic, minced
½ teaspoon sea salt
¼ teaspoon freshly ground pepper
½ cup olive oil
3 tablespoons finely chopped Italian flat-leaf parsley

1 pound peeled, cooked large shrimp, tails removed

Cut squid into 1/4-inch thick rings. Place in a shallow dish and mix with baking soda and sugar. Mix well, cover, and refrigerate for 2 hours. Rinse well, and drain.

Place lemon juice and oil in a 2-quart pot, over medium heat, and add squid rings. Mix well, cover, and cook for 2 minutes. Stir again, and test a squid ring to see if it is done; it should be opaque and tender. If not, cook for half a minute more. (Be careful not to overcook the squid rings or they will become rubbery.) Remove from heat and drain well.

To Prepare the Dressing:
In a bowl, whisk the lemon zest, lemon juice, Dijon mustard, garlic, salt and pepper to taste. Gradually whisk in olive oil, whisking constantly. Add the finely chopped parsley.

Arrange the shrimp and squid rings in a shallow round serving dish. Pour the dressing over them and toss well. Serve with a green salad.

eggplants with white cheese

Ege Usulü Patlıcan Silkme
Izmir

Eggplant is a delicious, fairly neutral, practically calorie-free vegetable, and it is very versatile in cooking. Turkish cooking has dozens and dozens of eggplant recipes, and this one is chock full of vegetables and cheese. Italian eggplants are small (about 4 to 5 inches long) and have very dark skin. Dutch eggplants can also be used for this recipe.

Serves 6

Water for soaking eggplant plus ⅓ cup
Freshly squeezed juice of 1 lemon
Sea salt
5 medium (about 2 pounds) Italian eggplants
2 large onions, thinly sliced into half circles
16 cloves garlic, slivered (quartered lengthwise)
2 green bell peppers, seeded, ribs removed, cut into ½-inch cubes
2 medium tomatoes, peeled, cut into ½-inch cubes
4 medium tomatoes, peeled and puréed
¾ cup extra-virgin olive oil
½ cup Turkish white cheese, Bulgarian cheese, or ricotta salata, cut into ¼-inch cubes
4 tablespoons finely chopped Italian flat-leaf parsley

157

Fill a large bowl with water and add the lemon juice and salt. Cut the stems off each eggplant. Leaving an inch of peel on the top and bottom, peel off 1/2-inch strips of skin, lengthwise, at 1/2-inch intervals, making a striped effect. Cut eggplant into 4 lengthwise slices and then cut them into 1-inch-thick crosswise pieces.

Place the eggplant pieces in the bowl of water and let sit for at least 30 minutes.

Line the bottom of a large skillet with the onion and garlic slices and top with the pieces of green pepper. Drain the eggplants, press them gently to get rid of any excess water, and lay them on the green peppers. Cover the eggplants with the cubed and puréed tomatoes.

Season with salt and add 1/3 cup water and the olive oil. Bring to a boil for one or two minutes, then turn heat to low, cover and continue to cook for 40 to 45 minutes, shaking the pan by the handles 3 or 4 times.

Arrange eggplants on a serving dish. When they are cool, add the cheese and parsley.

eggplant a la ayvalık

Çığırtma
Throughout the Aegean

This recipe is from Nur's dear friend Elvan Baransel's late mother-in-law Ceyda Baransel who lived in Ayvalık her whole life. The dish is simple but has a unique taste. The quality of the extra-virgin olive oil used in the recipes makes a big difference. Use vine-ripened tomatoes from a farmers' market or grocery store. Italian eggplants are curved, firm, small eggplants with deep purple skin.

Serves 4 to 6

6 medium (4- to 5-inch long) Italian eggplants
1 cup extra-virgin olive oil
4 large tomatoes, peeled and coarsely grated
10 cloves garlic, each cut into four lengthwise slices
Sea salt
Pinch of freshly ground pepper

Cut the stems off each eggplant. Leaving an inch of peel on the top and bottom, peel off 1/2-inch strips of skin, lengthwise, at 1/2-inch intervals, making a striped effect. Repeat until all the eggplants are striped.

Make four lengthwise slits into each eggplant starting an inch from the top and going to an inch from the bottom, but not deep enough to cut the eggplant into pieces. This allows all the flavors to penetrate the eggplants.

In a large skillet, heat the oil and fry the eggplants on all sides until golden brown. Add the tomatoes, garlic, and salt to taste and reduce heat to simmer. Cook, covered, until the eggplants are tender, about 30 to 35 minutes.

crustless zucchini pie

Fırında Mücver
Bodrum and Izmir

We love this hearty, vegetarian dish with zucchini, cheese, and fresh herbs. It can be made ahead so it is great for a party, brunch, potluck, or picnic.

Serves 6 to 8

Canola oil for greasing
1 bunch Italian flat-leaf parsley, washed, drained, dried, and finely chopped
1 bunch fresh dill, washed, drained, dried, and finely chopped
5 scallions, roots and damaged outer green leaves removed, finely sliced
1 cup crumbled white cheese (such as feta)
1 cup grated cheddar cheese
2 pounds unpeeled zucchini, grated coarsely
6 large eggs, beaten
1½ cups flour, sifted
½ cup olive oil
1 teaspoon baking powder
½ teaspoon Aleppo pepper

Preheat oven to 350°F. Grease a 9 x 13 x 2-inch baking pan.

In a large bowl, add parsley, dill, scallions, cheeses, and zucchini. Mix well.

Add eggs, flour, olive oil, and baking powder. Mix well.

Pour mixture into the prepared baking pan and spread evenly. Sprinkle with Aleppo pepper and bake 30 to 40 minutes until it has set. Remove from oven and let sit until it cools to room temperature. Cut into 2-inch squares and serve.

fresh okra with chickpeas

Nohutlu Bamya
Bodrum

This nourishing vegetarian dish is from Bodrum where Nur has a summer home. While shopping in the village vegetable market in Gündoğan, she purchased some very fresh okra and the vendor gave her this recipe. When she prepared it for her family, they loved it. Instead of cooking okra with chicken or lamb, the villagers of Bodrum use chickpeas, which makes the dish tastier and healthier.

Okra is a love/hate vegetable. Its flavor is a bit like eggplant mixed with green beans. Some people refer to okra as the "fuzzy" vegetable and many like it best when it is mixed with other ingredients. Native to Africa and Asia, Turkish okra is smaller than American okra. Okra is very perishable, so when you buy it, make sure it is as fresh as possible; make sure the pods have no bruises, and that they are tender but not soft. The best ones are only about 4 inches long.

Serves 4 to 6

½ cup extra-virgin olive oil
2 medium onions, finely chopped
4 to 5 cloves garlic, slivered (quartered lengthwise)
4 medium tomatoes, peeled, finely chopped or 1½ cups canned chopped tomatoes
2 teaspoons tomato paste
1½ pounds fresh medium-size okra
Freshly squeezed juice of 1 lemon
2 cups warm water
Sea salt
Freshly ground pepper
¾ cup canned chickpeas, rinsed and drained

Heat the olive oil in a large skillet over medium heat. Add the onions and garlic and sauté for 5 minutes, stirring constantly. Add the tomatoes and sauté for 7 to 8 minutes. Stir in the tomato paste, okra, lemon juice, and 2 cups of warm water. Season with salt and pepper to taste and bring to a boil. Lower heat, cover, and simmer for 30 to 35 minutes until the okra is tender. Stir in the chickpeas. Cook, covered, for 4 to 5 minutes. Remove from heat.

Arrange in a deep round serving dish and serve with tomato rice. Serve warm or at room temperature.

green tomato stew

Gök Domates
Aydın

This tasty dish is interesting because no water is used in the preparation. The vegetables cook in their own juices.

Serves 4 to 6

6 medium green tomatoes (about 1½ pounds)
¼ cup extra-virgin olive oil
1 large onion, finely chopped
2 green cubanelle peppers, stem, seeds, and ribs removed, finely chopped
2 medium red tomatoes, peeled and finely chopped
Sea salt
Freshly ground pepper
3 tablespoons medium-grain rice, washed and drained

Wash and drain the green tomatoes. Cut each tomato in half and each half into 3 equal pieces.

In a medium-size skillet, heat the olive oil and sauté the onions, stirring, for 5 to 6 minutes. Add the cubanelle peppers and red tomatoes and cook for another 3 to 4 minutes. Stir in the green tomatoes and season with salt and pepper to taste. Reduce heat and simmer, covered, 10 to 15 minutes. Stir in the rice. Cover and cook for another 15 to 20 minutes. Serve warm or cold.

cream pudding with coconut and walnuts

Afyon Kaymağı
Afyon

If you have never used mastic in your cooking you will be delighted by the subtle flavor it provides. This tasty make-ahead dessert uses coconut for added flavor. Coconut came to Turkey via the Silk Road.

Serves 4

1 piece of mastic
½ teaspoon sugar
8 tablespoons ground walnuts, divided
2 cups whole milk
⅜ cup sugar
¼ cup flour, sifted
½ cup heavy (or whipping) cream
2 tablespoons grated, flaked, or shredded coconut
1 teaspoon vanilla
2 teaspoons cornstarch mixed with 2 teaspoons water
Honey or maple syrup (optional)

163

Grind the mastic and sugar together in a mortar and pestle or spice mill. Set aside.

Line the bottom and sides of four 1/2-cup ramekins with plastic food wrap, pressing well with your fingertips along the bottom. Put 2 tablespoons of walnuts on the bottom of each ramekin (on top of the plastic wrap).

In a medium-size saucepan, combine the milk, sugar, flour, cream, coconut, vanilla, and ground mastic mixture in a medium-size saucepan. Cook over medium heat, whisking constantly. After 5 or 6 minutes, reduce heat to low and continue whisking.

When mixture begins to thicken, slowly whisk in the cornstarch mixture. Whisk for a few more minutes and, using a ladle, equally divide the pudding among the 4 ramekins. Let cool to room temperature, then refrigerate for 3 to 4 hours.

To serve, unmold puddings onto dessert plates, and drizzle with honey or maple syrup.

milk pudding with dried figs

Incirli Muhallebi
Izmir

This recipe is from Nur's close friend Dilek Altan. In this light but elegant dessert, dried figs of the Aegean are soaked until they are soft and arranged around the bottom of a dish before pudding is ladled over them. To avoid scorching the pot, rinse it in cold water without drying it before you add the milk. This dish is lovely for a buffet; you can use a large porcelain or ceramic baking dish instead of individual ramekins.

Serves 8

12 dried figs, soaked for 2 to 3 hours in cold water, drained
¼ cup water
4 cups milk
¼ cup cornstarch
1 cup sugar
1 teaspoon vanilla
2 to 3 small pieces of mastic, pounded with 1 teaspoon of sugar
4 tablespoons coarsely chopped pistachio nuts, for garnish

Rinse the soaked figs and place in a medium saucepan. Add 1/4 cup water and bring to a boil.

Reduce heat and simmer, covered, for 8 to 10 minutes. Drain well and let cool. Remove the stem and slice each fig into 4 pieces. Line up 8 individual ramekins or Pyrex bowls and arrange 6 pieces of sliced figs in each.

Rinse a large saucepan in cold water. Pour the water out but do not dry the pot. In a large saucepan, combine the milk, cornstarch, sugar, vanilla, and ground mastic. Cook over medium heat, whisking constantly, until the mixture thickens, about 10 to 12 minutes. Ladle the pudding into the ramekins, over the figs.

When cool, top with pistachio nuts and refrigerate until serving.

ricotta dessert

Lor Tatlısı
Ayvalık

This is a traditional dessert of the Ayvalık region and is made with semolina. Semolina is a meal consisting of the hard, coarse kernels of wheat, a by-product in the manufacture of fine flour. There are two types of semolina: durum is yellow in color and made from hard wheat. It is is used to make pasta, couscous, or bulgur; and soft wheat is white in color and used for cereals and desserts.

Serves 8 to 10. Makes 24 rounds.

Syrup:
3 cups water
3 cups sugar
¼ cup freshly squeezed lemon juice

1 pound ricotta cheese
⅓ cup plus 4 tablespoons semolina
⅓ cup plus 4 tablespoons flour, sifted
1 large egg, room temperature
1 teaspoon baking powder
1 or 2 teaspoons lemon zest
1 teaspoon vanilla

To Prepare the Syrup:
Bring 3 cups of water to a boil. Stir in the sugar; reduce heat to simmer, and cook for 5 to 6 minutes, stirring occasionally. Stir in the lemon juice, mixing well, and simmer another 2 to 3 minutes. Remove from heat and let cool.

Spray or lightly grease a jellyroll pan. Using a wooden spoon, combine the ricotta cheese, semolina, and flour in a large bowl. Stir in the egg, baking powder, lemon zest, and vanilla. You will have a very soft dough.

Divide dough into 24 small balls of equal size. On a lightly floured surface, flatten each ball with your fingertips into 2-inch rounds.

Arrange the rounds about 2 inches apart in the greased pan. Bake 30 to 35 minutes or until golden brown.

Remove from the oven and pour the cold syrup over the hot ricotta patties. If you desire, prick each patty with a toothpick to help absorb the syrup. Cover with aluminum foil and let stand overnight, turning the patties over from time to time.

orange curd

Portakal Peltesi
Izmir

If you love lemon curd, then you should definitely experience orange curd. This dessert is quick, easy, and elegant, and perfect for when you have unexpected guests; it uses ingredients that are usually on hand. It is also a nice comfort food for an upset stomach.

Serves 5 or 6

Freshly squeezed juice of 2 whole oranges or enough to make 1 cup
Zest of 1 orange
1¼ cups water
1 cup sugar
2½ tablespoons cornstarch
2 tablespoons coarsely chopped pistachio nuts

In a medium saucepan over medium heat, whisk together the orange juice, zest, water, sugar, and cornstarch. Whisk constantly for about 8 to 10 minutes, or until mixture thickens. Pour curd into 5 or 6 individual serving cups and top with chopped pistachio nuts. Let cool, then refrigerate for a few hours before serving.

167

Variation: In the city of Aydın, a similar dessert called *peluze* is made by using 2 1/2 cups of water, 1 tablespoon rose water, 1 cup sugar, 2 1/2 tablespoons cornstarch, and 2 tablespoons coarsely chopped almonds. Follow the same method used to prepare the orange curd.

syrupy walnut rolls

Samsa Tatlısı
Isparta

Called *samsa* dessert in Turkish, these rolls are made with puff pastry, a multilayered dough with butter in between each layer that is repeatedly folded and rolled out. This can be a very tedious and time-consuming process, so you can use ready-made puff pastry (usually found in the freezer aisle of the supermarket).

Serves 8. Makes 24 rolls.

Filling:
1 cup ground walnuts or almonds
4 tablespoons sugar
¼ teaspoon cinnamon
1 large egg white, lightly beaten

9 ounces (1 sheet) puff pastry,
    at room temperature
2 to 3 tablespoons milk for brushing

Syrup:
1½ cups sugar
1 cup plus 3 tablespoons water
Freshly squeezed juice of 1 lemon

168

Mix the ground nuts and sugar in a bowl. Sprinkle cinnamon over the mixture and stir in the beaten egg white. Set aside.

Preheat oven to 350°F. On a lightly floured surface, carefully unfold the puff pastry sheet and divide it into three equal-size rectangular pieces. Using a rolling pin, roll out one of the pieces of puff pastry until the sheet is 15 inches across by 5 inches wide. Repeat with the other two sheets of puff pastry.

Divide the nut filling into thirds. Place 1/3 of the filling along one long edge of each piece of puff pastry, leaving an inch clear around the edges. On each sheet, fold the short sides over towards the middle (about an inch or two). Starting from the nut-covered edge, tightly roll each pastry until you have a log. Cut each log into 8 equal pieces and arrange in a jellyroll pan. Brush the tops of the pieces with milk and bake for 30 to 35 minutes or until golden brown.

To Prepare the Syrup:
Combine sugar, water, and lemon juice in a medium saucepan. Bring to a boil. Reduce heat to medium and boil for 7 to 8 minutes.

When the pastries are done, remove from the oven and pour boiling syrup over them. (The syrup must be boiling when you pour it.) Turn syrup-covered pastries from time to time to coat each piece. Let cool and serve with ice cream and berries, allowing 3 per person.

Hint: Grind the nuts in a food processor with a teaspoon or two of the sugar (from the filling ingredients); the sugar absorbs the nut oil and keeps the ground nuts from clumping.

walnut spice cake with syrup

Tezpişti
Aegean, Marmara, and throughout Turkey

This is a version of a very popular cake that is served throughout Turkey and Greece all year round. In Turkey, it is very popular among the Sephardic Jewish community and a flourless version is typically prepared for Passover. Other versions of the recipe add cognac to the sugar syrup. For the best flavor, make the cake a day ahead. The combination of nuts, a moist cake, and syrup will have your guests begging for the recipe!

Serves 12

1 cup canola oil plus extra for greasing
1½ cups sugar
3 large eggs
3 teaspoons baking powder
½ teaspoon baking soda
1 teaspoon cinnamon
½ teaspoon ground cloves
2 cups flour
1 cup milk plus 1 teaspoon vinegar,
    mixed well
1 cup chopped walnuts

Syrup:
2 cups sugar
1 cup water
2 cinnamon sticks
1 teaspoon freshly squeezed lemon juice
2 tablespoons cognac or Metaxa
    (Greek brandy) (optional)

Preheat oven to 350°F. Grease and flour a 9 x 13-inch cake pan. Using a mixer set to medium speed, beat the oil with the sugar until well blended, about 3 minutes. Add eggs, one at a time, beating well after each addition. Add baking powder, baking soda, cinnamon, and cloves, mixing well.

Set the mixer to its lowest speed and gradually add the flour and milk in alternating batches. Stir in nuts and pour batter into the prepared pan. Bake for about 35 to 40 minutes or until a toothpick inserted in the center comes out clean. Cool in pan on a wire rack. Cut into diamond shapes.

To Prepare the Syrup:
Combine all the ingredients in a saucepan and bring to a boil. Boil on medium heat for 5 to 7 minutes, stirring constantly. If using, add the cognac or brandy, mixing well.

Pour hot syrup over cooled cake. Let cake sit for several hours to absorb the syrup.
Serve the diamonds in cupcake papers if desired.

mediterranean

mezze and salads

soups

pilafs, boereks, and bread

meat

fish

vegetables

desserts and sweets

Mark Antony is said to have given part of the Mediterranean coastline to Cleopatra as a wedding present. The weather is beautiful; the sun shines for ten months of the year. The Taurus Mountains rise up directly behind the coast, offering a landscape filled with pine forests and spectacular vistas.

Nowhere is the beauty of the region more evident than in the city of Antalya, capital of the Turkish Riviera, with its olive and citrus groves, and palm, avocado, kiwi, and banana plantations. Specialty dishes of the region include Tahini Sauce (page 185), White Bean Salad (page 186), a red lentil dish called *atsi*, a dish of lamb ribs stuffed with nuts, meat, rice, and vegetables, and *tandır* kebab (lamb cooked in a clay oven). The coast provides a rich source of seafood; grouper, red mullet, and monkfish are the most common varieties of Mediterranean fish, and these are baked, fried, grilled, or steamed.

To the west of the city of Antalya lies the city of Finike (ancient Phoenicus), which is surrounded by orchards and gardens known to have the best oranges—the pride and symbol of the town. To the east, the seaside resort city of Alanya is home to warm-weather sporting events, cultural festivals, and tourism. Alanya lies on a small peninsula, guarded by the Taurus Mountains. This positioning made the town an important stronghold for the Ptolemaic, Roman, Byzantine, and Ottoman empires. Though tourism is fast becoming its primary industry, the region is also known for the variety of fruits that grow there. Jams—including citrus, sour cherry, strawberry, apricot, watermelon, carrot, pumpkin, rose, and even eggplant—are a local specialty.

174

North of the Antalya province, the Burdur province is known for its clean and beautiful lakes and lovely beaches. The rose gardens of the Isparta province lie to the northeast, and their sweet aroma permeates the air. Rose jam and rose water (for cooking) and rose oil (for cosmetics) are produced with the roses grown in this region. The Isparta town of Eğirdir is named for the lake on whose shores it was built. As the second largest freshwater lake in Turkey, Lake Eğirdir has brought about local delicacies such as batter-fried white bass.

With its close proximity to Syria, Middle Eastern cooking and customs heavily influence the southeastern Mediterranean. Grains, yogurt, and a variety of kebabs are staples of this region. Many salads or mezze dishes combine vegetables with lemon juice, olive oil, and tahini. The southeastern Mediterranean is perhaps most famous for a meat and bulgur dish called Mothers and Daughters (page 285).

Mersin—a large and busy port city and the provincial center of the province of that name, lies midway on the eastern Mediterranean coast of Turkey. Spicy and sour (from pomegranates and sumac) are the prime tastes of Mersin's cuisine. A local dish of vegetables cooked with green lentils, garlic, and sour pomegranate is well worth trying. Fine bulgur salad with tomatoes, onions, parsley and basil is a typical lunch of the region, and *tantuni* and liver kebabs are also among the local specialties. Perhaps the most famous local delicacy, however, is *Cezerye (page 221)*, a confection made from grated carrots and walnuts and dusted with fine coconut (sometimes this dessert is known as carrot *lokum*). Varieties of halva are also popular.

Further south, banana plantations surround the town of Anamur, which lies at the southernmost point of Turkey in the province of Mersin. The temperature is at its hottest in Anamur, making it a prime location for tropical agriculture, including strawberries, papayas, avocados, pineapples, and of course, bananas, which grow in no other region of Turkey.

With a history of over 9,000 years, the Mersin district of Tarsus, with its fertile soil, has been an important center of trade for many civilizations. It is a meeting point of land and sea routes that connect the Çukurova Plain (the ancient region of Cilicia), Anatolia, and the Mediterranean Sea. At the heart of the Çukurova Plain is the city of Adana, the fifth most populous city in Turkey. The famous Adana Kebab (page 202)—a spicy kebab prepared with ground meat—reflects the Arabic influence of neighboring Syria. A local drink called *salgam*, which is made from dark turnips, usually accompanies the dish. Both are must-try delicacies for visitors to the region.

On the northeastern corner of the region, the city of Kahramanmaraş (also called by its older name, Maraş) is best known (throughout Turkey and beyond) for its distinctive ice cream. This is made from goat milk using a long-handled paddle and traditional methods. It has a chewy texture and resistance to melting thanks to mastic resin and *salep* (orchid-root flour), which is also produced in the region. Lamb, wheat, rice, medium-hot red peppers, vegetables, and fruits are also important elements of the cuisine of Kahramanmaraş.

To the southeast, in the Hatay province, the city of Antakya is the cradle of many ancient civilizations. The city lies on the Orontes River (in Turkish, *Asi Nehri*) in a fertile plain surrounded by mountains. Orchards of laurel trees surround the Harbiye waterfalls, located in the south of Antakya, and in the autumn the dates are ripe. Its close proximity to the Syrian city of Aleppo shows through its regional cuisine; warm hummus with pine nuts, Fresh Thyme Salad (page 180), walnuts with red peppers, stuffed vegetable dishes, pilafs, bulgur, boereks, and a dried, veined cottage cheese are a few of the dishes they share. Cumin, cinnamon, and allspice are the most commonly used spices. The city is famous for the Middle Eastern dessert, *Künefe (page 222)*, which is prepared with buttered shredded phyllo, mozzarella, and sweet syrup. Antakya has a distinctive cuisine of its own, however. Wheat, barley, rice, and most of Turkey's oranges, mandarins, and bananas are grown here. Local delicacies include a variety of *cezeriye*, and *biberli ekmek*, a small flatbread topped with a spicy meatless sauce.

177

Left: the city of Adana © Andre Klaassen; image of Alanya on p.175 © Tomas Marek.

baked shallot salad

Pişmiş Soğan Salatası
Adana

This delicious salad is often served as a condiment for grilled meat and chicken kebabs, particularly for the world-famous Adana Kebabs (page 202), which are made with lemon juice, sumac, Aleppo pepper, and pomegranate molasses. Shallots taste like a combination of onion and garlic, but are milder than both. They should be stored like onions, in a cool, dark place. They are low calorie, contain no cholesterol, and have very minimal sodium.

Serves 2 to 4

Cooking spray
Sea salt
1 pound (about 28 to 30) shallots, skins on
1 tablespoon freshly squeezed lemon juice
1 teaspoon dried sumac
½ teaspoon Aleppo pepper
1 teaspoon pomegranate molasses
4 tablespoons olive oil
1 tablespoon very finely chopped Italian flat-leaf parsley

Preheat oven to 350°F. Spray a baking dish with oil, and sprinkle with salt. Add the shallots and bake for 30 minutes. Remove shallots from the oven and let cool slightly, then peel the skins off and slice them lengthwise. Place shallots in a shallow bowl and mix with lemon juice, sumac, Aleppo pepper, pomegranate molasses, and olive oil. Toss to mix well. Sprinkle parsley on top and serve with grilled meat.

fine bulgur salad

Kısır
Antakya, Adana, and Mersin

Usually, the shallots in this recipe are raw, but Nur's grandmother always sautéed them for her father, who had stomach problems. Cooked shallots are easier to digest, and delicious in this recipe.

Serves 6 to 8

1½ cups fine bulgur
1½ cups hot water
4 tablespoons extra-virgin olive oil
2 shallots, very finely chopped
2 teaspoons tomato paste
2 teaspoons red pepper paste
Sea salt
1 teaspoon Aleppo pepper
½ red bell pepper, stem, ribs, and seeds removed, finely chopped
1 green cubanelle pepper, stem, ribs, and seeds removed, finely chopped
1 bunch Italian flat-leaf parsley, finely chopped
6 to 7 sprigs fresh mint, finely chopped
5 scallions, root end and damaged green leaves removed, thinly sliced crosswise
2 tomatoes, seeds removed, cut in ¼-inch cubes
Romaine lettuce hearts, separated, rinsed, and drained

Place the bulgur in a bowl and pour 1 1/2 cups of hot water over it. Mix well, cover, and let stand for 20 minutes.

Meanwhile, heat the oil in a small skillet and sauté the shallots until golden brown over low heat, 10 to 12 minutes. Stir in tomato paste, pepper paste, salt to taste, and Aleppo pepper. Mix well and add to the soaked bulgur, mixing well so all the bulgur is coated with the sautéed ingredients.

Stir in the red and green peppers, parsley, mint, scallions, and tomatoes. Gently stir to mix well. Heap onto a serving dish lined with the romaine leaves or stuff each leaf with salad and serve as individual portions.

fresh thyme salad

Zahter Salatası
Antakya

Nur first tasted this unusual vegetarian salad in a small family restaurant during a visit to Antakya. It was love at first bite! Fresh thyme leaves have a strong taste, so you can usually only eat 3 to 4 tablespoons of this salad as part of a mezze.

Serves 4 to 6

2 bunches fresh thyme, leaves separated from stems
1½ teaspoons sea salt
1 red onion, very finely chopped
2 medium tomatoes, seeds removed, very finely chopped
½ teaspoon minced garlic
½ bunch Italian flat-leaf parsley, finely chopped
1 tablespoon pomegranate molasses or freshly squeezed lemon juice (or more to taste)
3 to 4 tablespoons extra-virgin olive oil
½ teaspoon Aleppo pepper
Seeds of one pomegranate

Place thyme leaves in a bowl, sprinkle with salt, and rub them together with your fingertips for 5 to 6 minutes to remove bitterness. Rinse the leaves well, drain, and pat dry with paper towels.

In a medium-size bowl, combine onions, tomatoes, garlic, parsley, pomegranate molasses or lemon juice, and olive oil. Mix gently, taste, and add more pomegranate molasses or lemon juice if needed. Stir in the thyme leaves and toss well.

Arrange on a serving platter, sprinkle with Aleppo pepper and decorate with pomegranate seeds.

fried vegetables with vinegar and tomatoes

Şakşuka
Throughout Turkey

This vegetarian appetizer, in many variations, is popular throughout Turkey and other Mediterranean countries

In Turkey, vegetables are dried during the hot summer months to be rehydrated and used as needed during the winter. This dish can be served as an appetizer or dip. Serve it with crusty bread or warm pita to mop up the sauce. It can also be served with lemon wedges.

Serves 6

Sea salt
1 large Italian eggplant, cut into ½-inch cubes
2 medium zucchini, washed, drained, dried with paper towels, and cut into ½-inch cubes
2 medium golden potatoes, washed, drained, dried with paper towels, peeled,
    and cut into ½-inch cubes
1½ cups canola oil for frying

Sauce:
⅓ cup olive oil
1 large onion, very finely chopped
3 to 4 cloves garlic, finely chopped
2 thin green cubanelle peppers, finely chopped
2 large tomatoes, finely diced
2 teaspoons white vinegar
Sea salt
Freshly ground pepper

Sprinkle salt on the eggplant and let it sit in a colander for 30 minutes. Rinse, drain, and pat dry with paper towel. Make sure the zucchini and potatoes have also been dried well (they must be dry for frying).

In a large skillet, heat the oil and fry the potato cubes until light golden brown. Remove from pan with a slotted spoon, drain on a large plated covered with three layers of paper towel to absorb the oil. Repeat with the zucchini, and then with the eggplant.

To Prepare the Sauce:
Heat the oil in a medium-size pan; add garlic and onion and sauté for 4 to 5 minutes over medium heat. Reduce heat to medium-low. Add the pepper and cook, stirring, for another 3 to 4 minutes. Add the tomatoes and mix well. Cook, uncovered, stirring occasionally, for 10 to 15 minutes. Remove from heat and stir in vinegar, salt, and pepper.

Arrange vegetables on a serving platter, pour sauce over vegetables, and serve at room temperature.

potato salad with tahini

Tahinli Patates Salatası
Adana and Antakya

Instead of the familiar mayonnaise dressing, this salad uses a dressing made from tahini. It is a great dish for a buffet, and is usually served cold with chicken or fish dishes.

Serves 4 to 6

4 cups water
Sea salt
1 pound (about 6 medium) golden potatoes
½ cup tahini
Freshly squeezed juice of one lemon
3 to 4 cloves garlic, minced
4 tablespoons extra-virgin olive oil
½ teaspoon ground cumin
¾ teaspoon Aleppo pepper

In a 3-quart pot, place water, salt, and potatoes, and bring to a boil. Reduce heat and simmer, covered, for about 30 minutes or until potatoes are tender (test them by inserting a toothpick). Drain well and let cool.

Peel the potatoes and push them through a ricer, and then purée them. Add the tahini, salt, lemon juice, and garlic. Blend well with a wooden spoon, and slowly add the olive oil, cumin, and Aleppo pepper, mixing well. Place in a serving dish and sprinkle with some Aleppo pepper.

mixed herb and cheese fritters

Yumurta Öccesi
Adana

Turkish cooks love fresh herbs. They are an important part of most Turkish dishes, and they are delicious with salty cheeses like *hellim*. Better known here by its Greek name, *halloumi*, *hellim* cheese can be found in most Middle Eastern or specialty markets.

Serves 6. Makes 20 fritters.

1 bunch Italian flat-leaf parsley, washed, drained, finely chopped
½ bunch fresh mint, washed, drained, finely chopped
½ bunch fresh tarragon, washed, drained, finely chopped
6 scallions, root end and damaged green leaves discarded, finely sliced crosswise
3 cloves garlic, minced
1 teaspoon Aleppo pepper
Freshly ground pepper
1 cup grated *hellim* cheese
Sea salt, if needed
3 large eggs, lightly beaten
5 tablespoons flour
1½ cups canola oil for frying

In a large bowl, combine the parsley, mint, tarragon, scallions, garlic, Aleppo pepper, freshly ground pepper, and grated cheese; mix well. Taste and add salt if needed (the cheese is very salty). Mix in the eggs, and gradually mix in the flour.

Heat the oil in a large skillet and drop in 1 tablespoon of the batter. Continue making fritters, leaving a little space in between each one. Fry until golden brown on one side, then turn fritters over and fry on the other side. Remove from pan and drain on a plate covered with layers of paper towel to absorb excess oil. Repeat until all the batter has been used.

roasted eggplant dip

Ezme Patlıcan Salatası
Adana, Mersin, and Antakya

Similar to baba ghanoush, this eggplant and tahini mixture can be served as a dip, spread, or salad. Serve with pita bread.

Serves 6

3 pounds (2 to 3 large) eggplants
3 to 4 cloves garlic, minced
4 tablespoons freshly squeezed lemon juice (or to taste)
4 tablespoons extra-virgin olive oil
¼ cup tahini
Sea salt
Sprinkle of paprika for garnish

Roast the eggplants in a broiler, or directly over a gas flame, until skins are completely charred and the inside is creamy. Turn them every 4 to 5 minutes to make sure they cook evenly. Do not undercook them. Place on a baking sheet, let cool until you can comfortably handle them, and carefully peel off the charred skin. Place the peeled eggplants on a chopping board and finely chop into a purée. Place eggplant purée in fine sieve, over a bowl, and let drain for a few hours to remove any bitter juices. Place eggplant puree in a bowl, add the garlic, lemon juice, olive oil, tahini, salt to taste, and mix well. Cover and let chill in the refrigerator for a few hours.

Place in a shallow, round, serving bowl and sprinkle with paprika.

tahini sauce

Hibeş
Antalya

For over 40 years, Nur has treasured her friendship with her school friend, Ayşe Ataman. Happily, they meet in Ankara or in Bodrun in the summers. Many years ago, Nur's family had the pleasure of visiting Ayşe and her family at their farm, where Nur's children enjoyed picking and eating fruit right from the trees. This sesame-based spread, flavored with lemon juice and cumin, was always served in Ayşe's home. It is served with boereks, fish, steamed vegetables, salad, or with bread as a dip. It is a wonderful versatile dish that can be easily made in advance.

Serves 6. Makes about 1 cup.

½ cup tahini
⅓ to ½ cup lukewarm water
3 garlic cloves, pounded into a fine paste in a mortar and pestle with ½ teaspoon salt
Freshly squeezed juice of one lemon (or to taste)
3 tablespoons olive oil
½ teaspoon ground cumin
½ to 1 teaspoon Aleppo pepper

Place tahini in a bowl and whisk in water, mixing well. Stir in garlic paste, lemon juice, olive oil, cumin, and Aleppo pepper. Mix to a smooth, creamy paste. If needed, add a little water or lemon juice.

white bean salad with tahini

Fasulye Piyazı
Antalya and throughout Southern Turkey

This colorful vegetarian salad can be served as an appetizer or paired with warm, whole-wheat bread and served as a main course.

Serves 6

2 cups small dried white beans, soaked overnight and then cooked until tender or canned white beans, rinsed and drained
1 medium Spanish onion, halved and finely sliced
1 tablespoon finely chopped Italian flat-leaf parsley
4 cloves garlic, minced
2 to 3 tablespoons tahini
3 teaspoons freshly squeezed lemon juice
⅔ cup extra-virgin olive oil
1½ teaspoons sea salt, divided
1 teaspoon Aleppo pepper

Garnish:
Few lolo rosso leaves (curly red and green lettuce leaves)
2 medium tomatoes, halved and sliced
2 hard-boiled eggs, quartered and sliced
olives to garnish (optional)

Combine the cooked or canned beans with onions and parsley; mix well and set aside.

In a large bowl, combine the garlic, tahini, lemon juice, olive oil, salt to taste, and Aleppo pepper. Whisk well, add beans, and toss to mix. Let cool and taste for seasoning.

Arrange lolo rosso leaves on a large oval shallow dish or serving platter. Place bean mixture over the leaves and decorate with sliced tomatoes, eggs, and olives, if using. Sprinkle with Aleppo pepper.

Note: If using dried beans, heat 4 cups of water in a medium-size pan with 1/2 teaspoon salt. Bring to a boil, add the beans, reduce heat to simmer, and cook, covered, until the beans are tender, 30 to 60 minutes. Drain well to get rid of excess water.

red lentil mezze

Atsi
Antalya

This is an easy vegetarian appetizer made with red lentils, olive oil, onions, garlic, cumin, and Aleppo pepper. This dish can be served cold or at room temperature.

Serves 8

2 cups dried red lentils, rinsed and drained
5½ cups hot water, divided
Sea salt
Freshly ground pepper
½ cup extra-virgin olive oil
4 to 5 medium onions, halved and thinly sliced
3 to 4 cloves garlic, minced
1½ teaspoons ground cumin
1 teaspoon Aleppo pepper

Place the lentils in a 3-quart pan with 4 cups of water lightly seasoned with salt and pepper. Bring to a boil; reduce heat and simmer, covered, for 10 to 15 minutes, checking frequently. When all the liquid has been absorbed, add 1 1/2 cups of hot water and cook until all the liquid has been absorbed and lentils have cooked into a thick purée; the total cooking time should be about 25 minutes.

Meanwhile, in a medium frying pan, heat the oil and sauté the onions over medium heat for 5 to 7 minutes. Reduce heat and continue to cook the onions until they are light brown, about 15 more minutes. Stir in garlic, cumin, and Aleppo pepper. Season with salt and pepper to taste. Pour 3/4 of the fried onions into the lentils and mix well.

Grease a 9-inch round bowl and place the lentil purée in the bowl. Place the remaining onion mixture over the top of the lentils. Let cool.

chicken and rice soup

Tavuklu Pirinç Çorbası
Adana

The tomato paste, red pepper paste, mint, and chickpeas are what make this soup distinctly Turkish, and different from other chicken soup recipes. Light or heavy, cold or hot, Turkish cuisine offers a wide variety of soups, which are usually made from a chicken or meat stock. This one uses water as its base.

Serves 4 to 6

6 cups water, divided
2 whole chicken legs, rinsed and patted dry with paper towels
1 onion, halved
1 small carrot, peeled and halved
A few Italian flat-leaf parsley sprigs tied together
1 bay leaf
6 black peppercorns
Sea salt
½ cup uncooked medium-grain rice
1 tablespoon butter
2 tablespoons canola oil
1 teaspoon tomato paste
1 teaspoon red pepper paste
1 tablespoon flour
1 teaspoon dried mint
½ cup canned chickpeas, rinsed and drained
Lemon wedges, to garnish

189

In a 4-quart pot, place 5 cups of water and bring to a boil. Add the chicken, onion, carrot, parsley, bay leaf, peppercorns, and salt to taste. Reduce heat, cover, and simmer until chicken is tender, 40 to 45 minutes. Transfer chicken to a plate and let cool. Drain soup, reserving the cooking liquid. Once the chicken has cooled, remove skin and bones and shred into bite-size pieces. Set aside.

In a 3-quart pot, bring 1 cup water to a boil. Add rice, cover, and simmer until rice is cooked, 10 to 12 minutes. Add 4 cups of the reserved chicken stock (if there is not enough, add enough water to equal 4 cups) and shredded chicken. Cook for another 4 to 5 minutes.

Meanwhile, heat the oil and butter in a small skillet. Stir in the tomato and red pepper pastes, flour, and dried mint. Mix well and pour over the soup, mixing well. Stir in the chickpeas and cook for another 5 minutes. Serve hot with lemon wedges.

mixed grain soup

Kara Çorba
Adana

This soup, chunky with wheat berries, chickpeas, cranberry beans, cannellini beans, and green lentils, is a meal in itself, especially for vegetarians. The combination of grains and spices offers a unique taste. In Eastern Anatolia, this soup is made with different spices, making it ideal for the cold winter months. All of the beans can be soaked together.

Serves 8

10 cups water
½ cup shelled wheat berries, soaked in cold water overnight
½ cup dried chickpeas, soaked in cold water overnight
½ cup dried cranberry beans, soaked in cold water overnight
½ cup dried (white) cannellini beans, soaked in cold water overnight
Sea salt
Freshly ground pepper
½ cup dried green lentils, soaked in hot water for 2 to 3 hours
2 tablespoons butter
¼ cup canola oil
1 large onion, finely diced
1 teaspoon red pepper paste
1 teaspoon tomato paste
1 teaspoon Aleppo pepper
1 teaspoon ground cumin
Freshly squeezed juice of one lemon

In a 4-quart pot, bring 10 cups of water to a boil. Rinse and drain mixed beans and wheat berries and place in the pot. Reduce heat to simmer, slightly season with salt and pepper, and cook, covered, about 45 minutes. Drain green lentils and add to the pot. Mix well and cook for another 30 to 35 minutes.

Meanwhile, in a frying pan, heat the canola oil and butter. Sauté the onions over medium-low heat until golden brown, about 12 to 16 minutes. Stir in the red pepper and tomato pastes, mixing well. Then stir in the Aleppo pepper and cumin. Pour onion mixture into the soup, mix well, and cook for 5 minutes. Remove from heat and stir in the lemon juice. Serve hot.

swiss chard soup

Pazı Çorbası
Antakya

This is a tangy, healthy soup that uses Swiss chard stems. Nur was raised never to waste food so whenever she cooks with Swiss chard leaves, she sautés the stems or uses them in soups like this one. Swiss chard has been traced back to the famed Hanging Gardens of Babylon. Cook Swiss chard in a non-reactive pot since it contains an acid that will discolor your pot.

Serves 6 to 8

3 tablespoons canola oil, divided
1 medium onion, finely chopped
1 medium carrot, peeled and coarsely grated
8 cups chicken stock
1 medium potato, peeled and coarsely grated
½ cup dried green lentils, soaked in hot water for a few hours, drained
½ cup dried red lentils, rinsed and drained
3 cups Swiss chard stems, thick damaged parts removed, trimmed, and finely chopped
Sea salt
Freshly ground pepper
2 tablespoons butter
5 to 6 cloves garlic, minced
1 teaspoon dried mint
½ teaspoon ground cumin
1 tablespoon freshly squeezed lemon juice

In a 4-quart pot, heat 2 tablespoons canola oil and sauté the onion and carrot for 3 to 4 minutes, stirring. Add the stock and bring to a boil. Add the potato, green and red lentils, Swiss chard stems, and salt and pepper to taste. Reduce heat and simmer, covered, for 30 minutes.

In a small skillet, heat 2 tablespoons butter and 1 tablespoon canola oil. Add minced garlic and cook for 3 to 4 minutes until golden brown. Remove from the heat and stir in mint and cumin. Mix well and add to the soup. Cook for another 2 to 3 minutes and remove from heat. Stir in the lemon juice and mix well.

red lentil soup

Kırmızı Mercimek Çorbası
Antakya

This is a simple vegetarian soup. Lentils are thin-skinned so they don't need to be soaked in order to cook quickly, and they are very easy to digest.

Serves 6

7 cups water
Sea salt
Freshly ground pepper
1½ teaspoons ground cumin, divided
1½ cups dried red lentils, rinsed and drained
2 tablespoons butter
2 tablespoons canola oil
1 large onion, finely chopped
1 tablespoon flour
1 teaspoon Aleppo pepper
2 tablespoons freshly squeezed lemon juice

In a 4-quart pot, heat water. Season with salt and pepper to taste, add 1 teaspoon cumin, and bring to a boil. Add lentils, mix well, reduce heat, and simmer, partially covered, for 25 to 35 minutes. Check and stir periodically.

Meanwhile, heat butter and oil in a small skillet and sauté the onion for 12 to 15 minutes over low heat until golden brown. Stir in the flour and Aleppo pepper, mix well, and blend into the soup, mixing well. Stir in the lemon juice and serve.

wheat, chickpea, and red lentil soup with spinach

Maraş Çorbası
Kahramanmaraş (Maraş)

The distinction between soup and thin stew is not always clearly defined in Turkish cooking. This rich, hearty soup can also be made with eggplant diced into 1/2-inch cubes instead of the spinach.

Serves 6 to 8

10 cups chicken stock or water, divided
¾ cup shelled wheat berries, soaked overnight in hot water
½ cup dried chickpeas, soaked overnight in lightly salted cold water
¾ cup dried red lentils
Sea salt
Freshly ground pepper
1 tablespoon tomato paste
1 tablespoon red pepper paste
3 to 4 cloves garlic, minced
Freshly squeezed juice of one lemon
2 cups baby spinach leaves, washed, drained, finely chopped

Garnish:
2 tablespoons butter
1 tablespoon dried mint
½ teaspoon Aleppo pepper

In a large pot, bring 7 cups of chicken stock or water to a boil. Rinse and drain wheat berries and chickpeas. Add them to the pot; reduce heat to medium-low, and cook, covered, 45 to 50 minutes. Stir in 2 to 3 cups more of stock or water, along with the lentils. Season with salt and pepper to taste. Stir in tomato and red pepper pastes and mix well. Cover pot and simmer for another 20 to 25 minutes. Add the garlic, lemon juice, and spinach leaves. Mix well, cover, and cook for another 10 to 15 minutes. Remove from the heat, taste and adjust seasoning if needed. Place soup in a tureen or serving bowl.

To Prepare the Garnish:
Melt the butter in a small pan. When it sizzles, remove from heat and stir in the mint and Aleppo pepper. Mix well, and drizzle circles over the top of the soup.

bulgur pilaf with vermicelli

Şehriyeli Bulgur Pilavı
Adana

This is a hearty and healthful pilaf made with vermicelli, coarse bulgur, and black-eyed peas. As a variation, substitute spinach, zucchini, or fava beans for the vermicelli.

Serves 6 to 8

4 tablespoons canola oil, divided
½ cup small pieces of vermicelli
1½ cups coarse bulgur
¾ cup canned black-eyed peas or canned chickpeas, rinsed and drained (optional)
3 cups hot chicken stock
Sea salt
Freshly ground pepper
2 tablespoons butter
2 medium onions, finely chopped
1 teaspoon Aleppo pepper

In a 3-quart pan, heat 3 tablespoons of oil and fry the vermicelli over medium heat until brown. Stir in the bulgur, black-eyed peas (if using), and the chicken stock. Season with salt and pepper to taste, reduce heat, and simmer, covered, for 15 to 20 minutes.

Meanwhile, in a small skillet, heat 1 tablespoon of oil and the butter and sauté the onions over low heat for 10 to 15 minutes until golden brown. Mix in Aleppo pepper.

When the bulgur has absorbed all of the cooking liquid, remove from heat. Remove the lid, place a double layer of paper towels on top of the skillet, and replace the lid; set aside for 10 minutes. Pour over the fried onions, stir well, and serve with any vegetable, meat, or poultry dish.

Variation: One pound of spinach leaves, zucchini, or shelled broad beans can be substituted for the vermicelli. Just lightly sauté the vegetables and omit the chickpeas or black-eyed peas.

195

spinach or beef boereks on the griddle

Saç Böreği
Adana, Merin, and Antalya

These boereks are different because they are made with yogurt dough and are not baked or fried but rather cooked in a griddle or non-stick pan on the stovetop. This is a light lunch or teatime specialty of the southeastern Mediterranean, especially during Ramadan because it offers sustenance for the day of fasting ahead.

Serves 6 to 8. Makes about 7 or 8 large boereks.

Dough:
1 cup water
1 large egg
2 tablespoons plain yogurt
2 tablespoons canola oil
1½ teaspoons salt
2¾ to 3 cups flour

Spinach Filling:
2 tablespoons canola oil
1 onion, finely chopped
1 pound fresh spinach leaves
Sea salt
Freshly ground pepper
Butter for cooking

Ground Beef Filling:
10 ounces ground sirloin, 93% fat free
Sea salt
Freshly ground pepper
1 onion, finely grated
½ cup milk or water

Canola oil for cooking

To Prepare the Dough:
Place water, egg, yogurt, oil, and salt and whisk together. Gradually add flour until you have a soft dough. Cover and let rest in a warm place for 30 minutes.

196

To Make Spinach Boereks:

Prepare the filling: In a sauté pan, heat the oil on high and sauté the onion for 4 to 5 minutes. Add spinach and cook until it wilts, about 2 to 3 minutes. Season with salt and pepper to taste. Make sure all the cooking liquid has been absorbed and no liquid is left in the pan. Set aside.

Using a rolling pin, roll 6 tablespoons of dough out on a lightly floured surface until it is a 12 x 11 inch rectangle. Place 3 tablespoons of the spinach filling in the center of the dough, and spread it all over the dough. Fold a 1 1/2-inch-wide piece of dough from the left side all the way over the filling and repeat with the right side. Fold the remaining two sides over the spinach, slightly over-lapping each other, making a rectangle. Repeat with remaining dough and filling.

Heat a griddle over medium heat and lightly butter it. When butter is hot, place a boerek in the pan; cook each boerek on both sides until golden brown spots appear. Cut the boereks into quarters and serve hot with yogurt, fruit compote, and salad.

To Make Meat Boereks:

Prepare the filling: In a bowl combine the sirloin, salt and pepper to taste, and grated onion. Mix well, then stir in the milk or water (this keeps the meat moist and prevents clumping while cooking); make sure everything is well blended. Set aside.

Using a rolling pin, roll out a walnut-size piece of dough on a lightly floured surface until it is a circle about 7 or 8 inches in diameter. Spread 1 1/2 tablespoons of the meat filling across half of the circle of dough, leaving a 1/2-inch border that is not covered with meat. Fold the other half of the dough over the meat filling and, using a fork tine, crimp the edges to seal the boerek. Repeat with the remaining dough and filling.

Using a non-stick skillet, heat 3 tablespoons of oil and cook boereks 3 to 4 minutes per side to make sure the meat is cooked. If needed, add some oil and heat it between cooking each boerek. Cut the boereks into quarters and serve hot with yogurt, fruit compote, and salad.

tahini, walnut, and sesame rolls
Nokul
Isparta

These barely sweet vegetarian rolls are served for breakfast or at teatime. The filling is made with tahini, grape molasses, ground walnuts, cinnamon, and cloves.

Makes 24 rolls

2½ cups flour, sifted
½ cup warm water, divided
¼-ounce packet dry active yeast
1 teaspoon sugar
⅔ cup canola oil
½ cup plain yogurt

Topping:
2 tablespoons water
3 tablespoons sesame seeds

Spread:
¼ cup tahini
3 tablespoons canola oil
2 tablespoons grape molasses
½ cup coarsely ground walnuts
1 teaspoon cinnamon
¾ teaspoon ground cloves

Butter or oil for greasing the pan

Place flour in a large bowl and make a well in the center. In a small bowl, place 3 tablespoons warm water, dry yeast, and sugar. Mix until yeast dissolves. Pour yeast mixture into the center of the flour and cover over with flour. Cover with a towel and place in a warm spot to rise, about 10 to 20 minutes. Add the remaining water, oil, and yogurt. Mix and knead until a soft dough has formed. Cover again and keep in a warm place until mixture doubles in size, about 40 to 45 minutes.

Meanwhile, prepare the spread. Mix tahini, oil, and molasses in a cup and set aside. Mix coarsely ground nuts with spices and set aside.

Preheat oven to 350°F. Grease a jellyroll pan. On a floured working surface, divide the dough in half. Using a rolling pin, roll out half the dough until it is about 15 inches long by 14 inches wide.

Using a pastry brush or your hand, spread half of the tahini mixture all over the rolled dough. Sprinkle half of the walnut, cinnamon, clove mixture all over the dough. Cut the dough in half horizontally. Roll each half up horizontally into a log. Repeat with the other half of the dough and filling.

Mix 2 tablespoons water with 3 tablespoons sesame seeds. Using your hands, cover the top of the pastries with sesame seeds. (Using water helps prevent the seeds from falling off.) Cut each log into 2 1/2-inch rolls. Place rolls on the prepared pan and bake 30 minutes or until golden brown.

rice and eggplant turnover

Çevirme

Antakya

Sautéing the rice in butter before cooking is the secret to success in cooking Turkish pilafs like this one. The filling—meat, rice, currants, pine nuts, cinnamon, and allspice—reminds me of Spanish picadillo. Serve with a mixed green salad.

Serves 6 to 8

1½ pounds (7 or 8, 5 to 6-inch long) Italian eggplants
Sea salt
1 cup canola oil
2 tablespoons olive oil
½ pound ground sirloin
Freshly ground pepper
½ teaspoon Aleppo pepper
2 tablespoons pine nuts, dry roasted
3 tablespoons butter
1½ cups uncooked extra-long-grain rice, soaked in lightly salted warm water
    for 30 minutes, drained
3 tablespoons dried currants, soaked in water for 30 minutes
½ teaspoon cinnamon
¼ teaspoon allspice
1 teaspoon sugar
3 cups hot chicken stock or water
Spray for greasing

Cut the stems off the eggplants. With a vegetable peeler, peel the eggplants lengthwise in stripes 1/2-inch wide, leaving a 1/2-inch strip between stripes of removed skin. Repeat, making a striped effect. Slice eggplants lengthwise into 1/8-inch thick slices.

Sprinkle eggplants with salt and place them in a colander for 30 minutes. Rinse well, drain, and pat dry with paper towels. Preheat oven to 350°F.

In a medium-size frying pan, heat the canola oil and fry the eggplants in batches until golden brown, about 3 to 4 minutes. Place eggplants on a plate covered with a double layer of paper towel, and drain well.

In a 1-quart saucepan, heat the olive oil. Stir in the ground sirloin and cook until meat is browned and cooked, about 7 to 8 minutes. Add salt, Aleppo pepper, and pine nuts. Mix well. Remove from heat and set aside.

In a medium-size pan, heat the butter. Stir in the drained rice and sauté for 2 to 3 minutes. Stir in the currants, season with salt and pepper to taste, cinnamon, allspice, and sugar. Mix well and add 3 cups of hot chicken stock and cook, covered, for 15 to 20 minutes or until all the liquid has been absorbed and steam holes appear on the surface. Remove from heat. Remove lid, cover pan with paper towels, replace lid, and let stand for 10 to 15 minutes.

Grease an 8 x 2-inch round, ovenproof bowl. Line the bottom of the bowl with overlapping eggplant pieces, until the surface is completely covered. Place sautéed ground meat over the eggplant slices on the bottom, pat down gently with the back of a wooden spoon, and place the rice over the meat up to the top of the bowl. Gently pat down the rice with the back of a wooden spoon.

Bake for 10 to 15 minutes, remove from oven, and turn upside down onto a round serving dish.

201

adana kebab

Adana Kebabı
Adana

This is a world-famous kebab recipe made with lemon juice, sumac, Aleppo pepper, and pomegranate molasses. It is healthy, elegant, and quick to prepare.

Serves 4

1 pound ground beef, 85% fat free
1 onion, very finely chopped
Sea salt
¼ teaspoon black pepper
1 teaspoon Aleppo pepper
1 teaspoon red pepper paste
½ teaspoon paprika

Preheat oven to broil. Mix all the ingredients together in a bowl, kneading well with your hands.

Divide meat into four balls, and shape each into a burger. Place a flat, 13 x 3/4-inch skewer through the middle of one of the burgers. Wet your hands and gently stretch and pull the patty, lengthening and thinning until it is about 9 inches long and about an inch wide.

Repeat with the other burgers. Broil about 8 minutes, turning, until meat is done and begins to lightly char.

tantuni kebab

Tantuni Kebabı
Mersin

Lamb, onion juice, tomatoes, and seasonings flavor these delicious kebabs, which are wrapped in warm bread. The meat mixture in this recipe has to be refrigerated overnight so plan to make it a day ahead.

Serves 4

1 pound boneless leg of lamb, cut into 1-inch cubes, then sliced on the diagonal
    into ¼-inch wide slices
Juice of 1 medium onion (prepared by finely grating the onion, pressing through
    a fine sieve with the back of a wooden spoon, and reserving the liquid)
¼ teaspoon ground black pepper
¼ teaspoon Aleppo pepper
1 tablespoon canola oil
1 onion, peeled, halved, thinly sliced
1 teaspoon ground sumac
Sea salt
2 tablespoons butter
2 tomatoes, seeds removed, cut into ½-inch cubes
4 pieces lavash bread, pita bread, or tortillas, warmed

Place the lamb, onion juice, black pepper, Aleppo pepper, and oil in a bowl and mix well. Cover and refrigerate overnight. Remove sliced lamb from the refrigerator one hour before cooking.

In a small bowl, mix together the sliced onion, sumac, and salt to taste. Set aside.

Heat the butter in a frying pan until it sizzles; add lamb and sauté for 7 to 8 minutes. Season with salt to taste.

Place lamb in the center of a serving dish. Arrange the cubed tomatoes on one side of the lamb and the onion mixture on the other. Serve with warm bread, and make a wrap with bread, onions, tomatoes, and lamb.

mothers and daughters

Analı Kızlı
Adana, Mersin, and Antakya

This is a wonderful specialty of the southeastern Mediterranean. Two types of dough (made from bulgur and meat) are cooked in sauce. As the story goes, in Nur's grandmother's time, families were very large and cooking for the family took a lot of time. Daughters of all ages were expected to help their mothers. In doing so they learned to cook themselves. Mothers prepared the large stuffed shells, while daughters made the small, unstuffed balls, so the name Mothers and Daughters was given to this dish.

It is time consuming, but well worth the effort. Enlist your children to help! The filling can be made a day ahead and kept in the refrigerator. The finished dish is served either in a shallow soup bowl or pasta dish.

Serves 8

Filling:
3 tablespoons canola oil
½ pound ground sirloin
1 onion, finely diced
2 tablespoons coarsely chopped walnuts
    (optional)
Sea salt
Freshly ground pepper
2 teaspoons red pepper paste

Dough:
2 cups fine bulgur
1 cut water
10 ounces ground sirloin, 93% fat free
    (very important or dough won't hold)
1 medium onion, finely chopped
1 tablespoon red pepper paste or
    tomato paste
4 tablespoons flour
1 tablespoon semolina
1 large egg
Sea salt
Freshly ground pepper

Sauce:
3 tablespoons canola oil
1 medium onion, finely diced
2 heaped tablespoons flour
1 tablespoon tomato paste
1½ tablespoons red pepper paste
8 cups chicken stock (or 8 cups water
    with 1 chicken bouillon cube)
4 cloves garlic, minced, mashed into a
    paste with ½ teaspoon sea salt
1 cup canned chickpeas, rinsed and
    drained
2 tablespoons freshly squeezed
    lemon juice

Garnish:
3 tablespoons butter
1 tablespoon dried mint
1 teaspoon Aleppo pepper

To Prepare the Filling:

Heat the canola oil in a frying pan and stirring constantly, sauté the ground sirloin for a few minutes until the color changes. Add in the onions and continue to cook for 6 to 7 minutes, stirring constantly. Add walnuts, salt and pepper to taste, and red pepper paste; mix well. Remove from heat and set aside to cool. (This can be done a day ahead and kept covered in the refrigerator.)

To Prepare the Dough:

In a large bowl, soak the bulgur in the water for 10 minutes.

Stir in the meat, onion, red pepper paste, flour, semolina, and egg, and season with salt and pepper to taste. Mix and knead well. In batches (probably 3), process the dough in a food processor until it is well mixed and has formed a ball, about 2 to 3 minutes.

Divide the mixture in half; one half will be made into "daughters" and the other half will be filled to make the "mothers." To make the daughters, pinch off small pieces of dough and roll between your palms into a 1/2-inch round ball, wetting your hands between each ball.

Make the mothers using the other half of the mixture. Using your palms, roll a heaped tablespoon of the bulgur mixture into a ball. Carefully push your thumb into the center of the ball, turning it back and forth to expand the opening (making the sides thinner) until the opening is about 3/4 of an inch wide. Place a teaspoon of the meat filling in the hole. Wet your fingertips and gently smooth the opening closed so no filling is exposed. Wet your palms and roll the mother between your palms to smooth the surface, making sure there are no holes. Repeat until all the mothers have been made (you will have about 27). Now you are ready to cook!

To Prepare the Sauce:

In a 5 or 6-quart pot, heat 3 tablespoons of oil. Add the onion and sauté until translucent, about 5 to 6 minutes. Add the flour, mix well, and cook for another minute. Stir in the tomato and red pepper pastes and the chicken stock.

Bring to a boil and add the mothers. Reduce heat to medium and cook, covered for 5 minutes. Stir in the garlic, chickpeas, and the daughters. Season with salt and pepper, cover, and cook for another 12 to 15 minutes. Stir in the lemon juice during the last 5 minutes of cooking. Remove from the heat.

To Prepare the Garnish:

In a small skillet, heat the butter until it sizzles. Remove pan from the heat and stir in the mint and Aleppo pepper. Mix well and pour over the meat. Let rest 8 to 10 minutes before serving.

lamb shanks with wheat, chickpeas, and walnuts

Keşkek
Antakya

This recipe uses wheat berries, chickpeas, and lamb shanks. It has to be started the night before since some of the ingredients must be soaked overnight. It is similar to a chicken and wheat dish made in the Black Sea region.

Serves 4 to 6

1 large onion, peeled, halved, and sliced
1 cup shelled wheat berries, soaked overnight in water
½ cup dried chickpeas, soaked overnight in salted cold water
1½ pounds lamb shanks (about 2)
Sea salt
Freshly ground pepper
3 cups hot water
½ cup butter, divided
1 cup halved walnuts
1 teaspoon ground cumin
1 teaspoon Aleppo pepper

Spread the onion slices on the bottom of a 4-quart pot. Drain the wheat berries and chickpeas and place on top of the onions. Season the lamb shanks lightly with salt and pepper and place in the pot along with the hot water. Bring to a boil, reduce heat, cook, and remove any scum that accumulates on the surface with a slotted spoon or small strainer. Cover and simmer for 1 1/2 hours. Remove lamb shanks, cover the pot, and continue cooking.

When lamb shanks are cool enough to handle, remove skin and bones, separate the meat into small pieces, and return to the pot; cook for another 10 to 15 minutes. Remove from heat, and using a large wooden spoon or a pestle, stir in 4 tablespoons of butter. Using the back of a wooden spoon, stir and beat the mixture until the meat disappears into the wheat and forms a thick purée the consistency of oatmeal.

Place mixture on a shallow serving dish.

In a small skillet, heat 4 tablespoons of butter, add the walnut halves, and sauté for 2 to 3 minutes. Stir in the cumin and Aleppo pepper, mix well, and cook for another minute. Pour over the meat in swirls and serve hot.

stuffed rice kibbeh

Kubbe Halep
Antakya

Because of their close proximity, no visa is needed to travel between Antakya in Turkey and Aleppo in Syria; many people make the trip daily. The cultures and cuisines of the two cities have long influenced one another. This dish is Syrian in origin, and has been adapted into the cuisine of Antakya. The recipe was shared by Nur's friend Gulsen Kirdar. Kibbeh are made with many different types of dough. In this recipe, rice dough is stuffed with a meat and almond filling.

Serves 8. Makes 26 to 28.

Filling:
2 to 3 tablespoons water
½ pound ground sirloin
1 large onion, very finely chopped
1 tablespoon butter
½ tablespoon oil
Sea salt
Freshly ground pepper
½ teaspoon Aleppo pepper
4 tablespoons slivered and chopped almonds
A dash of cinnamon (optional)
2 tablespoons finely chopped
    Italian flat-leaf parsley

Dough:
3½ cups water
Sea salt
½ teaspoon turmeric
1 medium potato, peeled and
    chopped into small cubes
1½ cups basmati rice
1 large egg yolk

1½ cups canola oil for frying

To Prepare the Filling:
In a small skillet, heat the water and add ground sirloin. Stirring, sauté over medium heat until the color changes. Add onion, continue to cook for a few minutes, reduce heat, and cook uncovered for 15 to 17 minutes or until onions are translucent. Stir in the butter and oil, season with salt and pepper to taste, and add Aleppo pepper. Mix well and remove from heat. Stir in almonds, cinnamon if desired, and parsley. Mix well and set aside to cool.

To Prepare the Dough:
In a 3-quart pot, place 3 1/2 cups of water and bring to a boil. Season lightly with salt; add 1/2 teaspoon turmeric, potatoes, and rice. Mix well; reduce heat, cover, and simmer 15 to 20 minutes until all the liquid has been absorbed. Remove from heat and set aside, covered, for 10 minutes. Transfer rice mixture to a fine sieve (over a bowl) and let cool for a couple of hours. Place cooled rice mixture in a bowl, add egg yolk, and mash with a potato masher to form a sticky dough.

Wet your hands; place 2 tablespoons of rice dough into the palm of your hand. Flatten the dough with your fingertips forming a 2 1/2-inch round patty. Place 2 teaspoons of filling in the center of the patty and fold the sides over the filling to enclose it securely, making a 2 1/2-inch-long oval. Repeat until all the dough and filling have been used.

Heat the oil in a deep frying pan. Without crowding the pan, fry the kibbeh in batches until golden brown.

eastern mediterranean stuffed zucchini
Şıhıl Mahşi
Antakya and throughout the Eastern Mediterranean

Zucchini have a crisp, moist, flavorful flesh, and when cooked, they retain their firm texture. Nur's grandmother never threw away anything that could be used, so when she made stuffed zucchini she used the scooped out flesh to make frittatas. The red pepper paste gives this recipe its zing. Serve hot with garlic yogurt.

Serves 5

2 pounds pale green zucchini,
    each about 5 inches long
4 tablespoons canola oil
4 tablespoons olive oil, divided
1 onion, finely chopped
½ pound ground sirloin
2 teaspoons red pepper paste, divided
Sea salt
Freshly ground pepper
2 tablespoons pine nuts
1 cup hot water
½ tablespoon tomato paste

Garlic Yogurt:
2 cloves garlic, minced and mashed into
    a paste with ½ teaspoon sea salt
1 cup plain yogurt

Wash the zucchini and scrape the outer peel, making a striped design. Cut the tops and bottoms off the zucchini. Starting at one end, scoop out the insides with a long corer, leaving a 1/4-inch-thick shell. Rinse well and drain.

Heat the canola oil in a frying pan. Lightly fry the zucchini on all sides without letting the color change, about 2 to 3 minutes. Transfer zucchini to a plate covered with paper towels to drain; set aside to cool.

In a small pan, heat 2 tablespoons of olive oil. Add the onion and sauté, stirring, 4 to 5 minutes. Add the ground sirloin and cook until the color has changed and meat is cooked, 4 to 5 minutes. Stir in 1 teaspoon red pepper paste, salt and pepper to taste, and pine nuts.

Mix well and remove from heat. Let mixture cool to room temperature. Using a teaspoon, stuff the zucchini with the meat mixture.

Place zucchini side-by-side in a 10-inch skillet. In a small bowl combine hot water, tomato paste, remaining teaspoon of pepper paste, salt and pepper to taste. Stir in 2 tablespoons of olive oil and pour the mixture over the stuffed zucchini. Bring to a boil, reduce heat, cover, and simmer for 25 minutes.

Blend the garlic paste with the yogurt and serve alongside the hot, stuffed zucchini.

baked grouper with mediterranean flavors

Akdeniz Usulü Laos Balığı
Mersin

Grouper is a Mediterranean fish known for its tasty and tender flesh. You can roast it as kebabs, bake, poach, or steam it. Here the fish is baked with garlic, shallots, tomatoes, cubanelle peppers, and mushrooms.

Serves 4

4 (½-pound) grouper fillets
Sea salt
Freshly ground pepper
1 tablespoon oil or butter to grease baking dish
6 to 7 cloves garlic, halved
4 shallots, peeled and quartered
3 medium tomatoes, quartered
2 to 3 green cubanelle peppers, stems, ribs, and seeds removed, halved,
      and cut into 2-inch lengths
½ pound small button mushrooms, cleaned with a damp cloth, stems removed
1½ tablespoons butter, melted
1 tablespoon fresh thyme leaves
2 to 3 bay leaves

211

Preheat oven to 350°F. Season grouper fillets with sea salt and pepper to taste. Grease a 12-inch round clay dish or heavy baking dish with 1 tablespoon butter.

Place the seasoned fillets in the prepared pan, leaving space in between them. Arrange garlic cloves, shallots, tomatoes, cubanelle peppers, and mushrooms around the sides of the fish fillets. Drizzle 1 1/2 tablespoons of melted butter over the fish and vegetables. Sprinkle with thyme and add bay leaves. Bake until cooked, about 20 minutes. (Test by inserting a toothpick into the fish; if needed, cook for a few more minutes.)

Remove fish from oven and let sit 6 to 7 minutes. Remove bay leaves and serve hot with lots of warm crusty bread.

fried red mullet

Barbunya Tava
Antalya

Red mullet *(barbunya balığı)* is plentiful in the Aegean and Mediterranean seas because of the warm climate. Small-boned red mullet has a firm texture and a delicate and unique, buttery flavor. In Turkey, it is usually available between July and October. It is the Ilkin family's favorite summer fish. Since it is not a fatty fish, it is best when fried, baked, or steamed. It is hard to find in the United States, although you may come across it at your local fishmonger from time to time. This dish is lovely with arugula salad.

Serves 3 to 4

2 pounds (about 7 or 8 pieces) red mullet with heads left on, cleaned by a fishmonger
5 to 6 tablespoons flour
½ teaspoon sea salt
1¼ cups canola oil for frying
Lemon wedges for serving

Wash and drain the fish and pat dry. Place flour on a flat plate and mix with salt. Dip fish in the flour mixture until it is well coated on all sides.

Heat the oil in a medium frying pan. Fry fish in batches for 3 to 4 minutes on each side. Drain well on paper towels and serve with lemon wedges.

grilled swordfish steaks

Izgara Kılıç Balığı
Antalya

Swordfish is a firm fish that won't fall apart, making it great for grilling. Live fish can reach 15 feet in length and have swords that extend as much as 5 feet! They are a favorite fish in eastern Mediterranean cooking.

Serves 4

4 (½-pound, 1-inch thick) swordfish steaks

Marinade:
¼ cup olive oil
2 tablespoons freshly squeezed lemon juice
Sea salt
Freshly ground pepper
2 cloves garlic, minced

Sauce:
¼ cup olive oil
1½ tablespoons freshly squeezed lemon juice
Sea salt
Freshly ground pepper
1 tablespoon finely chopped Italian flat-leaf parsley
2 scallions, roots removed, sliced thin, with about 2 inches of green
1 tablespoon capers (optional)

Lemon wedges for serving

Rinse fish steaks, drain, and pat dry with a paper towel. Arrange in a shallow dish.

In a bowl, combine marinade ingredients, mixing well. Pour the marinade over fish and cover. Refrigerate for 3 to 4 hours, turning fish over from time to time. Remove from the refrigerator 30 minutes before cooking and bring to room temperature.

Meanwhile, in another bowl, combine all the ingredients for the sauce and mix well. Set aside.

Preheat broiler or place a cast iron plate or griddle over high heat. Place steaks on a broiler pan or in the cast iron plate and cook for 4 to 5 minutes on each side; be careful not to overcook the fish.

Arrange the fish on a serving platter with lemon wedges. Pour the sauce over the top and serve hot with baked potatoes and green salad.

monkfish kebabs

Fener Balığı Şiş
Antalya

Firm monkfish (*baliği* in Turkish) is excellent for making kebabs. Monkfish are the best known of the anglerfish genus, which has over 150 species. Serve hot with a salad and lemon wedges.

Serves 5 to 6

2½ pounds monkfish fillets

Marinade:
1 teaspoon fresh thyme leaves
¼ cup freshly squeezed lemon juice
3 cloves garlic, minced
1 bay leaf
6 tablespoons extra-virgin olive oil
Sea salt
Freshly ground pepper

10 to 12 small button mushrooms, cleaned, stems removed
1 red bell pepper, ribs, stem, and seeds removed, cut in 1½-inch squares
1 green bell pepper, ribs, stem, and seeds removed, cut in 1½-inch squares
Olive oil to brush fish
Lemon wedges to serve

Cut away the thin membrane that covers the flesh of the monkfish. Rinse the fillets in cold water. Drain well, pat dry with paper towels, and cut into 1 1/2-inch squares.

To Prepare the Marinade:
In a bowl, combine the thyme, lemon juice, garlic, and bay leaf. Gradually whisk in the olive oil and season with salt and pepper to taste. Place fish in the marinade and toss to coat well. Cover and refrigerate for two hours.

Remove from the refrigerator at least one hour before cooking. Thread the fish onto skewers, alternating the fish with mushrooms, and green and red peppers. Place the broiler rack about 3 inches from the heat and brush with oil. Place the kebabs on the rack side by side, leaving some space between them.

   Broil the kebabs for about 5 to 6 minutes on each side, brushing with leftover marinade after you turn them.

eggplant stew with lentils

Şeyh Mualla
Antakya

This stew uses green lentils, eggplants, onions, bell peppers, and tomatoes. Living in the same apartment building and coming from neighboring cities (Antakya and Gaziantep), Nur and her dear late friend Sevinç Üstün shared and cooked many recipes together. This vegetarian recipe is one of Sevinç's. Nur recalls her (and her food) fondly.

Serves 6 as an entrée

¾ cup green lentils
Water for soaking
6 (4- to 5- inch) Italian eggplants
Sea salt
½ cup canola oil for frying
¾ cup extra-virgin olive oil, divided
4 medium onions, finely diced
6 to 7 garlic cloves, finely diced
1 large red bell pepper, finely diced

1 large green bell pepper, finely diced
4 large tomatoes, peeled and diced
Freshly ground pepper
1 tablespoons pomegranate molasses
½ teaspoon cumin
1¾ cups water
2 tablespoons freshly chopped Italian
    flat-leaf parsley
1 teaspoon dried mint

215

In a large bowl soak the lentils in water to cover for two hours. Then cook them, covered, until tender, 20 to 25 minutes. Drain well.

Wash the eggplants. Leaving an inch of peel on the top and bottom, peel off 1/2-inch strips of skin, lengthwise, at 1/2-inch intervals, making a striped effect. Repeat until all eggplants have been striped. Starting just below the 1-inch uncut space at the top of the eggplants, make four, evenly spaced, lengthwise cuts, forming four equal size pieces that are connected at the top but separate at the bottom; be careful not to cut the eggplants into individual pieces. Place the eggplant pieces in a colander and generously salt them. Let eggplants stand for 30 minutes, then rinse and drain well. Pat eggplants dry with paper towel.

Cover a plate or cookie sheet with layers of paper towel for draining the eggplants after frying. Heat canola oil in a deep frying pan and fry the eggplants on both sides until golden brown. Drain well on the paper towels.

In a medium-size saucepan, heat 1/2 cup of the olive oil over medium heat. When hot, add the onions and garlic, stirring constantly. Add the red and green peppers and mix well. Continue to sauté for 3 to 4 minutes. Add the tomatoes and the lentils. Mix well and cook for 4 to 5 more minutes, then turn off the heat. Stir in the salt, pepper, molasses, and cumin and mix well.

Arrange the eggplants in a large skillet. Gently place the lentil mixture in between the cuts of each eggplant, fanning them out to hold the filling. Pour water and remaining olive oil over and around the eggplants, cover, and cook over medium heat for 25 to 30 minutes. Arrange on a serving platter and sprinkle with chopped parsley and dried mint. Serve warm or at room temperature.

chickpea patties

Nohut Köftesi
Throughout the Mediterranean

Similar to falafel, this vegetarian entrée is a unique way to use chickpeas. It is served with a delicious yogurt sauce.

Serves 2 to 3. Makes about 10 patties.

1½ cups (15.5 ounces) canned chickpeas, rinsed and drained
1 large egg
5 tablespoons flour
Sea salt
Freshly ground pepper
2 to 3 cloves garlic, minced
2 tablespoons finely chopped Italian flat-leaf parsley
½ teaspoon Aleppo pepper
3 scallions, root end and damaged green leaves removed, thinly sliced crosswise
¼ cup canola oil for frying

Yogurt Sauce:
1 cup plain yogurt
2 cloves garlic, minced, mashed into a paste with ½ teaspoon sea salt
½ teaspoon dried mint

Place the chickpeas, egg, flour, salt and pepper to taste, garlic, parsley, Aleppo pepper, and scallions in the food processor and pulse until well blended. Place the mixture on a plate. Wet your hands and make (about 10) 2-inch round patties.

Heat the oil in a frying pan and fry patties for 2 to 3 minutes, turning them over, until golden brown.

Prepare yogurt sauce: Mix all the ingredients together in a bowl. Serve patties with the sauce.

green lentil stew with spinach roots or zucchini

Ekşili Ispanak Başı
Mersin

This vegetarian dish uses spinach roots, green lentils, and a few other ingredients. It can also be prepared by substituting zucchini (diced into 1-inch cubes) for the spinach roots. (The cooking time has to be increased by 5 minutes, and another 1/4 cup of water may be needed.)

Serves 6

1½ pounds spinach with roots
1½ cups dried green lentils, soaked in hot water for 3 to 4 hours
¼ cup extra-virgin olive oil
2 medium onions, finely chopped
Sea salt
Freshly ground pepper
1 tablespoon tomato paste
3 cups water
2 to 3 cloves garlic, minced
2 to 3 tablespoons freshly squeezed lemon juice

Prepare spinach by discarding damaged outer leaves and stems. Cut off roots that come from underneath the soil. Do not separate the stems from the pink roots; these are the tastiest part. Cut the stems and pink roots into 2-inch-long pieces and soak in water, changing the water several times until there is no more sand (keep the leaves for stir fries or salads). Drain soaked green lentils.

In a medium-size skillet, heat the oil and sauté the onions for 5 minutes, stirring. Season to taste with salt and pepper, stir in tomato paste, and 3 cups of water. Bring to a boil, and stir in the drained green lentils. Reduce heat, cover, and simmer for 15 minutes. Stir in spinach roots; mix well, and cook, covered, 9 to 10 minutes. Combine the garlic and lemon juice and stir into stew during the last 5 minutes.

Adjust seasoning if needed and serve warm or at room temperature.

bulgur patties with tomato and garlic sauce

Sarımsaklı Bulgur Köftesi
Adana

This is a hearty vegetarian dish that can easily be made ahead. The patties are complemented by a wonderful sauce made with tomatoes and plenty of garlic.

Serves 8

2 cups fine bulgur
6¼ cups water, divided
1 medium onion, finely grated
Sea salt
Freshly ground pepper
1 teaspoon Aleppo pepper
1½ teaspoons red pepper paste
    or tomato paste
1 large egg, lightly beaten
1 cup sifted flour

Garlic sauce:
½ cup extra-virgin olive oil
5 to 6 cloves garlic, minced, mashed into
    a paste with ½ teaspoon sea salt
4 medium tomatoes, peeled and grated
Sea salt
Freshly ground pepper
½ teaspoon Aleppo pepper
1 teaspoon ground cumin
2 teaspoons red pepper paste
2 tablespoons finely chopped Italian
    flat-leaf parsley

In a large bowl, combine the bulgur with 1 cup of hot water. Cover and let sit for 10 to 15 minutes. Stir in onion, salt and pepper to taste, Aleppo pepper, and pepper paste. Using your hands, knead the mixture for 3 to 4 minutes, blending the ingredients. Add the lightly beaten egg, and gradually add the flour, kneading with each addition. Knead for 10 minutes, forming a smooth dough.

Divide the mixture into 2 parts and pulse each part in the food processor until well blended. If the dough is too hard, add 2 tablespoons of water to each part. Place mixture on a plate. Wet your hands; using your palms, form a ball from 1 tablespoon of the mixture. Press your thumb into the center of the ball, making a slight indentation. Repeat until all the mixture has been used, making sure to wet your hands before forming each patty.

In a 4-quart pot, place 5 cups of water and a pinch of salt, and bring to a boil. Reduce heat and add the patties to the pot. Cook for 15 to 20 minutes, uncovered. Remove with a slotted spoon to a serving bowl or platter.

To Prepare the Garlic Sauce:
In a small saucepan, heat the oil and sauté the garlic for 2 minutes, stirring. Add the tomatoes and continue to cook for 6 to 7 minutes. Add salt and pepper to taste, Aleppo pepper, cumin, and red pepper paste. Continue to cook for another 2 to 3 minutes and remove from the heat.

Transfer the sauce to a large skillet, heat it, and add the koftas; cook with the sauce until they are hot. Arrange on a serving platter and sprinkle with parsley.

carrot and walnut slices

Cezeriye
Mersin

This dessert is made from carrots, which are native to Afghanistan. The name of the dish derives from the Arabic word, *cezer*, meaning carrots. In southern Turkey, *cezeriye* refers to all the desserts prepared with carrots, and there are many. The carrots in Turkey are delicious, sweet, and rich in vitamins A and B. They range from reddish-pink to purple in color. Since 1949, *cezeriye* has been prepared in what is now Mersin. Its popularity is worldwide. Finely ground coconut is available in Middle Eastern and organic markets, or you can make it by chopping shredded or grated coconut in your food processor.

Serves 8 to 10

1 pound (about 5) carrots, peeled and coarsely grated
2 cups sugar
1 cup plus 2 tablespoons water
1 tablespoon cornstarch
1½ cups coarsely chopped walnuts or hazelnuts
¼ cup finely ground coconut, or more to taste

221

In a 3-quart pan, combine the carrots, sugar, and 1 cup of water. Cook over medium-low heat until all the liquid has been absorbed, 55 to 60 minutes (or longer if necessary).

When the liquid is just about absorbed, mix together the cornstarch and 2 tablespoons of water and stir into the carrot mixture. Using a potato masher, mash the carrots well for 3 to 4 minutes. Stir in the walnuts and remove from heat.

Sprinkle an 8 x 6-inch Pyrex pan with the coconut (you can use an 8 x 8-inch pan but the slices will not be as thick). Put carrot mixture into the prepared pan, and even out the top by gently pressing on it with your fingertips. Sprinkle the top with coconut. Cover and let cool at room temperature for 3 to 4 hours.

Cut into 1-inch squares and cut every square into 4 equal slices. Lay slices on one side and sprinkle with more coconut.

kataifi with cheese

Künefe
Throughout the Mediterranean

We learned this marvelous recipe from Hayri Karakas, whose father was also a cook. It is best if you can use an 11-inch round pan and an 11 3/4-inch pan, since the dessert is turned over into the bigger pan before the cooking is finished. Serve hot, immediately after you prepare this recipe; it does not reheat well. Kataifi is a shredded phyllo pastry that looks like shredded wheat. You can find it in the freezer section of Mediterranean markets and some supermarkets.

Serves 10 to 12

Syrup:
2 cups water
1½ cups sugar
½-inch-thick slice of lemon

4 ounces butter, melted, cooled to room temperature
10½ ounces kataifi phyllo (we used Apollo brand), defrosted and at room temperature
12 ounces fresh, unsalted mozzarella cheese, sliced into 1/8-inch thick slices
2 tablespoons chopped pistachio nuts

To Prepare the Syrup:
In a small pot bring the water, sugar, and lemon slice to a boil over high heat. Stir to dissolve the sugar, and then stir occasionally for 15 to 20 minutes. Syrup is done when a drop placed on your fingernail firmly holds its shape (and does not spread). Let syrup cool to room temperature.

Preheat oven to 375°F. Grease an 11-inch round pan (3/4-inch high) and a round 11 3/4-inch pan with 1 or 2 teaspoons of the melted butter.

Place kataifi in a large pan or bowl. Using your fingers, toss and separate the strands. Then toss with all of the remaining melted butter. Evenly spread half of the kataifi in the smaller pan, gently pressing down with your fingers. Cover the kataifi with the slices of mozzarella, leaving about 1 inch around the edges free of cheese. Cover the cheese with the remaining kataifi. Press gently all around the pan with your hands. Place the dish in the refrigerator for 10 minutes.

Remove from the refrigerator and bake until golden brown, 30 to 40 minutes; use a spatula to lift up a section to check if the bottom has browned. Remove from the oven.
Place the larger pan over the smaller pan and carefully flip them over so the dessert ends up in the larger pan. Bake for another 5 to 8 minutes.

While the kataifi is baking, fill a large bowl with ice. Place the cooled syrup into a small bowl that fits comfortably into the ice. Let the syrup sit in ice until chilled.

Remove the dish from the oven and carefully ladle the cold syrup over the hot kataifi a little at a time so it can be absorbed. Sprinkle the top with pistachio nuts, cut into wedges, and serve.

molasses halva with walnuts
Pekmez Helvası
Isparta

During a visit to Isparta, the İlkins were served this dessert with coffee. It is a slightly rich sweet that takes no time at all to prepare. During her childhood, Nur was given grape molasses before going to school in winter to give her energy and strength. Grape molasses and wheat starch are available in Turkish, Mediterranean, or Middle Eastern markets.

Serves 6

¾ cup wheat starch or cornstarch
¾ cup water
1 cup grape molasses
½ tablespoon butter
½ cup coarsely chopped walnuts
6 tablespoons ground walnuts, divided

In a medium-size pan, combine the wheat starch and water, mixing well until blended. Place on medium-low heat and slowly add the molasses, stirring constantly with a wooden spoon. Continue stirring, making sure there are no lumps, until the mixture thickens, about 10 to 12 minutes. Be careful not to let mixture burn; if necessary, lower the heat. Stir in the butter and mix well. Stir in 1/2 cup of coarsely chopped walnuts. Remove from the heat.

Line the bottom and sides of a shallow, 6-inch round dish or bowl with plastic wrap. Gently spread and press 3 tablespoons of the ground walnuts on the bottom of the dish with your fingertips. Spoon the molasses mixture over the ground nuts and spread it evenly with a metal spatula. Sprinkle the remaining 3 tablespoons of ground walnuts evenly over the top. Let cool, cover, and refrigerate for at least 6 to 7 hours. Unmold the mixture onto a plate or round dish and gently remove the plastic wrap. Cut into 6 equal pieces and serve with coffee.

semolina dessert with tahini

Tahinli İrmik Tatlısı
Adana

You don't usually think of tahini as being a dessert ingredient, but it is in this dish. For added sweetness, serve this with ice cream and berries.

Serves 8

Syrup:
1¾ cups sugar
1¾ cup water
1 tablespoon freshly squeezed lemon juice

½ cup tahini
1 cup plain yogurt
⅓ cup melted butter, cooled a little
½ cup sugar
2 cups semolina
1 teaspoon vanilla
Butter or oil for greasing the pan
⅓ cup unsalted peanuts or hazelnuts, to decorate the top

To Prepare the Syrup:
Cook the sugar and water in a small pot over medium heat, stirring constantly, for 10 minutes. Add lemon juice, reduce heat and cook for another 5 minutes. Remove from heat and set aside to cool.

Preheat oven 350°F. In a large bowl, combine tahini, yogurt, melted butter, and sugar. Mix well and slowly add the semolina and vanilla, stirring well to blend the ingredients.

Grease a 10-inch round baking dish, and spoon the semolina mixture into the dish, flattening with a spatula to even. Decorate the top with peanuts or hazelnuts. Bake until the top is golden brown, about 40 minutes. Remove from oven and pour cold syrup all over. Let dessert cool and absorb the syrup.

semolina halva with cheese

Peynirli İrmik Helvası
Adana

The name halva comes from Arabic word *halwa* (sweet), and it is one of the oldest Turkish desserts. It came to Anatolia before the Turks, and is still very popular today. It is served on special occasions such as Ramadan, Kandil, and other holy days, but is also used to honor birth and death. There are several versions of halva, and a variety of ingredients can be used to make it.

Semolina halva is a loose granular pudding made with semolina and sweet hot milk. Semolina, with its sugar-like consistency and mildly nutty flavor, is the inner endosperm of wheat. In baking, it is prized for its special texture as well as its thickening properties. Note that leftovers need to be reheated before serving.

Serves 8

2 cups milk
1 teaspoon vanilla
4 tablespoons butter
1 cup semolina
1¼ cup sugar
10 ounces fresh unsalted mozzarella, coarsely grated
Dash of cinnamon (optional)

Boil the milk and vanilla in a small pan. In a medium pan, heat the butter. Stir in the semolina and sauté, stirring, for 8 to 10 minutes. Stir the boiled milk into the semolina and continue stirring until all the liquid has been absorbed and no lumps remain. Add the sugar and grated cheese, mixing with a wooden spoon until well blended, about 6 to 7 minutes. Remove from heat. Cover pan with a kitchen towel, cover with pan lid, and let rest for 10 to 15 minutes.

Turn halva upside down onto a round serving dish and sprinkle with cinnamon if desired. Serve hot.

semolina milk pudding

İrmik Muhallebisi
Antakya

Semolina is golden-yellow in color. Many cuisines use it in fillings to help absorb excess liquid.

Serves 8 to 10

4 cups milk
1 cup sugar
2 pieces of mastic, pounded with 1 teaspoon sugar
1 teaspoon vanilla
3 tablespoons semolina
1 tablespoon butter
2 tablespoons finely ground or shredded coconut
1 cup dried currants, soaked in water for 30 minutes, rinsed, and drained well
3 tablespoons coarsely chopped pistachio nuts

Place the milk and sugar in a 2-quart pan and bring to a boil. Reduce heat to medium, add mastic and vanilla, and stir well. Slowly add the semolina and whisk constantly until mixture thickens, 6 to 7 minutes. Stir in the butter, coconut, and currants.

Run water all over the inside of a 9-inch round Pyrex pie pan, and pour out the water, without drying the pan; this will prevent the pudding from sticking. Pour the pudding into the pan and let cool. Sprinkle top with nuts. Refrigerate, covered, for at least 6 hours. Turn pudding out onto a serving platter, and serve.

central anatolia

mezze and salads

Yogurt 236
Strained Yogurt 237
Garlicky Yogurt 237
Beet Salad with Bulgur and Garlicky Yogurt 238

soups

Green Bean Soup with Green Lentils and Bulgur 239
Green Lentil Soup with Noodles and Mint 240

pilafs and bread

Anatolian Flatbread 242
Mevlana's Rice 243
Rice Pilaf with Lamb, Chickpeas, and Jumbo Raisins 245

meat

Ankara Rice with Lamb 246
Lamb Loin and Eggplant Stew 247
Baked Koftas 248
Stuffed Quinces 248
White Beans with *Pastırma* in a Clay Pot 249

vegetables

Tomato Stew with Bulgur 251
Chickpea Stew 252

desserts and sweets

Diamonds with Tahini and Walnuts 254
1, 2, 3, 4 Spoon Halva 255
Noah's Milk Pudding 255
Saffron Rice Pudding 257
Sweet Rounds with Almonds 258

The arid highlands of Central Anatolia form the heartland of Turkey. The vast plain has been settled for over 8,000 years, and has seen the rule of the Hattis, Hittites, Phrygians, Lydians, Persians, Greeks, Galatians, Romans, Byzantines, and the Seljuk and Ottoman Turks. It wasn't until the 11th century that Turks migrated from the East and made the plateau their own. Central Anatolian cuisine is a mosaic of centuries of these inhabitants, each adding distinctive ingredients and flavors.

The Turks were first introduced to rice and numerous fruits and vegetables in their new homeland, and these ingredients were quickly incorporated into their cuisine. Drying fruits and vegetables and using them to prepare pickles and molasses for winter are traditions that continue today. Stuffing all types of vegetables, even okra and cherry leaves, was typical of the Turks of Central Anatolia, and is still a common practice. These dishes are called *dolmas*.

Today, over half of the land is used for agriculture and farming. Wheat is the principle source of nutrition in the Central Anatolian diet. Originally, the Turks cultivated wheat and used it to prepare leavened and unleavened breads, noodles, boereks, *mantı* (ravioli-like dumplings), shelled wheat, cracked wheat, and more. Goat cheese and traditional cheeses prepared in clay pots or pitchers (*çömlek peyniri* or *testi peyniri*) are also produced in the area. Yogurt is an integral part of everyday life throughout Anatolia and it is considered Turkey's most important culinary gift to the world.

At the heart of Asia Minor, the ancient city of Ankara was declared Turkey's capital in 1923. Its history can be traced as far back as the Bronze Age. Although its name changed frequently, it has remained a center of trade and commerce for the surrounding region. Such delights as copperware, traditional crafts, fresh produce, spices, nuts, and varieties of dried fruits can be purchased here. Ankara has been famous for its pears, honey, and muscat grapes, as well as a breed of goat prized for its wool. Special dishes of the region include *Ankara tavası*, Ankara Rice with Lamb, (page 246) and a variety of kofta baked in copper (page 248). Its cuisine is enriched by local wheat, beans, corn, and tomatoes that are grown in the neighboring province of Çankiri.

Konya, once the capital of the Seljuke Empire, is a cultural center with a rich, distinctive cuisine that has been developed over centuries. Konya's cuisine reached its zenith during the Mystic Mevlana Celalettin Rumi Period. The shrine of the 13th-century Sufi mystic and poet Mevlana Jalal al Din Rumi lies in Konya and has become a place of pilgrimage. Wheat, fruits, grains, vegetables, and meats were the main source of nutrition during this period, and many luxurious dishes emerged. Numerous soups, and an opulent pilaf called *Mevlevi Pilavı*, Mevlana's Rice (page 243) have remained a part of the local cuisine.

During the 14th and 15th centuries, woven carpets from the region became a symbol of luxury and wealth throughout Europe; they appear in many famous paintings. Today, Konya is known for a lamb dish called *tandır*, which is baked in a clay oven by the same name (the famous Anatolian flatbread—page 242— is also prepared in this way). A variety of boereks and *pide* (flatbread) topped with ground meat are also regional specialties as well as many varieties of halva, a sweet consisting of flour, butter, sugar, and milk.

Though historically less important, the city of Aksaray is revered for its local cuisine. As in Konya, flour and syrup-based desserts are popular here, along with many varieties of toasted boereks. The Silk Road trade route passed through the province of Aksaray, infusing the culture with foreign ingredients and cultures. The fertile soil provides grains, meat, and dairy and many kinds of fruits and vegetables.

Central Anatolia is also well known for its viticulture; the province of Nevşehir predominantly relied on its grape production for income—before the onset of the tourist industry. Historic Cappadocia, largely in this province, is home to the geological wonder, the fairy chimneys, which have drawn many tourists to the region. The cityscapes offer monasteries, caravanserais, and the beautiful churches of Göreme (a city also known for the production of fine chickpeas and wheat). Nevertheless the fine-quality grapes of the region are still a boon to both local and international wine producers and the quality of Turkish wines is constantly improving. The city of Ürgüp is the wine-producing center of the province and hosts an annual international wine festival in October.

Other fruits flourish in this part of the region as well; the nearby cities of Nidğe and Kirşehir are rich with orchards that produce the best quality apples and quinces. These are often stuffed with ground meat and grape molasses, combining the flavors of the region. Many of these fruits are dried or made into jams for the winter. A rare truffle called *keme* can be found in this area and is used to give stews, sautés, and kebabs a distinct local flavor.

In the eastern part of the region, the beautiful city of Kayseri is a popular tourist destination en route to historic Cappadocia. It is flanked by the Zamantı River and Mount Erciyes, which characterize the landscape and draw adventure travelers to the region. The city is known for such culinary delights as *mantı* (ravioli-like dumplings) and *pastırma*—dried cured beef coated with garlic and spices. Popular dishes include *Pehli*, Lamb Loin and Eggplant Stew (page 247), and White Beans with Pastırma in a Clay Pot (page 249).

Clay pots have been used in Turkish cooking for hundreds of years, and these methods are popular in the region. In the northwest, the Eskişehir province has a longstanding clay-pot making tradition that has influenced the regional cuisine. In some villages in Eskişehir this pottery is made using Neolithic techniques, including the use of open-fire kilns. The city of Eskişehir provides a stark contrast to the provincial villages that surround it. A booming industrial metropolis, Eskişehir is a center of cultural amalgamation and has populations of Crimean Tatars and Turks who emigrated from Bulgaria, Romania, Bosnia, and Sandzak. These cultures introduce diversity to the local cuisine.

The northeast of the region is populated by moderately sized cities and small, rural villages. The economy relies on agriculture and the industry of the cities. The thermal springs of Sivas, which are believed to have healing powers, draw many visitors to the city, a significant rail junction. The Sivas Province is a large producer of cereal products, and many of the local dishes include these grains. Examples of these include *Fasulye Çorbası*, Green Bean Soup with Green Lentils and Bulgur (page 239), and a fragrant dish popular for weddings called *Alatlı Pilavı*, Rice Pilaf with Lamb, Chickpeas, and Jumbo Raisins (page 245). The neighboring Yozgat province has a history of trade, agriculture, and animal husbandry. *Pancar Cacığı* (page 238), a hearty beet and bulgur salad with a garlic yogurt sauce, comes from this province.

yogurt

Yoğurt
Central Anatolia and throughout Turkey

Yogurt, which is made from milk fermented with living bacterial cultures, plays an important role in Turkish cuisine, particularly in Anatolia, where it is an integral part of everyday life. It is used in everything from sauces to soups, desserts, and drinks. Yogurt can be made from almost any full fat, low-fat, or fat-free milk, including goat's milk, cow's milk, sheep's milk, and even soy milk; but whole milk yields a sweeter, thicker, creamier yogurt than its low-fat counterparts.

Makes 1 quart (4 cups)

1 quart (4 cups) milk
3 tablespoons plain yogurt, at room temperature

Fold an old blanket or a bath towel into four and place it in the corner of a kitchen counter; this will be a nest for your yogurt. Place a large glass bowl in the middle of the blanket or towel.

Place the milk in a large pot and heat until it reaches just under boiling point (190°F to 210°F), about 5 to 10 minutes. (This temperature destroys undesirable organisms that could prevent coagulation.)

The milk will bubble around the edges and a film or skin will form on the top. Remove pan from the heat and carefully pour milk into the bowl. Let sit, uncovered, until it cools to about 110°F to 115°F (it is hot to the touch but not burning). This is the ideal temperature for adding the yogurt starter. (If the temperature is lower, the bacteria in the starter is less active and takes longer to grow; temperatures over 120°F will destroy the bacteria.)

Stir a little of the warm milk into the yogurt to thin it, making it easier to blend into the milk. Use a wooden spoon to make a well in the center of the milk. Pour the thinned yogurt starter into the well and stir well. Cover the bowl with plastic wrap, and completely cover the bowl with the sides of your blanket or towel. Leave undisturbed at room temperature for at least 12 hours; this time allows the yogurt to develop its slightly tangy taste. After this time, place the yogurt in a container, cover with 4 layers of paper towel to absorb excess whey, and refrigerate for about 12 hours (or as desired) before using. The yogurt can be stored in the refrigerator for up to 1 1/2 weeks. Change the paper towels often during the first few days to absorb excess whey.

strained yogurt

Süzme Yoğurt
Central Anatolia and throughout Turkey

Strained yogurt is sometimes referred to as Greek yogurt or *labneh*.

Makes 1½ to 2 cups

4 cups (32 ounces) good quality, plain yogurt

Line a colander or strainer with a double layer of cheesecloth, allowing the edges to hang over the sides; place over a large bowl. Pour the yogurt into the colander and let sit at room temperature for at least 4 to 5 hours, checking periodically and draining the whey (liquid) as it accumulates in the bowl.

To speed up the draining process or yield a thicker result, you can tie the edges of the cheesecloth over the top of the yogurt. It can then be pressed with a heavy weight or can. You may also gently squeeze the cheesecloth bag to get rid of more whey. The longer the yogurt drains; the thicker it will become. When you are satisfied with the consistency, transfer the strained yogurt to a container, cover, and refrigerate until use.

237

garlicky yogurt

Sarımsak Yoğurt
Central Anatolia and throughout Turkey

1½ cups plain yogurt
3 to 4 cloves garlic, minced with ½ teaspoon sea salt

Mix the yogurt and garlic paste in a bowl. Serve as a sauce or dip.

beet salad with bulgur and garlicky yogurt

Pancar Cacığı
Yozgat

This is a typical dish prepared in the poorer rural villages in the heart of Anatolia. It is a tasty meal rather than just a salad. Beets are easy to grow, lend themselves to both hot and cold dishes, and can be eaten cooked or raw. Just remember that they bleed and stain when you work with them. A helpful hint is to cover your chopping board with plastic wrap to protect it from stains. Cookbook author Janet Ballantyne taught me to leave about an inch of stem, the taproot, and the skin intact to reduce the bleeding; but the beets still bleed some.

Serves 4

1 pound fresh beets, preferably of equal size
4 cups water
¼ teaspoon sea salt
1 tablespoon butter
3 tablespoons canola oil
1 large onion, finely chopped
½ cup coarse bulgur
1¼ cups chicken or vegetable stock
Freshly ground pepper
Garlicky Yogurt (page 237)

Wash beets and cut the greens away; these can be reserved for use in salads. In a medium saucepan, heat water. Add the beets and bring to a boil. Add salt and simmer, covered, over low heat for approximately 40 minutes or until beets are cooked. Drain well and let cool. Peel off the skin under cold running water. Cut beets into 1/2-inch-thick cubes.

In a medium-size skillet, heat the butter and oil. Stirring constantly, sauté the onions over low heat until golden brown. Add the cubed beets, bulgur, and stock. Mix well and cook, covered, until all the liquid has been absorbed, about 15 to 20 minutes. Remove from heat, remove lid, and cover the skillet with a double layer of paper towels. Replace the lid and set aside for 10 to 15 minutes. Season with salt and pepper to taste. Arrange on a serving dish.

Serve the salad with Garlicky Yogurt.

green bean soup with green lentils and bulgur

Fasulye Çorbası
Sivas

This exceptional, chunky soup makes use of the local produce of the Sivas Province. Nur's grand-mother told her "everything that grows together at the same time goes together when cooking." As a vegetarian variation, substitute vegetable stock or water for the chicken stock.

Serves 6 to 8

5 tablespoons canola oil
1 large onion
9 ounces (2 cups) fresh green beans, ends trimmed, rinsed, drained,
     cut crosswise into ½-inch pieces
2 green cubanelle peppers, stem, ribs, and seeds removed, finely chopped
2 medium tomatoes, peeled and finely chopped
8 cups warm chicken stock
½ cup green lentils, soaked in water for 3 to 4 hours, drained
⅓ cup medium-coarse bulgur
½ tablespoon tomato paste
1 teaspoon red pepper paste (optional)
Sea salt
Freshly ground pepper
2 tablespoons butter
½ tablespoon dried basil

In a 5-quart pot, over medium heat, heat oil and sauté onion for 4 to 5 minutes. Stir in beans, and continue to cook for 6 to 7 minutes. Add green peppers and tomatoes and cook for another two minutes, mixing well. Add the warm chicken stock and bring to a boil. Add drained lentils, bulgur, tomato paste, red pepper paste if using, and salt and pepper to taste. Reduce heat to medium-low. Cover and cook until beans are tender, 45 to 50 minutes. Taste for seasoning and add more salt or pepper if needed.

In a small skillet, heat butter until it sizzles. Remove from heat and stir in dried basil. Mix well and pour over soup.

239

green lentil soup with noodles and mint

Yeşil Mercimekli Erişte Çorbası
Central Anatolia and throughout Turkey

This is a common soup throughout Anatolia. The combination of noodles and green lentils is unusual, and dried mint adds a unique taste. In Turkey, noodles are often homemade. If you don't want to make your own, you may find homemade noodles in some specialty food markets, but Nur likes to use angel hair pasta or fettuccine in this recipe.

Serves 6

8 cups chicken stock, divided
1 cup dried green lentils, soaked for 3 to 4 hours, drained
Sea salt
Freshly ground pepper
½ tablespoon tomato paste
½ tablespoon red pepper paste
¾ cup noodles, angel hair pasta, or fettuccine, broken into matchstick-size pieces
2 tablespoons butter
1 tablespoon canola oil
1 tablespoon dried mint
½ teaspoon Aleppo pepper

In a 4-quart pot, bring 6 cups of chicken stock to a boil. Add drained green lentils, salt and pepper to taste, tomato paste, red pepper paste, and mix well. Cover, reduce heat, and simmer for 20 to 25 minutes. Add 2 more cups of stock and the noodles. Mix well, replace cover, and continue to cook for another 10 to 15 minutes. Transfer soup to a tureen.

Heat butter and oil in a small skillet. Remove from heat and stir in dried mint and Aleppo pepper. Mix well and pour over the soup in swirls.

anatolian flatbread

Bazlama
Throughout Central Anatolia

This thick, round flatbread is traditionally baked in a *tandır* (a clay oven) or between two thin hot iron plates. Bread is a staff of life in Turkey and served with almost every meal. This is a tasty, basic bread.

Makes 16 to 18 flatbreads

2 (¼-ounce) packages active dry yeast, at room temperature
1 teaspoon sugar
2 cups warm water (about 105°F to 115°F; do not heat the water too much or it
    will kill the yeast)
3 tablespoons canola oil plus more for greasing the bowl
2 teaspoons salt
5½ cups sifted all-purpose or bread flour, plus more if necessary, divided

Place yeast and sugar in a large bowl and add water. Mix well to dissolve and let stand for about 10 minutes to proof or until foam forms on the top. (If it does not foam, your yeast may be dead and the recipe will not work.) Whisk in the oil, salt, and 2 cups of flour and mix until blended and smooth. Add another cup of flour and blend well; then add another cup, blending well until mixture is smooth. Using your hands, mix in the last 1 1/2 cups of flour. The dough may be somewhat sticky; if it is, add extra flour by the tablespoon as you knead the dough.

On a lightly floured work surface, knead the dough until it has formed a smooth, elastic ball of dough, about 8 to 10 minutes. Lightly grease a large bowl and place the ball of dough in it, turning the ball so all sides are lightly greased. Cover bowl with a clean kitchen towel. Set aside in a warm, draft-free place to rise until it has doubled in bulk, about an hour.

Flour your hands and punch down the dough. Divide dough into 16 to 18 balls. Place a ball on the lightly floured surface, flatten the ball, and then pat back and forth between the palms of your hands a few times, to stretch the disk. Using your thumb and index finger, push the edges of the disk, stretching from the center out until it is about 5 inches across and a 1/2-inch thick. Continue until all balls of dough have been stretched.

Lightly grease a large non-stick skillet. Fry as many disks as fit without touching each other in the skillet. Cook over medium heat until puffed and lightly golden brown on the bottom. Turn over and cook until top is just lightly golden. Remove from pan and repeat with the remaining disks. Serve warm with jam, olives, yogurt, or your favorite dip.

Variation: To bake instead of fry, place the disks on a lightly greased baking sheet, covered with a clean kitchen towel, and set aside to rise for another hour in a warm, draft-free place. Preheat oven to 500°F, remove towel, and bake for about 7 minutes or until puffed and brown. (Adapted from a recipe by Gilda Angel, *Sephardic Holiday Cooking: Recipes and Traditions*)

mevlana's rice
Mevlevi Pilavı
Konya

This rich main course is made with expensive ingredients like pine nuts, currants, chestnuts, and pistachio nuts, and your first taste will make it worthwhile! This time-honored dish takes its name from the 13th-century Sufi mystic and poet Mevlana Jalal al Din Rumi, whose followers founded the Mevlevi Order of the Whirling Dervishes in Konya. It was once cooked in Mevlana's own kitchen. Konya was at that time the capital of the Seljuk Sultanate, which controlled most of Anatolia. This era shaped the rich and elaborate cuisine of Konya that is popular today.

Serves 8

4 tablespoons canola oil, divided
4 tablespoons butter, divided
1½ pounds boneless leg of lamb, cut into 1-inch cubes
2 medium onions, finely chopped
3 cups hot water
Sea salt
Freshly ground pepper
3 medium carrots, peeled and coarsely grated
3 tablespoons pine nuts
2 cups uncooked extra-long-grain rice, soaked in lightly salted warm water for 30 minutes
3 tablespoons dried currants
1 cup canned chickpeas, rinsed and drained
1¾ cup roasted and peeled chestnuts
1 teaspoon allspice
¼ cup shelled pistachio nuts, dry roasted
¼ cup shelled almonds, dry roasted

In a 3-quart pan, heat 2 tablespoons canola oil and 1 tablespoon butter. Add the lamb and sauté until the color changes, 4 to 5 minutes. Let the meat release its juice and cook until all the juice has been absorbed. Then add the onions and cook for another couple minutes. Add hot water, salt and pepper to taste, and mix well. Cover, reduce heat, and simmer until the lamb is tender, 40 to 45 minutes. Drain lamb and onions, reserving the cooking liquid. Measure the reserved cooking liquid and add enough hot water to bring liquid to 4 cups. Set aside.

Meanwhile, in a 4-quart pan, heat remaining canola oil and butter. Add the carrots and pine nuts and sauté for 4 to 5 minutes. Add drained rice and currants, mix well, and cook for another few minutes. Stir in the chickpeas, chestnuts, drained lamb, and onions. Pour reserved cooking liquid over the rice, check seasoning and adjust if needed. Stir in the allspice and bring to a boil.

Lower heat to simmer and cook, covered, until steam holes appear on the surface and all the liquid has been absorbed, 20 to 25 minutes. Remove from heat, uncover, and place a double layer of paper towels over the pan. Replace the lid and let stand for 10 to 15 minutes. Stir with a wooden spoon and arrange on a platter. Serve with a fruit compote.

Note: To dry roast nuts, place nuts in a non-stick skillet or pan over medium heat. Cook for 5 to 7 minutes, shaking the pan so they don't burn.

rice pilaf with lamb, chickpeas, and jumbo raisins

Alatlı Pilavı
Sivas

This healthful, hearty dish is served at weddings in Central Anatolia. We love the combination of pepper, cloves, and allspice. Jumbo raisins are big yellow raisins found in specialty food stores or Middle Eastern markets. Each raisin is almost half an inch long. The whole cloves and allspice berries add a subtle, mellow flavor to the dish.

Serves 6 to 8

4 tablespoons butter, divided
1½ pounds boneless leg of lamb, cut into ½-inch cubes
5 black peppercorns
3 cloves
3 allspice berries
3 cups hot water plus more if needed
2 tablespoons canola oil
1 medium onion, finely chopped
2 cups extra-long-grain rice, soaked in lightly salted warm water for 30 minutes
1 cup canned chickpeas, rinsed and drained
¾ cup jumbo golden raisins
Sea salt
Freshly ground pepper

In a 2-quart pan heat 2 tablespoons of butter and sauté the lamb over medium-high heat, until the color changes and all the juices have been absorbed, 4 to 5 minutes.

Tie the peppercorns, cloves, and allspice in a small muslin bag, a piece of cheesecloth, or a spice infuser. Add this and 3 cups of hot water to the pan. Reduce heat, cover, and simmer 40 to 45 minutes or until lamb is tender. Drain lamb cubes, reserving the cooking liquid to cook the rice.

In another 4-quart pan, heat the remaining butter and the canola oil. Add the onion and sauté 10 to 12 minutes until golden brown. Stir in the drained rice and continue to cook for another minute or two. Add the chickpeas, raisins, cooked lamb, and season with salt and pepper to taste.

Measure the reserved cooking liquid and if needed, add enough hot water to measure 4 cups of liquid. Stir into the rice mixture, bring to a boil, reduce heat to simmer, cover and cook for 20 minutes or until all the liquid has been absorbed and steam holes appear on the surface.

Remove from the heat, remove lid, and place a double layer of paper towels or a clean kitchen towel over the top of the pan. Replace the lid and let stand for 10 to 15 minutes. Stir with a wooden spoon then arrange on a serving platter. Serve with a salad.

ankara rice with lamb

Ankara Tavası
Ankara

Nur's daughter-in-law Beste is one of many generations of her family from Ankara; this dish is a family recipe that was passed on to her. It is traditionally served on special occasions such as weddings and funerals. It is a Turkish custom that after a burial ceremony, close relatives prepare lunch for the deceased's family in their home, to share in their sorrow and relieve them of the cooking. Friends send food for several days or even weeks after the funeral, including sweets and rice dishes like this one. This dish has been a part of both the joyful and sorrowful occasions in Nur's life, from her mother's passing to her son's engagement.

Serves 6

2 tablespoons canola oil
4 lamb shanks (with meat)
1 large onion, quartered
1 bay leaf
8 to 10 black peppercorns
7 cups water plus more if needed
4 tablespoons butter
3 medium tomatoes, finely diced
1 cup uncooked extra-long-grain rice, soaked in salted warm water, 30 minutes, drained
Sea salt
Freshly ground pepper

In a large pot, heat the oil and sear the lamb shanks, turning, until all sides change color. Add the onion, bay leaf, peppercorns, and water. Bring to a boil and remove any scum or foam that appears on the surface with a slotted spoon or small strainer. Reduce heat to simmer, cover, and cook 1 1/2 hours or longer, until meat is done. Transfer lamb shanks to a plate. Strain the cooking liquid. You will need 3 1/2 cups of this stock; if you don't have enough, add more hot water.

In a large skillet, heat the butter and stir in the tomatoes. Cook over medium heat for 5 to 6 minutes. Add the rice and cook for another minute or two, mixing well. Season with salt and pepper to taste.

Add the hot stock, place the lamb shanks on the rice, cover, and cook over medium-low heat until all the liquid has been absorbed and holes appear on the surface, about 20 minutes. Remove from heat. Remove the lid and place a kitchen towel over the top of the skillet. Replace the lid and let sit for 10 to 15 minutes. Arrange on a serving platter and serve warm with a green salad.

lamb loin and eggplant stew

Pehli
Kayseri

Lamb loin chops usually contain sections of both the loin and tenderloin, which lies just behind the rib (similar to a beef T-bone). This section is a mild tasting, leaner piece of meat. This Central Anatolian dish is traditionally served on holidays and other special occasions. Turkish baldo rice is a recommended accompaniment.

Serves 6

2 or 3 (about 2 pounds) large eggplants
Sea salt
3 tablespoons canola oil
2 tablespoons butter
12 lamb loin chops (with the bone)
2 onions, finely chopped
6 to 7 cloves garlic, finely chopped
4 green cubanelle (or bell) peppers, stems, seeds, and ribs removed, coarsely chopped
4 large ripe tomatoes, peeled and finely chopped
Freshly ground black pepper
1½ cups hot water
1 tablespoon tomato paste

Using a vegetable peeler, peel the eggplants in 1/2-inch lengthwise stripes, leaving 1/2-inch intervals of skin between each stripe. Cut each eggplant into 1 1/2-inch cubes. Generously salt the eggplant and place in a colander for at least 30 to 40 minutes. Rinse well and drain.

In a large skillet, heat the oil and butter and sauté each lamb chop on each side for 3 minutes. Add the onions, garlic, peppers, tomatoes, and salt and pepper to taste. Mix 1 1/2 cups of hot water with the tomato paste and pour over the meat mixture.

Cook, covered, over medium heat for 10 minutes. Reduce heat and simmer until lamb chops and eggplant are tender, about 30 to 35 minutes, shaking the pan occasionally, using the handles.

baked koftas

Mücirim Köftesi
Ankara

This old recipe is usually made in a *mücirim*, a copper pan that is similar to a pancake pan with indented cups. Nur prepared it in mini-muffin pans; it worked fine, and looked cute. Served with a green salad or Yogurt and Swiss Chard Salad (page 278), this dish is wonderful for brunch.

Serves 4. Makes 12 koftas.

2 tablespoons canola oil
½ pound ground sirloin
½ teaspoon Aleppo pepper
Sea salt
Freshly ground pepper
3 tablespoons finely chopped Italian flat-leaf parsley
2 to 3 tablespoons seasoned herb breadcrumbs
3 large eggs, beaten
Spray for greasing

Preheat oven to 350°F. In a small saucepan, heat the oil and sauté the meat over low heat for 10 to 15 minutes. Place cooked meat in a bowl and season with Aleppo pepper and salt and pepper to taste. Stir in the parsley, breadcrumbs, and beaten eggs. Mix well.

Spray a 12-cup mini-muffin pan and pour mixture evenly into the cups. Place muffin pan on a cookie sheet and bake for about 15 minutes, or until set.

stuffed quinces

Ayva Dolması
Niğde and Kırşehir

This is a family recipe from Hürriyet Silsüpür and her husband, who works for the Turkish mission at the United Nations. Quince are scooped out and stuffed with rice, allspice, cinnamon, and molasses to make this lovely side dish.

Serves 6

6 quinces, washed
Freshly squeezed juice of 1 lemon
3 tablespoons canola oil

9 ounces ground sirloin
⅓ cup uncooked medium-grain rice, soaked in warm water for 30 minutes, drained
Sea salt
Freshly ground pepper
⅛ teaspoon cinnamon
⅛ teaspoon allspice
½ cup grape molasses
1½ cups water plus more if needed
3 tablespoons butter

Peel and halve the quinces lengthwise, reserving the peel. Core and scoop out the pulp with a melon-baller or spoon, leaving a 1/3-inch-thick shell. Be careful not to break this shell. Place the quinces in a large bowl and cover with water and the lemon juice (to prevent discoloring).

In a small pan, heat the oil and sauté the ground sirloin over medium-low heat for 10 to 15 minutes. Remove from heat and transfer to a shallow dish. Add drained rice, salt and pepper to taste, cinnamon, allspice, and molasses. Mix well and stuff quince halves with the mixture.

Line bottom of a large skillet with quince peel. Place stuffed quinces side by side, stuffed-side up, on the bed of quince peel.

In a small pan, boil 1 1/2 cups of water. Add the butter, stir to melt, and pour over the quinces. Cook the quince 30 to 35 minutes, covered, until both quince and rice are tender. If needed, add more water and cook a little longer. Serve with rice.

white beans with pastırma in a clay pot
Güveçte Pastırmalı Kuru Fasülye
Kayseri

Clay pots are the oldest of cooking vessels. They have been used in Turkey for hundreds of years, and cooking with clay pots is still popular today. Traditional pottery production continues in many areas of Turkey, including Avanos, Cappadocia, and Beypazarı in Central Anatolia; Gümüşhane and Kastamonu in the Black Sea region; and Balıkesır in Marmara. The village of Kınık (in the Bilecik province on the border of the Central Anatolia and Marmara regions) is famous for its pottery, which is sold all over Turkey and exported globally.

Pastırma or *basturma* is a dried cured beef, powerfully flavored with spices and a garlic paste-like coating (which must be removed before chopping). It is available in Middle Eastern shops. *Pastırma* is distantly related to pastrami. If you substitute pastrami, add cumin, garlic, and red pepper to the recipe.

Serves 6 to 8

1½ cups dried white navy beans, soaked overnight in water to cover
Sea salt
2 tablespoons butter
2 tablespoons canola oil
2 medium onions, finely chopped
4 to 5 cloves garlic, finely chopped
4 green cubanelle peppers, seeds, ribs, and stem removed, finely chopped
4 tomatoes, peeled and finely chopped
½ tablespoon tomato paste
½ tablespoon red pepper paste
1¾ cup chicken or vegetable stock plus ¼ cup more if needed (or water)
Freshly ground pepper
5 ounces *pastırma* (rind removed), finely chopped

Drain the beans. Preheat oven to 400°F. In a medium saucepan, heat about 4 cups of lightly salted water. Add the beans; reduce heat to medium, and cook, covered, for 10 minutes. Drain well.

Meanwhile, heat the butter and oil in a sauté pan, and sauté the onions and garlic for 4 to 5 minutes. Add the cubanelle peppers and tomatoes. Cook for a few more minutes and stir in the tomato and pepper pastes and 1 3/4 cups hot stock. Mix well and add drained beans. Season with salt and pepper to taste.

Place in a medium-size (8-cup) clay pot. Cover tightly with aluminum foil and bake in the oven for 1 1/2 hours. Lower the oven to 350°F, uncover the pot, and add the chopped *pastırma*. If needed, add another 1/4 cup of water or stock.

Cook for 15 minutes. Turn off the oven and let stand for another 15 to 20 minutes. Serve for lunch with rice and a green salad.

tomato stew with bulgur

Galeta Baskısı
Akşehir, Konya

Nur and Baki first tasted this recipe at a small boutique hotel where they were staying in historic Cappadocia. They enjoyed it so much that Nur wanted the recipe. It makes a lovely light summer appetizer, lunch, or side dish. It is best when the tomatoes are ripe and in season. The tomatoes should be very ripe, so they give off a lot of liquid. This is a great way to use up tomatoes from your garden.

Serves 6 as an appetizer

2 tablespoons butter
2 tablespoons extra-virgin olive oil
2 medium onions, finely chopped
3 to 4 cloves garlic, chopped
2 pounds tomatoes, peeled, seeded, and cut into quarters
3 tablespoons coarse bulgur
⅓ cup water, if needed
Sea salt
Freshly ground pepper
2 tablespoons chopped Italian flat-leaf parsley

251

In a 3-quart pot, over medium heat, heat the butter and olive oil over medium heat. Sauté the onions and garlic, stirring constantly, 4 to 5 minutes. Add the tomatoes and continue to cook for 10 minutes, then add the bulgur, and salt and pepper to taste. Mix well; if there is not about 1/2 cup liquid in the pot from the tomatoes and onions, add water. Reduce heat to medium-low, cover, and cook for 15 to 20 minutes.

If all the liquid has been absorbed and the bulgur is not cooked, add 1/4 to 1/3 cup of water and cook for another 8 to 10 minutes, covered, over low heat.

Remove from heat and place the stew in a shallow serving dish. Adjust seasoning if desired. Sprinkle with parsley. Serve with Garlicky Yogurt (page 237) and whole wheat bread.

chickpea stew

Nohutlu Yahni
Central Anatolia and throughout Turkey

Chickpea stew is one of the principle dishes of Anatolia. It can be prepared with chicken, lamb, or vegetables. Here, chickpeas are simmered with lamb, onions, garlic, bell peppers, and seasonings. The chickpeas must be soaked overnight but if you are in a rush, quick-soak (page xxvii). Cooking times vary depending on the type of legumes you use and the length of time they have been stored. The older the legumes, the longer they take to cook, so it is not advisable to combine newly purchased legumes with those already on your shelf.

Serves 6 to 8

9 cups water, divided, plus more if necessary
2 cups dried chickpeas, soaked
3 tablespoons canola oil
1 pound boneless leg of lamb, cut into ¾-inch-thick cubes
2 tablespoons butter
2 medium onions, finely chopped
3 cloves garlic, minced
1 small red bell pepper, stem, seeds, and ribs removed, coarsely chopped
1 small green bell pepper, stem, seeds, and ribs removed, coarsely chopped
Sea salt
Freshly ground pepper
½ teaspoon Aleppo pepper
1 tablespoon tomato paste
½ tablespoon red pepper paste
4 cups hot water plus ½ to ¾ cup more if needed

In a 4-quart pot, bring 5 cups of water to a boil. Drain the chickpeas, add to the boiling water, and cook over medium heat, uncovered, for 13 to 15 minutes, skimming off any foam that collects on the surface. Remove from heat, drain, and set aside.

In another 4-quart pot, heat the canola oil and sauté the lamb until the color changes and the meat starts to release its juice. Continue to cook until all the liquid has been reabsorbed, about 7 to 10 minutes. Add the butter, onions, and garlic. Mix well and cook for 3 to 4 minutes. Add the peppers and season with salt and pepper to taste. Mix well and cook for another minute. Add drained chickpeas, Aleppo pepper, tomato and red pepper pastes, and 4 cups of hot water. Mix well and bring to a boil.

Cover, reduce heat, and simmer for 55 to 60 minutes or until the lamb and chickpeas are tender. If all the liquid has been absorbed but the lamb and chickpeas are not tender, add another 1/2 to 3/4 cup hot water and continue to cook until done. Serve with rice or bulgur pilaf.

diamonds with tahini and walnuts

Nevzine
Kayseri

The dough for this dessert is unusual since it is made with walnuts, tahini, yogurt, and flour. To make tahini, sesame seeds (*sesam* in Turkish) are crushed into a smooth paste. The word is an adaptation of the Arabic word *tahana*, meaning "to grind."

Serves 8 to 10. Makes 24 diamonds.

Syrup:
1½ cups water
1 cup sugar
Freshly squeezed juice of ¼ lemon

Dough:
½ cup plus ½ tablespoon butter, melted
  and cooled
¾ cup ground walnuts
3 tablespoons tahini
3 tablespoons plain yogurt
2½ cups flour, sifted
2 teaspoons baking powder
1 tablespoon canola oil

Garnish:
4 tablespoons coarsely chopped walnuts
3 tablespoons grape molasses

Butter or spray for greasing

254

To Prepare the Syrup:
In a medium-size pan, bring water and sugar to a boil, stirring constantly. Reduce heat to medium and continue to cook for 7 to 8 minutes, stirring occasionally. Add lemon juice and cook for another 6 to 7 minutes. Remove from heat and let the syrup cool to room temperature.

Preheat oven to 375°F. Grease an 8-inch square baking pan. In a bowl, combine butter, walnuts, tahini, yogurt, flour, baking powder, and oil. Using your hands, mix well and knead ingredients together until a hard dough has formed. Place dough into the prepared pan, gently flattening it with your fingertips to make sure it is evenly spread. Using a sharp knife, cut the dough diagonally in both directions, making 24 diamond-shaped pieces. (If you prefer, you can cut it into squares instead.) Bake for about 35 minutes, or until golden brown.

Remove from the oven and slowly pour the syrup over the diamonds.

Let the diamonds sit at room temperature for 2 to 3 hours, until they have cooled and all of the syrup has been absorbed. Arrange on a serving platter and sprinkle with walnuts.

Drizzle with grape molasses right before serving.

1, 2, 3, 4 spoon halva

Kaşık Helvası
Central Anatolia and throughout Turkey

Usually prepared in winter, halva is a sweet dessert, most commonly made with flour or semolina, butter, sugar, milk, and nuts. It is traditionally considered a poor man's dessert since it uses inexpensive ingredients. One needs patience to prepare halva since there is a lot of stirring involved, but the result is worth the time and effort.

Serves 6 to 8

1 cup unsalted butter
2 cups flour
3 cups sugar
4 cups water
Chopped nuts to decorate (optional)

Melt the butter in a heavy pan over low heat. Using a wooden spoon, stir in the flour and stirring constantly, cook until the flour begins to brown, 50 to 60 minutes.

Meanwhile, in a medium-size pot, combine the sugar and water and bring to a boil. Remove from heat, cover, and let stand until the flour mixture is ready. (You may need to reheat the syrup before pouring it over the halva.)

Add the hot syrup to the flour mixture, stirring constantly until all the liquid has been absorbed. Place a kitchen towel over the top of the pan and cover with the lid. Let stand, undisturbed, for 20 to 30 minutes.

Spoon the halva into a serving dish. Sprinkle with nuts (if desired) and serve warm.

noah's milk pudding

Süt Aşureşi
Kayseri

This pudding is a variety of *aşure*—the most beloved of Turkish puddings. It is said that Noah made this pudding from all of his leftovers on the ark. In Turkey, it is prepared on holidays and special occasions, particularly the Islamic holiday, *Yaumu-l 'Ashurah*, the 10th day of the holy month of Muharram. Each region—from Indonesia to the Carribean—has local customs to mark this day. This recipe is from Nur's dear friend Hamra Onart, who is from Kayseri. This is her family specialty.

Serves 6

4 cups milk, divided
¼ cup flour
¼ cup sugar (or to taste)
⅓ cup dried black currants, rinsed well, soaked in cold water, drained well, patted dry
⅓ cup ground walnuts

Place 3 1/2 cups of milk in a 3 to 4-quart pan and bring to a boil. Meanwhile, place the remaining milk in a small bowl. Whisk 1/4 cup flour into the bowl and mix well. When the 3 1/2 cups of milk comes to a boil, reduce heat and slowly whisk in the flour mixture. Stirring constantly, cook for 10 minutes. Next, whisk in the sugar and continue to cook for 40 to 45 minutes. (Hamra uses a hand mixer to make the whisking easier.) Remove pan from the heat and continue whisking until the mixture is cool.

Divide mixture among 6 individual dessert cups and decorate the top with the currants and walnuts. Set aside to cool and thicken.

saffron rice pudding
Zerde
Central Anatolia and throughout Turkey

This golden-colored rice pudding is scented with rosewater, which is used in many Turkish desserts. It is traditionally served at weddings and on religious holidays. This is an adaptation of a recipe I had in Safranbolu (a town on the border of Central Anatolia and the Black Sea regions). When Nur's grandmother made this dish, she half filled the serving cups, cooled them overnight, and filled them with plain rice pudding before garnishing the tops, creating a two-toned dessert. Rosewater is available in many markets, spice stores, and Middle Eastern markets.

Serves 8 to 10

3 heaped tablespoons pine nuts
1 teaspoon saffron, soaked for 24 hours in 6 cups of water
½ cup medium-grain rice
½ cup cornstarch
Scant 2 cups sugar
Zest of ½ to 1 orange
½ cup orange juice
4 tablespoons rose water
3 heaped tablespoons dried currants (optional)

Preheat oven to 350°F. Place pine nuts on a small baking sheet and bake for 3 to 4 minutes until just lightly browned. Be careful not to let them burn. Set aside to cool, and store, covered, until use.

Wash the rice several times, soak in water for 30 minutes and drain. In a saucepan, bring the water and saffron to a boil. Reduce heat to simmer and add the rice and cornstarch. Cook for 20 to

25 minutes, stirring occasionally. The mixture should begin to coat a wooden spoon. Add sugar, orange zest, juice, and rose water. Mix well, and cook for a minute, stirring.

Pour the pudding into small individual ramekins or bowls and garnish with pine nuts and currants. Refrigerate overnight until firm and well chilled. Serve cold.

sweet rounds with almonds

Şekerpare
Central Anatolia and throughout Turkey

I first tasted these fabulous Turkish cookies at one of Nur's luncheons. I pigged out on them, and then begged for the recipe. I'm sure you will add these to your dessert repertoire, too.

Makes about 4 dozen cookies

Syrup:
1 cup water
2 cups sugar
Slice of lemon

1 cup (2 sticks) plus 2 tablespoons butter, softened
2 large eggs
4 cups flour plus more if needed
¾ cup plus 1 tablespoon sugar
1 heaped teaspoon baking powder
Zest of 1 orange
1 teaspoon vanilla (optional)
50 whole blanched almonds
Oil or spray for greasing (optional)

To Prepare the Syrup:
Bring water to a boil. Add the sugar and boil for 3 to 4 minutes, stirring constantly. Reduce heat and simmer, stirring occasionally, for 10 minutes. Add the lemon and simmer for another minute. Remove from heat, pour syrup in a bowl, and let cool.

Place oven shelf in the top third of the oven. Preheat oven to 350°F. Lightly grease two jelly roll pans.

In a large bowl, combine the softened butter, eggs, flour, sugar, baking powder, orange zest, and vanilla if using. Work the mixture with your hands until a ball of dough has formed. Break off a walnut-size piece of dough and roll it between your palms or on a work surface to form a log. Place on a cutting board and cut into 1-inch rounds. Roll each piece between your palms to form a ball. Gently, with your fingertips, slightly flatten each ball, and place on a jelly roll pan. Repeat until all of the dough has been used.

Using your thumb, make an indentation in the top of each round and fill it with a nut.

Bake in the top third of the oven until the bottoms have lightly browned, 12 to 14 minutes. Break one of the rounds in half to be sure the insides are baked; if not, continue to bake, but watch carefully to make sure the bottoms do not burn.

Remove from oven and pour syrup over the rounds. Set aside for a few minutes, then flip the cookies so that they evenly absorb the syrup (if the nuts fall out, just replace them when you turn the rounds over again).

eastern anatolia

mezze and salads

Cottage Cheese Salad 266

Fresh Dill Salad 266

soups

Wheat Berry Soup with Green Beans and Meatballs 268

Noodle Soup with Meatballs and Chickpeas 269

bread

Tea Time Walnut Rolls 270

meat

Fried Koftas with Bulgur 271

Beef and Bulgur Koftas with Walnuts or Pomegranate Rice 273

Beef and Bulgur Koftas in Tomato Sauce 274

Stuffed Cucumbers 275

Apricot Stew with Lamb 277

vegetables

Yogurt and Swiss Chard Salad 278

Young Leeks with Eggs 280

desserts and sweets

Rose Dessert 281

Buttered Apricots with Walnuts 283

Mosque entrance, Erzurum, © Alexander Zotov

Eastern Anatolia is one of the most geographically diverse regions in Turkey. Most striking perhaps is the contrast between the mountains and the flat plains and plateaus that characterize the region. Adorned in snow in the winter and masses of wildflowers in the spring, the mountains of Eastern Anatolia provide breathtaking scenery all year round. Forests, waterfalls, green pastures, the famous Mount Ararat, and Lake Van (the largest lake in Turkey) are just some of the sights that the region has to offer.

Its altitude and distance from the sea gives Eastern Anatolia temperatures that are uncharacteristic of Turkey—long, harsh winters, and short summers. The cuisine of the region reflects this climate; wheat and animal products are the staple ingredients and many dishes feature dried fruits, vegetables, and grains, which can be stored for the cold winter months.

The main cities in Eastern Anatolia are: Malatya, Elazığ, Tunceli, Erzincan, Bingöl, Muş, Bitlis, Van, Erzurum, Kars, Ardahan, and Iğdır. Located on a high plateau, Erzurum is the largest city in East Anatolia. It has at times been ruled by the Ancient Armenian, Persian, Roman, Seljuk Turk, and Ottoman Empires, and the architecture of the city provides hidden remnants of its history. Apple orchards surround the city, and a wide variety of dishes are prepared using these local delicacies, including stuffed apples, apple and lamb kebabs, stews, and many sweets. Dried apples are used as well. Bordering Erzurum to the north, the city of Kars played an important role in Turkish history when it became an epicenter in the Turks Russian war. Thus some Russian influence can be found in the local cuisine, most notably in its cheese production.

To the west of Erzurum, the Erzincan province is an important rail and road junction in eastern Anatolia. Erzurum is best known for the production of tulum cheese or *tulum Peyniri*, a crumbly cheese prepared in sheepskin bags. Bulgur, green flat beans, shelled wheat, lamb, eggplants, and apricots are some of the ingredients that are most common of the local cuisine.

The ancient city of Muş lies to the south of Erzurum. It has at times been home to Urartu, Median, Persian, Armenian, and Byzantine, civilizations. Pickles and cabbages are commonly used; *cort*, a stew of lamb, cabbage, and wheat is a famous local specialty. Lake fish is also popular here. South of Muş, the city of Bitlis also consumes a lot of lamb and wheat products. Stuffed Cucumbers, with ground meat and fine bulgur (page 275), and Stuffed Beef and Bulgur Koftas (page 274) are two of the well-known dishes of this area.

The nearby Bingöl province is surrounded by mountains and glacial lakes that provide water for the surrounding areas. Bingöl is known for cottage cheese, cheese with herbs, rich grains, vegetables, legume soups, and of course, yogurt. The city of Van lies in the southeast of the region on a plain that extends from the shores of the famous Lake Van. Its beauty, and that of the surrounding landscapes, has earned the city the nickname the "Pearl of the East." The lakes and rivers of the province provide trout, and Van is known for its production of a Gruyere-type cheese, and cheese with herbs. Where other Turkish provinces specialize in kebabs or desserts, Van prides itself in its breakfast dishes. Beyond the lakes and plains of Van, in the southeastern corner of the country, the mountainous province of Hakkari depends on wheat and animal products. It is located at the juncture of Iraq and Iran, countries that have heavily influenced Turkish food.

In the southwest of the region, the fertile province of Malatya is famous for its apricots, which are recognized as the best in the world. These are mostly grown and sun-dried by family-run orchards. Famous dishes of Malatya include numerous varieties of kofta, which are prepared from fine bulgur. Stuffed vegetables are another local specialty and versions even use cherry and beet leaves (sugar beets are also produced here). Mulberries are grown in this area, and used fresh, dried, or in the form of molasses.

Bordering Malatya to the east, the province of Elazığ has been settled for centuries, its numerous rivers and lakes providing for local communities. The source of the Euphrates River lies in this province. Now, it is known for its grape production. Elazığ grapes are very large in size and have their own special aroma. They are used in the production of good-quality red wine, most notably, full-bodied Buzbağ.

Lake Van in January © Alexander Zotov

cottage cheese salad

Çökelek Salatası
Malatya

In Turkish cooking, some dishes are called salads, but they really are appetizers served with salad greens. Fresh herbs complement this simple cheese appetizer. The cottage cheese must be drained overnight. (See the recipe on page 13 if you want to make your own.)

Serves 4

3 cups cottage cheese, drained overnight in a colander lined with cheesecloth
5 scallions, root ends removed, rinsed, finely chopped
½ bunch fresh Italian flat-leaf parsley, washed, drained, dried, thick stems removed, finely chopped

½ bunch fresh dill, thick stems removed, washed, drained, dried, finely chopped
½ teaspoon Aleppo pepper
Sea salt
Freshly ground pepper
⅓ cup extra-virgin-olive oil

In a shallow bowl, combine the cottage cheese, scallions, finely chopped parsley, and dill. Sprinkle with Aleppo pepper, and salt and pepper to taste. Drizzle with olive oil. Toss well. Serve as an appetizer with warm bread and a green salad.

266

fresh dill salad

Dereotu Salatası
Malatya

This healthful and unique salad has a fresh, tangy taste, and exemplifies the Turkish love of fresh greens. Use fresh dill whenever possible; it is sweeter than dried dill.

Serves 4 to 6

2 bunches fresh dill
¼ bunch fresh Italian flat-leaf parsley
Sea salt
1 tablespoon freshly squeezed lemon juice

5 tablespoons olive oil
¼ teaspoon Aleppo pepper
2 hard-boiled eggs, sliced crosswise

Remove the thick stems from the dill and parsley. Wash, drain, and dry with a salad-spinner. Finely chop, place in a bowl, and sprinkle with a little salt.

In a small bowl, combine lemon juice and olive oil and drizzle over the salad. Sprinkle Aleppo pepper over the top and decorate with sliced eggs.

wheat berry soup with green beans & meatballs

Yarma Çorbası

Erzincan

Because this soup is so rich and filling, in Turkey it is called a "soup meal," or a one-pot meal, and it is perfect for lunch on a cold winter day. Wheat berries are very healthful but little known in the West. Wheat berries are the unprocessed wheat seed, also known as the kernel. They include the whole grain—endosperm, bran, and germ—and that's what makes them so good for you; they contain the fiber, vitamins, minerals, and phytonutrients that are removed during the refinement process used to make standard white flour. Wheat berries have a nutty, crunchy texture. The longer you cook them, the softer they get. They are available in health food stores and in some supermarkets. If you can't find wheat berries, you could substitute barley.

Serves 6 to 8

2 tablespoons butter
3 tablespoons canola oil
1 large onion, finely chopped
9 ounces fresh green beans, ends trimmed, rinsed and drained, cut into ½-inch
    pieces, crosswise
2 medium tomatoes, peeled and finely chopped
8 cups warm chicken stock
⅓ cup shelled wheat berries, soaked in warm water to cover overnight
1 small onion, grated
½ pound ground beef
Sea salt
Freshly ground pepper
3 to 4 tablespoons flour for dusting meatballs
2 tablespoons finely chopped Italian flat-leaf parsley

In a 4-quart pot, heat the butter and oil and sauté the chopped onion for 6 to 7 minutes. Add green beans and tomatoes and continue cooking for another 6 to 7 minutes. Add warm chicken stock and bring to a boil. Stir in wheat berries, cover, reduce heat to medium, and cook for 10 minutes. Lower heat and simmer for 45 to 50 minutes.

Meanwhile, place grated onion, ground beef, and salt and pepper to taste in a bowl and knead well until blended.

Dust a jelly roll pan with flour. Using tiny amounts of the meat mixture, make chickpea-size meatballs and place on the jelly roll pan (the flour prevents them from sticking). When all the meat mixture has been used, gently shake the pan from side to side to coat the meatballs with flour on all sides.

Turn heat to medium, add the meatballs to the soup, and cook for 10 minutes. Reduce heat to medium-low and cook for another 10 to 15 minutes. Add finely chopped parsley and remove from heat. Serve with warm bread.

noodle soup with meatballs and chickpeas

Kesme Çorba

Erzincan

Almost every Eastern Anatolian household makes or buys noodles for use throughout the winter. This healthful soup traditionally uses noodles made from a simple dough. These are cut into matchstick-size pieces, dried, and stored in cotton bags for the winter. Vermicelli or angel hair pasta can be used instead.

Serves 8

1 small onion, grated
½ pound ground beef
Sea salt
Freshly ground pepper
4 to 5 tablespoons flour, divided
8 cups chicken stock
15.5-ounce can (1½ cups) chickpeas,
　　rinsed and drained
¾ cup 1-inch pieces of noodles, vermicelli,
　　or angel hair pasta

3 cups plain strained yogurt (page 233)
1 large egg
2 tablespoons butter
1 tablespoon canola oil
1 tablespoon dried mint
½ tablespoon Aleppo pepper

269

In a medium-size bowl, mix and knead the grated onion, ground beef, and salt and pepper to taste.

Sprinkle 3 to 4 tablespoons flour on a jelly roll pan. Using tiny amounts of the meat mixture, make chickpea-size meatballs and place on the jelly roll pan (the flour prevents them from sticking). When all the meat mixture has been used, gently shake the pan from side to side to coat the meatballs with flour on all sides.

Bring stock to a boil in a 4-quart pot. Add the meatballs, and cook, covered over medium heat for 10 minutes. Add the chickpeas, cover, and continue to cook for another 5 minutes. Add the noodles; cover, reduce heat to medium-low, and continue to cook for another 15 to 20 minutes.

While soup is cooking, combine yogurt, egg, and 1 tablespoon flour into a medium pan. Whisk constantly and cook over medium-low heat until mixture bubbles. (Cooking these ingredients together prevents curdling and gives a creamy texture to the soup.)

Gradually add the yogurt sauce to the soup and cook for 4 to 5 minutes, whisking constantly. Pour soup into a tureen.

In a small skillet, heat butter and oil; when it sizzles, stir in dried mint and Aleppo pepper. Mix well and remove from heat. Drizzle over the center of the soup in swirls and serve.

tea time walnut rolls

Cevizli Açma
Erzurum

As a delicious alternative to cinnamon buns, try these—only slightly sweet—treats with cheese and homemade jam.

Makes 14 rolls

½ cup warm water
1 teaspoon sugar
1 (¼-ounce) envelope active dry yeast
½ cup milk
½ cup canola oil
½ cup plain yogurt
1 large egg
2 heaped teaspoons salt
4½ cups sifted flour
Oil or butter for greasing

Filling:
4 ounces butter, melted
1 cup finely chopped walnuts

Egg Wash:
1 large egg yolk plus 1 tablespoon water

In a small bowl, combine warm water, sugar, and dry yeast. Whisk well, cover, and let rise in a warm place for 20 to 30 minutes.

In a large bowl, combine the milk, oil, yogurt, egg, and salt. Whisk, and gradually add the yeast mixture, mixing well. Gradually whisk in flour to make a smooth dough. Cover the bowl with a towel and let rise in a warm place until it has doubled in size, about 50 to 60 minutes.

Preheat oven to 350°F. Lightly spray or grease two baking pans. Place the dough on a lightly floured work surface and divide it into 14 equal pieces. Using a rolling pin, roll out one of the pieces until it is a circle about 10 to 12 inches across. Brush the circle with melted butter and sprinkle with 1 1/2 tablespoons finely chopped walnuts. Starting from one side, roll the circle into a log. Place a hand on each end of the log and carefully stretch the dough.

Coil the stretched log into a pinwheel. Place the pinwheel on the prepared baking pan, and repeat with the remaining dough. (Leave two inches between each pinwheel on the pan.) Brush the tops of each coil with the egg wash and bake for 30 to 35 minutes.

fried koftas with bulgur
Bulgurlu et Köftesi
Bingöl

In this dish, a mixture of ground beef, bulgur, and seasonings are shaped into oval patties, coated, and fried. It is typically served with a salad and Garlicky Yogurt (page 237). Bulgur is an important part of central and eastern Turkish cuisines, and used throughout the Middle East (most famously in vegetarian dishes like *tabouleh*). Bulgur is wheat grain that is hulled, steamed, cracked, and dried. It is available in different textures from fine to coarse.

Serves 4 to 5. Makes 18 to 20 patties.

Batter:
1 large egg
½ cup water
1 to 2 tablespoons flour

Patties:
1 cup fine bulgur
¾ cup hot water
¾ pound ground sirloin
1 large onion, very finely chopped
2 tablespoons chopped Italian flat-leaf parsley, washed, drained, dried
1 teaspoon sea salt
Freshly ground pepper
¼ teaspoon red pepper paste
¼ teaspoon Aleppo pepper

Canola oil for frying

To Prepare the Batter:
In a bowl, combine the egg, water, and flour. Whisk well, pour into a shallow dish, and set aside.

To Prepare the Patties:
In a bowl, combine the bulgur with the hot water. Cover and set aside for 15 minutes. Mix in the ground sirloin, onion, parsley, salt, freshly ground pepper to taste, red pepper paste, and Aleppo pepper. Mix well and shape into oval patties about 2 1/2 inches long and 1 1/2 inches wide.

    Heat enough oil to cover the bottom of a large frying pan. Dip the patties in the egg mixture and fry in the hot oil. Drain well.

271

beef and bulgur koftas with walnuts or pomegranate rice

Bitlis Köftesi

Bitlis and Muş, Eastern Anatolia and Siirt, Southeastern Anatolia

Filling and delicious, this dish is popular in the neighboring provinces of Bitlis, Muş, and Siirt. There are numerous regional variations, including these two delicious stuffings.

Pomegranates are native to Persia, where they have been cultivated for thousands of years. They are one of the seven fruits mentioned in the Old Testament. They can be identified by their distinctive shape and leathery pink or crimson skin. Each of their many ruby-red seeds is encased in a thin membrane surrounded by white pith. The best way to seed pomegranates is under running water: Cut off the crown and gently scoop out some of the center white core with a spoon. Score through the outer rind, marking the fruit into quarters, place your thumb in the center of the core, and gently pull apart the sections. Peel away the white pith and discard, turn the skin inside out and pop out the seeds. Place the sections in a bowl of cold water and gently swish around to remove any remaining white pith (Aliza Green's *Field Guide to Produce*). Avoid cooking pomegranate seeds in aluminum pans since this can turn the juice bitter.

Serves 4. Makes about 18 to 20.

Rice Stuffing:
¼ cup canola oil
2 medium onions, finely chopped
¼ cup medium-grain rice
¾ cup water
Sea salt
Freshly ground pepper
3 to 4 tablespoons pomegranate seeds

Walnut Stuffing:
¾ cup coarsely chopped walnuts

Shells:
1 cup plus 2 tablespoons fine bulgur
½ cup water plus more if needed
9 ounces ground sirloin (93% fat free)
1 large egg
Sea salt
Freshly ground pepper
½ teaspoon Aleppo pepper
2 cups water
4 tablespoons olive oil
½ tablespoon tomato paste

To Prepare the Rice Stuffing:
In a small pan, heat the oil and sauté the onions for 15 minutes over low heat.

Stir in the rice, cook another minute or two, add water and season with salt and pepper to taste. Cook covered, until all the liquid is absorbed and the rice is cooked. Set aside to cool. Stir in pomegranate seeds.

To Prepare the Shells:
In a large bowl, soak bulgur in 1/2 cup and 1 tablespoon of cold water, cover, and let stand for

Fried koftas with bulgur

10 minutes. Add ground sirloin, egg, salt and pepper to taste, and Aleppo pepper. Using your hands, mix and knead for a few minutes. Divide the mixture in half.

Place one half in the food processor and pulse until mixture forms a ball (2 to 3 minutes) adding a tablespoon of water from time to time (not more than 3 to 4 tablespoons). Place mixture in a shallow dish, cover with a damp cloth to prevent drying out. Repeat with the remaining half of the mixture.

Flatten a walnut-size piece of meat in your palm. In the center, place 1 1/2 tablespoons of the stuffing of your choice. Wrap the meat dough around the filling, forming a ball.

In a pan, place 2 cups of water and bring to a boil. Arrange meat and bulgur balls in a steamer basket, and place in the pan. Cover and cook over medium heat, 15 to 20 minutes. After 10 minutes, shake the pan from side to side, using the handles. Transfer meatballs to a plate.

In a skillet, heat the oil and tomato paste. Sauté steamed bulgur and meatballs for a minute or two.

beef and bulgur koftas in tomato sauce
Yumru Köfte
Malatya

These meat and bulgur patties are found in Eastern and South Eastern Anatolia, and many varieties of the dish can be found, including some very unusual ones. Koftas are a filling, healthy, and inexpensive meal. In the past, the hardest part of preparing this dish was the kneading. Now, thanks to the food processor, preparation is very easy, and no longer time consuming. These patties can be served warm or cold and are great for picnics.

Serves 6. Makes about 27.

1 cup plus 2 tablespoons fine bulgur
1¾ cups plus 1 tablespoon water, divided
1 medium onion, finely chopped
½ bunch Italian flat-leaf parsley, washed, drained, dried, finely chopped
1 cup ground sirloin (93% fat free)
1 tablespoon tomato paste
Sea salt
Freshly ground pepper
4 tablespoons extra-virgin olive oil
½ teaspoon Aleppo pepper

Place bulgur in a bowl and add 1/2 cup and 1 tablespoon of cold water. Cover and let sit for 10 minutes, and then mix in onion, parsley, meat, and salt and pepper to taste. Knead with your hands for a few minutes, mixing well.

Divide the meat mixture in half. Place one half in the food processor and pulse for a minute or until the mixture is well blended and it forms a ball. Repeat with the remaining half of the mixture. Place meat in a shallow bowl and cover with a damp cloth to prevent it from drying out.

Place about a cup of water in a small bowl to use for wetting your hands when forming the patties. Wet your hands and form a walnut-size piece of meat into an oval patty. Repeat wetting your hands between each patty. You should have 25 to 27 oval patties.

In a large skillet, mix together 1 1/4 cups water, tomato paste, salt and pepper to taste, olive oil, and Aleppo pepper. Bring to a boil, reduce heat to simmer, place patties in the sauce, cover, and cook for 15 to 20 minutes or until all the liquid has been absorbed.

Cook for another minute or two, shaking the pan from side to side. Serve with yogurt and a salad.

stuffed cucumbers

Salatalık Dolması
Bitlis

You may have had stuffed zucchini, but wait until you taste stuffed cucumbers! They are a delicious Eastern Anatolian dish. You never know where you are going to discover a wonderful new recipe; this *dolması* recipe was given to Nur by her friend Elvan Baransel, who discovered it on a trip to Bitlis. It is a light, satisfying main course. You will need a handful of toothpicks for this recipe.

Serves 6

4 (12- to 13-inch) English cucumbers, washed

Filling:
9 ounces ground beef
1 large onion, finely chopped
1 cup fine bulgur
3 to 4 cloves garlic, minced
Sea salt
Freshly ground pepper
½ teaspoon Aleppo pepper
1 teaspoon dried basil

1½ cups hot water
2 tablespoons butter, melted
Garlicky Yogurt (page 237)
3 tablespoons olive oil or 2
   tablespoons melted butter
½ teaspoon Aleppo pepper

Peel the cucumbers with a vegetable peeler in long strips or ribbons; set aside the peels. Divide each cucumber into three 4-inch-long pieces. Scoop out the inside with a vegetable corer, melon baller, or spoon, leaving a 1/4-inch-thick shell. Sprinkle salt over the cucumbers and place in a strainer or colander. Let stand for 15 to 20 minutes, rinse well, and drain.

Meanwhile, in a bowl, combine the ground beef, onion, bulgur, garlic, salt and pepper to taste, Aleppo pepper, and basil. Mix well. Place mixture in a food processor and pulse a few times until mixture is well blended and forms a ball.

Stuff the cucumbers with the meat and bulgur mixture. Form the leftover meat mixture into small (2 teaspoon) balls. Flatten the balls and wrap with the long strips of cucumber peel. Place a toothpick through the meat and peel to prevent it from opening. Repeat until all the meat filling has been used.

Line the bottom of a large saucepan with the remaining peels. Add the stuffed cucumbers and arrange the wrapped balls on top of them. Pour hot water, melted butter, and salt and pepper to taste into the pan. Place a cut parchment circle over the contents of the pan. Bring liquid to a boil, reduce heat, cover the pan and cook over medium-low heat for about 40 minutes.

In a small bowl, make the Garlicky Yogurt. In another small bowl, mix the olive oil (or butter) and Aleppo pepper.

Arrange the stuffed cucumbers on a shallow serving dish, and pour garlic yogurt sauce over the top. Drizzle the Aleppo pepper mixture over the yogurt and serve.

apricot stew with lamb

Kayısı Yahnisi
East and Central Anatolia

The combination of lamb, apricots, and molasses gives this stew a unique, fruity flavor. In Anatolia, cooking lamb with dried fruit is popular, especially during the cold winter months. A very similar dish with dried prunes and golden raisins was very popular in the Ottoman court. This one-pot stew can easily be made in advance.

Serves 4 to 6

1½ pounds boneless leg of lamb, cut into 1-inch cubes
3 tablespoons butter
1 large onion, finely chopped
¼ teaspoon freshly ground pepper
2 cups hot water
1½ pounds dried apricots, soaked overnight in 2½ cups cold water
½ cup grape molasses or ½ cup brown sugar
Sea salt

Rinse the lamb cubes, drain well, and pat dry. Heat a 3-quart pot over medium heat; add the lamb and stir until the color changes. Reduce heat, cover, and cook until the meat releases and reabsorbs its juices, about 10 to 12 minutes. Add butter and sauté until the meat browns.

Add onion and pepper, and cook for another 2 to 3 minutes. Add 2 cups of hot water, cover, and simmer for 30 minutes.

Drain apricots, reserving the soaking liquid. Arrange the apricots over the lamb in the pot. Add the molasses or sugar and season with salt to taste. Add 1 cup of apricot soaking liquid. Cook, covered, over medium-low heat for 20 to 30 minutes. Check meat to make sure it is tender. Serve with rice.

277

vegetables

yogurt and swiss chard salad
Pazı Cacığı
Malatya

This wonderful, low calorie side dish is a version of *cacık*, a yogurt-based dish often served along-side kebabs or kofta.

The white stems of Swiss chard are not bitter like the red ones, and are often used in soups and sautés when the leaves have been used in other recipes. Otherwise, the stalks and leaves are cooked together because their tastes complement each other. The red-stemmed variety—more common in the United States—is bitter, but it is not available in Turkey. Swiss chard is a nutritious, rich source of vitamins and minerals, especially calcium.

Serves 6

2 bunches Swiss chard with white stems
3 cups water
Sea salt
3 cups plain strained yogurt (page 237)
5 to 6 cloves garlic, minced with 1 teaspoon salt
4 tablespoons extra-virgin olive oil
½ teaspoon Aleppo pepper

278

Separate the chard leaves from the stems. Do not soak; rinse well under cold running water just before slicing (this preserves the nutrients). Evenly stack the leaves and cut into 1/2-inch strips. Slice white stems into 1/2-inch slices and set aside for a later use.

In a large pan, place 3 cups of water and 1 teaspoon salt. Bring to a boil and add Swiss chard leaves. Cook for 3 to 4 minutes. Drain and rinse under cold water to stop further cooking. Drain again, and gently squeeze out as much water as possible, and finely chop leaves.

Meanwhile, in a bowl, mix together the yogurt and garlic and adjust salt if needed. Mix well with the chard and place on a serving platter.

Place olive oil in a small bowl and stir in Aleppo pepper. Drizzle mixture over the salad.

young leeks with eggs

Çiriş
Erzurum

Similar to frittata, this dish is traditionally made in the spring. Young leeks, which are a little thicker than scallions, are the first vegetables to come up in the Eastern part of Turkey after the heavy, snowy winters. This dish makes a nice breakfast on a cold early-spring morning or you can serve it as a light lunch with a green salad. Leeks are sometimes called "the poor man's asparagus," and have been in use since 3000 BC. Aliza Green suggests buying leeks with rounded rather than flattened bottoms, which she says are an indication of age. Aleppo pepper gives this tasty vegetarian dish a nice kick!

Serves 2

¼ cup canola oil
1 pound young leeks, root ends removed, thinly chopped crosswise, washed and drained
1 large onion, finely chopped
1 large tomato, very finely chopped
Sea salt
Freshly ground pepper
½ teaspoon Aleppo pepper, or to taste
4 large eggs

In a medium-size skillet, heat the oil over medium heat. Add leeks and onion and sauté for about 15 minutes, stirring from time to time. Stir in the chopped tomatoes and cook for another 5 minutes, stirring occasionally. Season with salt, pepper, and Aleppo pepper to taste.

Using the end of a wooden spoon, poke four holes in the mixture and break the eggs into the holes. Cover the skillet. Cook for another three minutes and remove from heat. Serve immediately.

rose dessert

Gül Tatlısı
Erzurum

This lovely recipe from Semra Yildiz is prepared with yogurt, semolina, and hazelnuts topped with sugar syrup. The dough is shaped to resemble roses when it is baked.

Serves 10. Makes 20 roses.

½ cup (1 stick) plus 2 tablespoons butter,
    melted and cooled to room temperature
½ cup plain yogurt, at room temperature
½ cup canola oil
½ cup semolina
1 large egg
1 teaspoon baking powder
1 teaspoon vanilla
2½ cups flour, sifted
20 unsalted hazelnuts

Syrup:
½ cup water
1½ cups sugar
1 teaspoon freshly squeezed lemon
    juice

281

In a large bowl combine the butter, yogurt, oil, semolina, egg, baking powder, and vanilla. Gradually stir in the flour, making a soft dough. Cover bowl and let rest for 30 minutes.

To Prepare the Syrup:
Place water in a small pan with sugar. Bring to a boil over medium heat, stir, and cook for about 10 minutes. Reduce heat to medium-low and stir in the lemon juice. Mix well, and cook for another 5 minutes. Remove from heat and set aside. (The syrup must be hot when it is poured over the roses so it may need to be reheated.)

Preheat oven to 350°F. Lightly grease a jelly roll pan. Pull off a handful of dough and roll it out on a lightly floured work surface, until it is 1/8-inch thick. Using a 3-inch cookie cutter, cut the dough into circles. Place the scraps of dough back in the bowl to be re-rolled.

    Lay a circle of dough on the work surface and lay another circle under the first, so that it overlaps the first circle by half. Repeat until you have a vertical row of 5 overlapping circles (about 10 inches long). Starting at the top of the first circle, carefully roll up the row (from top to bottom), ending up with a 3-inch-wide log. Cut the log in half vertically and place the two "roses" cut-side down on the prepared pan. Repeat using remaining dough. Place a hazelnut in the center of each rose and bake for 35 to 40 minutes or until golden brown.

    Meanwhile, reheat the syrup. Remove pan from the oven and immediately pour the hot syrup over the roses. Turn a few times so they absorb all the syrup. Serve at room temperature.

buttered apricots with walnuts

Kayısı Tatlısı
Erzincan

Turkish creativity really shines in this simple, elegant dessert. It is a wonderful dish to prepare in winter when fresh fruits are out of season. Nur and I both love apricots, and as far as we're concerned, you can't have enough apricot recipes. Here they are paired with walnuts and cream. Yum!

Apricots, a relative of peaches, originated in China and have been in use for over 4,000 years. In many countries, they are available in a variety of colors. Turkish apricots are white, black, gray, and pink in color but are also available in the orange-yellow variety that is common in the United States.

Serves 6

1 pound (about 26 to 28) dried apricots
½ cup sugar
1 cup water
2 tablespoons butter
½ cup coarsely chopped walnuts or slivered almonds
1 cup whipped cream

Wash and drain the apricots and place in a medium-size skillet. Sprinkle with the sugar and 1 cup water and bring to a boil. Reduce heat and simmer, covered, for 20 to 30 minutes or until all the cooking liquid has been absorbed. Remove the cover and stir in butter. Cook for a minute, shaking the skillet carefully from side to side to make sure the butter coats all of the apricots. Cover the pan again, remove from the heat, and let stand for 5 to 10 minutes. Arrange on a serving platter and sprinkle with nuts. Serve with whipped cream.

southeastern anatolia

The Euphrates River in Southeastern Turkey. Photo © Thomas Cannon

mezze and salads

Walnut and Red Pepper Spread 291

Antep Salad 292

Egg Salad 292

Grandmother's Purslane Salad 293

soups

Mung Bean Soup 294

Sour Red Lentil Soup with Eggplant 295

Wheat, Chickpea, and Green Lentil Soup with Tarragon 296

pilafs, boereks, and bread

Saffron Rice Boereks 298

Olive Boereks 299

Green Wheat Pilaf 300

Cheese-Topped Flatbread 302

Spinach-Filled Anatolian Flatbread 304

Veiled Rice with Ground Beef 306

meat

Ali Nazik Kebab 307

Kilis Kebab 308

Baked Leg of Lamb 310

Quince Stew with Lamb 311

vegetables

Zucchini with Chickpeas and Vegetables 313

Purslane with Beans, Lemon, Garlic, and Mint 314

desserts and sweets

Grandmother Fatma's Grape Pudding 315

Nightingale's Nest 316

Southeastern Anatolia has a rich history, geographic diversity, and distinctive cultural traditions. Sharing borders with Syria, Iraq, Iran, and the Azerbaijani exclave of Nakhichevan, the region was historically a center of cultural integration, and a junction in the trading route from East to West. It is split by mountainous southern and central landscapes and the flat, fertile plains of the east. The Euphrates (*Fırat*) and Tigris (*Dicle*) Rivers provide minerals and water for the land, and agriculture is a central part of the Southeastern Anatolian economy. Thanks to the Southeastern Anatolia Project (GAP)—the largest development project in Turkey—the region has become an active hub of sustainable development, restoring Southeastern Anatolia to its former glory. The project includes irrigation, hydraulic energy production, agriculture, urban and rural infrastructure, forestry, education, and health. The largest hydroelectric dams and plants are situated in Şanlıurfa (formerly Urfa) on the Euphrates River. The population of Southeastern Anatolia is a diverse mix, predominantly of Kurds, Turks, and to a lesser degree, Arabs and Assyrians, whose influences enrich the regional cuisine. The major cities in the region are Gaziantep, Adıyaman, Şanlıurfa, Diyarbakır, Batman, Mardin, and Siirt.

Gaziantep (also referred to as Antep) is the culinary capital of Southeastern Anatolia, located in the southwestern tip of the region on a fertile plain that is cultivated with olive groves, vineyards, and pistachio trees. It is a center of pistachio production in Turkey, and an important center of agriculture. Arab elements are especially evident in the local cuisine, especially in mezze dishes such as *Baba Ghanoush* and *Muhammara*, and local olives and olive oil are used frequently. Gaziantep is also famous for its rich variety of sweets made from phyllo dough and local pistachios; baklava from this province is world-renowned. Other local specialties include soups, bulgur dishes, yogurt, lamb kebabs, chickpea and lamb stews with a variety of vegetables, as well as sweet and sour stews called *tava*, which are made with lamb and fruits or vegetables such as apples, prunes, pearl onions, sour cherries or quinces. The provinces of Gaziantep and Kilis (formerly part of Gaziantep) share borders with Syria. It is this proximity that accounts for the Arab influences evident in many of the regional dishes. Kilis is undoubtedly most famous for its kebabs, simply known as Kilis Kebabs (page 308).

The cityscape of Şanlıurfa is a charming combination of old and new. Cobbled backstreets contrast starkly with the city's modern architecture. In the old quarter, villagers from the province convene to sell their wares and produce in an ancient bazaar and gather to play folk music. The cuisine is typical of southeastern Turkey, but many of the dishes are flavored with *isot*, a local smoked red pepper. The city is also known for Urfa cheese, a kind of *hellim* or *halloumi* that tastes very much like fresh mozzarella (when unsalted). Kebabs, bread, yogurt, and eggplant dishes are common. Local specialties include rice with green lentils, vermicelli, lamb, and eggplant pilaf, and stuffed lamb ribs.

On the northern border of the region, the fast-growing city of Diyarbakır is famous for its culture, folklore, and huge, sweet watermelons. These local delicacies are prized for their sweetness, their thick skins (allowing them to store longer than most other varieties), and for their lack of seeds. The local

Mardin stone homes © Sinan Durdu

cuisine is typical of the region, with varieties of twisted cheese, lamb dishes, and bulgur pilafs. Vegetables stuffed with ground meat and bulgur and dishes flavored with sumac are also very popular here.

To the west, the city of Siirt and the surrounding province is known for its traditional goat-hair blankets. It also has a rich culinary culture, including such local delicacies as floral honey and large pistachio nuts.

The city of Mardin, built into the rocky mountains that overlook Syria, is best known for its Arab architecture, built with the local golden stone. Mardin's cuisine developed as an accumulation of the different civilizations that passed through. Today, the province remains a diverse mix of cultures and the local cuisine includes a variety of distinctive flavors and spices. Stuffed lamb ribs with rice, Baked leg of lamb or *Dobo* (page 310), lamb stews with eggplants, stuffed kibbeh, and wheat soup with yogurt and bulgur are examples of popular dishes. Almond desserts, roasted chickpeas, grape molasses pudding, (page 315) and varieties of halva are local specialties.

289

walnut and red pepper spread

Muhammara
Gaziantep

When Nur was little, fresh red bell peppers were available only during the summer months. During the winter, her family made this delicious red pepper paste with dried Aleppo peppers. It can be served as a dip with toasted bread, as a canapé spread, as part of a mezze, or as an accompaniment to raw or cooked vegetables. It is great for a party! Pomegranate syrup is available in Mediterranean, Persian, and other markets. Because it is sour, Nur always adds brown sugar to the recipe.

Serves 4 to 6 as part of a mezze. Makes 1½ to 1¾ cups.

1 cup shelled walnuts
4 to 5 slices (2-day-old) stale white bread, crusts removed, processed into
    breadcrumbs, dry roasted in a Teflon skillet over medium heat for 3 to 5 minutes
4 ripe, red bell peppers, ribs and seeds removed, chopped or 4 fire-roasted canned
    red peppers, chopped
3 to 4 cloves garlic, finely chopped
Sea salt
4 teaspoons pomegranate syrup (or 2 tablespoons freshly squeezed lemon juice
    mixed with 2 teaspoons brown sugar)
4 teaspoons brown sugar
6 tablespoons extra-virgin olive oil

291

Heat a skillet; add walnuts and dry roast over medium heat for 6 to 7 minutes, shaking the pan so the nuts do not burn. Remove from heat and let cool. Place the walnuts in a food processor and process to breadcrumb consistency. Add breadcrumbs and process or pulse a few times. Add the red bell peppers, garlic, salt to taste, pomegranate syrup, brown sugar, and olive oil. Blend well until a rough paste has formed. Transfer paste to a bowl, cover, and refrigerate until serving.

antep salad

Ezme Salata
Gaziantep

This juicy salad is made from fresh, ripe tomatoes, onions, peppers, parsley, and mint, which are chopped very finely, giving it an unusual texture; it is so juicy that it is best eaten with a spoon! This salad is usually served with grilled or roasted meat dishes because it adds moisture and flavor to the meat.

Serves 4 to 6

5 large ripe tomatoes, finely chopped
2 medium onions, finely minced
3 green cubanelle or bell peppers, seeds, ribs, and stems removed, finely chopped
½ bunch Italian flat-leaf parsley, finely chopped
1 teaspoon dried mint
½ teaspoon Aleppo pepper
Freshly squeezed juice of 1 lemon
Sea salt
1 teaspoon pomegranate molasses
1 teaspoon brown sugar
1 tablespoon olive oil

In a shallow dish, combine the tomatoes, onions, green peppers, parsley, mint, Aleppo pepper, lemon juice, salt to taste, pomegranate molasses, and brown sugar. Toss to mix well. Arrange on a serving platter and drizzle with olive oil to give the dish a shiny appearance.

egg salad

Yumurta Salatası
Gaziantep

This egg salad—dressed with olive oil—is much lighter than the popular American favorite. This Turkish version is usually served wrapped in flatbread. If you are watching your cholesterol, you can make this dish with egg whites.

Serves 4

5 whole hard-boiled eggs, diced into ¼-inch cubes
5 scallions, trimmed, leaving about 1 to 2 inches of the green part, thinly sliced crosswise
1 bunch fresh Italian flat-leaf parsley, thick stems removed, washed, drained, finely chopped
½ teaspoon Aleppo pepper

Sea salt
Freshly ground pepper
4 tablespoons extra-virgin olive oil

Place the diced eggs in a bowl and top them with the scallions and parsley. Season with Aleppo pepper and salt and pepper to taste. Drizzle olive oil over the top and toss well.

grandmother's purslane salad
Semizotu Salatası
Gaziantep

When Nur was a child, her grandmother loved to dry vegetables. In the summer, the first vegetable her grandmother dried was purslane, which she stored in cotton bags to eat during the winter. Rehydrated, purslane has a stronger flavor, and is even more delicious! This salad can be made with fresh or rehydrated purslane and is garnished with toasted bread like the Italian *panzella* or the Lebanese *fatoush* salads.

Sumac (*sumak* in Turkish) is a spice made from the burgundy-red fruits of the sumac shrub (a relative of the cashew tree). The fruits are dried and ground into a coarse, deep-burgundy powder, which is used for its strong, tart, lemony flavor. Sumac is available in Middle Eastern markets.

293

Serves 4

3 cups purslane leaves and tender stems (roots and thick or damaged stems and
    leaves removed)
2 medium tomatoes, cut into ½-inch-thick chunks
1 medium cucumber, peeled and cut into ½-inch cubes
1 green bell pepper, cut into ½-inch cubes
¾ cup Italian flat-leaf parsley leaves, washed and dried
½ cup fresh mint leaves, washed and dried
5 scallions, roots removed, white and tender green stems thinly sliced crosswise
4 to 5 thick slices of country bread, toasted and cut into ½-inch cubes
Sea salt
1 teaspoon sumac
2 tablespoons freshly squeezed lemon juice
6 tablespoons extra-virgin olive oil

Rinse the purslane thoroughly and break into 2-inch-long pieces. Wash in cold water a few times in order to get rid of any sand or soil, and dry on towels or in a salad spinner.

Place purslane in a large bowl. Add the tomatoes, cucumber, green pepper, parsley, mint leaves, and scallions. Mix well; add bread cubes, salt to taste, and sumac. Mix again. Finally add the lemon juice and olive oil. Toss and set aside for 10 to 15 minutes before serving.

mung bean soup

Maş Çorbası
Gaziantep

The Turkmen people originally migrated to Turkey from Central Asia, and settled in Gaziantep where Nur's family comes from. They brought mung beans and numerous recipes to Southeastern Anatolia, including this one. When Nur was young, no one knew about mung beans in other parts of Turkey. Now, its popularity as a health food has spread. In the United States, mung beans can be found in organic and health food markets.

Serves 6 to 8

1¼ cups mung beans, picked over, washed and drained
4 cups water
6 cups chicken stock
2 medium onions, sliced, cut into half-moon-shape pieces
¼ cup medium-grain rice, washed and drained
1 whole dried red pepper
½ tablespoon tomato paste
Sea salt
Freshly ground pepper
2 tablespoons butter
2 tablespoons canola oil
1 tablespoons dried tarragon
½ teaspoon Aleppo pepper

In a 4-quart pot, bring 4 cups of water to a boil and add mung beans. Reduce heat and simmer, uncovered for 20 minutes, removing any scum with a slotted spoon or small strainer. Add chicken stock, bring to a boil, and add onions, rice, dried pepper, tomato paste, and salt and pepper to taste. Bring to a boil; reduce heat, cover, and simmer for 40 minutes, stirring occasionally. Check to make sure that the mung beans are tender and remove from heat.

In a small skillet, melt the butter and oil, and when it sizzles, stir in the dried tarragon and Aleppo pepper. Pour over soup in swirls and serve.

sour red lentil soup with eggplant

Ekşili Mercimek Çorbası
Kilis

Nur grew up eating all types of lentil dishes. During World War I, lentils were the most luxurious food available, and this hearty soup was Nur's grandmother's favorite.

The recipe uses dried eggplant and Swiss chard, giving it a distinctive flavor. In Nur's home, spinach was substituted for the Swiss chard. Diced, fresh eggplant can be used instead of dried.

Lentils have a mild earthy flavor and are low in fat and high in protein and fiber. They taste best if they are cooked with assertive flavorings. Lentils should be cleaned before use (rinse them and pick out any stones or debris). They do not need to be soaked but they will cook more slowly if cooked with salt or acidic ingredients. Older or bigger lentils take longer to cook so try to use fresher ones. They should only be stored for up to a year in a cool, dry place.

Serves 6 to 8

8 cups chicken stock
1¼ cups dried red lentils, cleaned and drained
¼ cup medium-grain rice, rinsed and drained
1 tablespoon tomato paste
Sea salt
Freshly ground pepper
1 (½-pound) eggplant, diced into ½-inch pieces, salted for 30 minutes, rinsed and drained
1 cup Swiss chard or baby spinach leaves, washed, drained, finely chopped
Freshly squeezed juice of 1 lemon
3 tablespoons olive oil
5 to 6 cloves garlic, quartered lengthwise
1 tablespoon dried mint
½ teaspoon Aleppo pepper

In a 4-quart pot, bring 8 cups of chicken stock to a boil. Add lentils, rice, tomato paste, and salt and pepper to taste. Mix well, reduce heat to medium-low, and skim off any foam that appears on the surface with a slotted spoon or small strainer. Cover and cook for 20 to 25 minutes. Stir in diced eggplant, Swiss chard or spinach, and lemon juice. Mix well, cover, and cook for another 20 minutes. Remove from heat. Pour soup into a soup tureen.

In a small skillet, heat the olive oil and sauté the garlic over low heat for 5 minutes or until golden brown. Add dried mint and Aleppo pepper. Remove from heat. Pour over soup in swirls.

wheat, chickpea, and green lentil soup with tarragon

Alca Çorba
Gaziantep

Nur's father comes from Gaziantep. As a youngster, Nur learned to love this very well known, traditional soup, which is hearty and nutritious and has a spicy, tangy taste. She serves it for lunch with warm, crusty bread. The wheat berries and chickpeas must be soaked overnight.

Serves 6 to 8

10 cups chicken stock or water, divided
¾ cup shelled wheat berries, soaked in warm water overnight
½ cup dried chickpeas, soaked in salted cold water overnight
2 tablespoons red lentils, rinsed and drained
⅓ cup dried green lentils, soaked in water for 3 to 4 hours, drained
2 red bell peppers, stems, ribs, and seeds removed, cut into ¼-inch cubes
2 large onions, quartered and sliced thinly crosswise
1 whole dried red chili pepper (optional)
Sea salt
Freshly ground pepper
3 tablespoons butter
1 tablespoon dried tarragon
½ teaspoon Aleppo pepper

In a 5-quart pot, bring 6 cups of stock or water to a boil. Drain the wheat berries and chickpeas, and add to the pot. Boil for 4 to 5 minutes. Using a slotted spoon or small strainer, remove any foam that appears on the surface. Reduce heat to medium-low, and cook, covered, for 55 to 60 minutes. Add the drained red and green lentils, the red peppers, onions, chili pepper (if using), and salt and pepper to taste. Add 4 more cups of stock or water; mix well, cover, and continue to cook for another 30 to 35 minutes. Remove from heat and transfer soup to a soup tureen.

In a small skillet, heat the butter until it sizzles, then stir in dried tarragon and Aleppo pepper, mixing well. Pour over soup in swirls and serve.

pilafs, boereks, and bread

saffron rice boereks

Pirinçli Börek
Gaziantep

If properly made, these boereks should be light and crispy without a trace of excess oil. They can be served with light soups, or just served on their own.

Saffron is believed to have originated in Iran, and was known to King Solomon over 4,000 years ago. Saffron comes from the dried stigmas of the saffron crocus (*Crocus sativus*), and has been the most expensive spice throughout history. Seventy thousand flowers, picked and cleaned by hand, make just a pound of dried saffron. It has a luxurious, somewhat bittersweet flavor and is used as a seasoning, fragrance, dye, and even as a medicine.

Serves 8 to 10

Stuffing:
1 cup plus 4 tablespoons hot water, divided
¼ teaspoon saffron threads
Sea salt
½ cup uncooked extra-long-grain rice
6 ounces ground sirloin
1 tablespoon butter
1 tablespoon canola oil
1 medium onion, finely chopped
Freshly ground pepper

Dough:
2 large eggs
½ cup plain yogurt
Sea salt
2½ cups plus 2 tablespoons flour,
    sifted, plus 3 to 4 tablespoons
    for rolling
1 teaspoon baking powder
4 tablespoons olive oil

1½ cups canola oil for frying

In a medium-size pan, place 1 cup of hot water and the saffron. Mix well and let sit for 30 minutes. Add salt, and bring to a boil. Add the rice, reduce heat to simmer, cover, and cook until all the liquid has been absorbed. Let rest for 10 minutes, stir with a wooden spoon, and transfer mixture to a bowl to cool.

In a sauté pan, heat 4 tablespoons of water. Add the ground meat and cook, stirring constantly, until the color changes and the water has been absorbed. Add the butter, oil, and onion, and sauté until the onions are translucent. Remove from heat and add the meat mixture to the rice. Add freshly ground pepper to taste, and adjust seasoning if needed. Set aside.

In a large bowl combine the eggs, yogurt, and salt, mixing well. Gradually add the flour and baking powder and mix until a hard dough has formed. Knead the dough, slowly adding olive oil until it softens and all the oil has been absorbed. Separate the dough into 20 equal pieces.

Lightly flour a work surface. Roll out a piece of dough into a circle about 5 inches in diameter. Place 2 tablespoons of stuffing onto one half of the circle. Fold the dough over the filling, forming a "D" shape. Pinch the edges securely to seal the boerek. Repeat using the remaining dough.

In a large frying pan, heat the canola oil and fry each boerek until golden brown, about 2 to 3 minutes on each side. Serve warm.

olive boereks

Zeytin Böreği
Gaziantep

These boereks are stuffed with a combination of ground beef, cracked green olives, walnuts, and parsley, and flavored with a little pomegranate molasses, making this dish a winner. They are usually prepared in autumn after the olives are harvested. They can be made a few days ahead, making this dish perfect for fall buffets.

Makes 10 boereks

Filling:
3 tablespoons water
½ pound ground sirloin
3 tablespoons extra-virgin olive oil
1 medium onion, finely diced
1 cup cracked green olives, pitted & chopped
½ cup walnuts, coarsely chopped
4 tablespoons finely chopped Italian
    flat-leaf parsley
3 scallions, root ends, damaged green leaves
    removed, thinly sliced crosswise
Sea salt
1 teaspoon Aleppo pepper
2 teaspoons pomegranate molasses

Dough:
½ cup lukewarm water
1 teaspoon sugar
1 (14-oz) envelope active dry yeast
½ cup milk
1 large egg
1 tablespoon butter, melted & cooled
1½ teaspoons sea salt
2¾ cups flour, sifted plus 3 to 4
    tablespoons for rolling

Egg wash:
1 large egg yolk plus 1 tablespoon
    water

To Prepare the Filling:
In a medium saucepan, heat water. Add the ground meat and sauté, stirring constantly, until all the liquid has been absorbed. Add the olive oil and onions and sauté over low heat until the onions are cooked, about 4 to 5 minutes. Stir in the chopped olives and cook for 7 to 8 more minutes. Stir in the walnuts and continue to cook for another minute or two. Remove from heat and stir in the parsley, scallions, salt if needed (the olives are salty), Aleppo pepper, and pomegranate molasses. Mix well and set aside.

To Prepare the Dough:
In a large bowl combine the lukewarm water, dry yeast, and sugar. Mix well and cover; set aside in a warm spot for 20 to 25 minutes. Add milk, egg, butter, and salt; mix well and gradually add the flour. Knead well until the dough is smooth. Cover the bowl with a kitchen towel and set aside in a warm place until the dough has doubled in size, about 50 to 60 minutes.

Preheat oven to 375°F. Lightly spray or grease a baking sheet. Lightly flour a work surface and separate the dough into 10 equal-size balls. Roll out one ball until it is a 6-inch-wide x 8- to 9-inch long oval. Place 2 1/2 tablespoons of the olive filling along one long edge, spreading it over half of the dough. Fold the other half over the filling, making a narrow "D" shape. Pinch and seal the edges securely. Repeat with the other balls of dough.

Place the boereks on the prepared pan, brush with egg wash, and bake for about 25 minutes or until golden brown. Serve warm.

green wheat pilaf
Firik Pilavı
Gaziantep

Roasted green wheat, or *freekeh*, is an ancient food that is perfect for today's healthy lifestyle. This delicious, very nutritious grain has an earthy, smoky taste. Because it is harvested while it is still young, *freekeh* retains most of its protein, vitamins, and minerals. It is low in carbohydrates, high in fiber, and rich in probiotics. In Turkey, it is never cooked by itself, but rather mixed with other ingredients to mellow its strong flavor. Nur's grandmother never rinsed *freekeh* or bulgur since she felt this changed their taste. Nur remembers watching her grandmother stand on the balcony with a tray of *freekeh*, tossing and blowing the grains to get rid of dirt and chaff.

In Nur's hometown, green wheat is often combined with chickpeas, bulgur, and lamb or chicken; this can be served as a pilaf or used to stuff vegetables. The combined ingredients mellow its strong taste. *Freekeh* can be found in many health food, Mediterranean, and specialty stores.

Serves 4 to 6

2 cups *freekeh* (roasted green wheat)
2 tablespoons canola oil
3 tablespoons butter
1 large onion, finely chopped
1 pound chicken tenderloins,
    cut into 1-inch cubes
Sea salt

Freshly ground pepper
1 teaspoon Aleppo pepper
4½ cups hot chicken stock
1 tablespoon red pepper paste
¾ cup canned chickpeas, rinsed and drained
1 cup coarse bulgur

Arrange *freekeh* on a jelly roll pan; carefully sift through it with your fingers to remove tiny stones or grit. Place it in a colander and shake it from side to side so that any unwanted pieces will fall through the mesh.

In a 4-quart pan, heat the oil and butter. Add the onion and sauté for 4 to 5 minutes. Stir in the diced chicken and continue sautéing until the color changes. Season with salt and pepper to taste, and Aleppo pepper. Mix well. Add the hot chicken stock and red pepper paste; mix well and bring to a boil. Stir in the *freekeh*, chickpeas, and bulgur. Adjust seasoning if needed. Cover and simmer for 15 to 20 minutes or until all the liquid has been absorbed. Remove the pan from the heat, uncover, and place a double layer of paper towel over the pan. Replace the lid and let stand for 10 to 15 minutes.

Stir with a wooden spoon and arrange on a serving platter. Serve as a main course with a salad and plain yogurt.

cheese-topped flatbread

Peynirli Pide
Southeastern Anatolia and throughout Turkey

These spring pizza-like pastries are prepared when the first fresh cheeses are made and before they are salted. Fresh green garlic and tarragon also become available at this time. In Gazientep, every household prepares their own favorite filling and sends it to the baker who makes it into flatbread. This recipe looks a little tricky, but it is not as complicated as it seems; the end result is a boat-shaped boerek with an opening down the middle where the cheese filling shows through.

Hellim (halloumi, in Greek), is a semi-hard, mild white cheese similar to mozzarella but usually made from sheep or goat's milk.

Makes 10 flatbreads

Dough:
½ cup lukewarm water
1 (¼-ounce) packet active dry yeast
1 teaspoon sugar
½ cup milk
1 large egg
1 tablespoon butter, melted and cooled
1½ teaspoons sea salt
2¾ cups flour, sifted plus 3 to 4 tablespoons for rolling

Filling:
½ pound fresh, unsalted mozzarella, coarsely grated
½ pound *hellim* (*halloumi*) cheese, coarsely grated
½ bunch fresh Italian flat-leaf parsley, wash, drained, dried, finely chopped
4 scallions, roots and damaged green leaves removed, thinly sliced crosswise
4 green (spring) garlic bulbs, root end and damaged leaves removed,
    thinly sliced crosswise (or substitute 4 to 7 cloves garlic, minced)
½ bunch fresh tarragon or 1½ teaspoons dried tarragon
2 teaspoons Aleppo pepper
Sea salt
Freshly ground pepper
2 large eggs, lightly beaten

Egg wash:
1 large egg yolk plus 1 tablespoon water

302

To Prepare the Dough:

In a large bowl, combine the lukewarm water, dry yeast, and sugar. Cover and place in a warm spot to rise for 20 to 25 minutes. Add milk, egg, butter, and salt and mix well; gradually add the flour. Knead well to make a smooth dough. Cover the bowl with a kitchen towel and set in a warm place to rise until it has doubled in size, about 50 to 60 minutes.

To Prepare the Filling:

In a large bowl, combine the cheeses, parsley, scallions, garlic, tarragon, Aleppo pepper, sea salt, and freshly ground pepper. Mix well. Check seasoning and adjust if needed. Add the beaten eggs.

Preheat oven to 375°F. Lightly grease baking sheets. Separate the dough into 10 equal-size balls and place on a lightly floured work surface. Using a rolling pin, roll out one ball into a 10-inch by 5-inch oblong.

Mix the beaten eggs into the cheese filling and place 3 tablespoons of filling in the middle of the oblong. Spread it around using a metal spatula, leaving a one-inch border around the edges without any filling. Fold the long sides of the dough over the filling, leaving them unconnected in the middle. Using both hands, pinch the short ends together, making a boat-like shape. Repeat using all the dough and filling.

Place on the prepared pans and brush with egg wash. Bake 25 to 30 minutes or until golden brown.

303

spinach-filled anatolian flatbread

Ispanaklı Gözleme
Central Anatolia, Black Sea, and throughout Turkey

This dish originated in Central Anatolia, but it is popular throughout Turkey and I first had it in Safranbolu, a gem of a town dating back to 3000 BC. I had traveled to the larger Turkish cities numerous times to enjoy the history, culture, and marvelous food, but I had never experienced and the time-honored traditions of provincial Turkish life until I visited Safranbolu. The town was named from the native saffron flower that grows in the area. Located between Ankara and the Black Sea, it is a preserved UNESCO historic town, where modern structures are prohibited. It comprises historic neighborhoods of preserved half-timbered houses and shops, along with the traditional artisans working at traditional Turkish crafts in their workshops, and bazaars. The friendly people and their warm hospitality ensured my desire to return to this lovely place, but most of all, Sabranbolu was a culinary adventure. I dined in many of the marvelous restaurants and coffee houses, which offer a huge variety of authentic Ottoman and Anatolian dishes, reflecting the rich cuisine of the civilizations that lived there for many centuries.

This dish is very popular in the area around Safranbolu, which neighbors Central Anatolia. It is traditionally made over a wood-burning fire, but your stovetop will do just fine. No salt is added because the cheeses are very salty. If you don't want to make your own dough, the filling can be enclosed in circles cut from *yufka* pastry leaves (found in Mediterranean markets).

You will need an *oklava* rolling pin or dowel (22 inches long and 1/2 inch wide); without one, it is difficult to roll the proper circles. I learned this rolling technique from Hacer karadag, whom I met at Lezzett, (a Turkish market and café in Rockville, Maryland). Hacer makes *gözleme* with meat filling, sweet potato filling, cheese filling, and spinach filling (my favorite). Her spinach filling is made from uncooked, fresh torn spinach, some diced red bell pepper, grated kashkaval cheese, and crumbled feta. Kashkaval cheese is similar to pecorino Toscana or Parmesan, but tastes much better in this recipe. It can be found in Mediterranean markets and some supermarkets.

Makes 2 large or 4 smaller flatbreads

Filling:
1 bunch scallions, whites and about 2 inches of the greens, finely sliced
    (a large onion, finely chopped can be substituted)
1½ cups fresh spinach leaves, washed, dried, and coarsely chopped
    (you can use a 10-ounce box of frozen spinach, defrosted, if you wish but
    nothing tastes as good as fresh spinach!)
Freshly ground pepper to taste
2 to 3 tablespoons feta cheese, rinsed in cold water (to remove some of the salt),
    crumbled (or more to taste)

3 to 4 tablespoons grated kashkaval cheese
¼ cup chopped red bell pepper (optional)
¼ cup chopped green bell pepper (optional)

Dough:
2 cups flour plus more if needed
½ teaspoon yeast
1 teaspoon salt
About 1 cup water

¼ cup melted butter (optional)

To Prepare the Filling:
In a large bowl combine the scallions, spinach, pepper, feta and kashkaval cheeses, and bell peppers if using. Taste and adjust seasoning if needed.

To Prepare the Dough:
Combine the flour, yeast, and salt in a large bowl. Make a well in the center with your fingers and gradually add water, mixing well; using your fingers, work the flour and liquid together until a ball of dough begins to form. Add a small amount of flour if dough is too sticky. Knead the dough in the bowl or on a lightly floured surface for about 10 minutes. Divide the dough into 2 or 4 equal pieces, shape them into balls, place them on a lightly floured surface, and cover with a slightly dampened cloth. Let dough rest for about 5 to 10 minutes.

On a floured surface, using an *oklava* rolling pin, roll out each ball of dough into circles about 10 to 12 inches in diameter. The secret to rolling these into thin circles is to hold the right side of the rolling pin with your right hand outside the circle of dough. The heel of your left palm rolls the dough into a circle that gets wider and wider. Keep flouring the surface if needed, and turn the dough to keep it even. Turn it over once or twice. The dough should be as close to paper-thin as possible.

Divide spinach mixture into 2 or 4 equal parts. Spread one part over half of each circle of dough. Leave a 1/2-inch between the edge of the filling and the edge of the dough. Fold the other half over the filling, making a half-moon shape. Using your fingertips, press gently all the way around the edges to seal in the filling. (Alternatively, the dough can be folded like an envelope.)

Heat a large griddle or a nonstick skillet over medium-high heat (set electric griddles to 300°F) and cook the *gözleme*, leaving space in between each. Using a non-stick spatula, carefully turn the *gözleme* over as soon as golden-brown spots appear on the bottoms. They cook very quickly so watch carefully! Cook until small spots appear on the other sides. If desired, using a pastry brush, apply a thin coat of melted butter to the topside of the finished *gözleme*. Remove from heat and serve immediately; I like to fold them like a wrap.

veiled rice with ground beef

Duvaklı Pilav
Siirt and Diyarbakır

In this dish, rice is veiled with ground meat. It is a specialty of Siirt and popular in the surrounding provinces. It has a decidedly Middle Eastern influence, and also features in Syrian and Egyptian cuisine. It is usually served as a side dish, but can also be a main course.

Serves 8 to 10 as a side dish or 6 to 8 as a main course

4 tablespoons canola oil, divided
4 tablespoons butter, divided
1 medium onion, finely chopped
2 cups uncooked extra-long-grain rice, soaked in warm, lightly salted water for 30 minutes
4 cups hot chicken stock
Sea salt
Freshly ground pepper
6 tablespoons water
1 pound ground sirloin
1 cup blanched almonds, dry roasted

In a 4-quart pot, heat 2 tablespoons of oil and 2 tablespoons of butter. Add the onion and sauté until golden brown, 10 to 12 minutes. Drain and add rice. Cook for another two minutes, mixing well. Add hot chicken stock and season with salt and pepper to taste. Remove from the heat when all the liquid has been absorbed and steam holes appear on the surface. Remove lid and cover the pot with a double layer of paper towels. Replace the lid and let rest 10 to 15 minutes.

Meanwhile, heat 6 tablespoons of water in a medium-size skillet. Add the ground beef and cook, stirring constantly, until all the liquid has been absorbed. Mix in 2 tablespoons canola oil, 2 tablespoons of butter, and salt and pepper to taste. Remove from heat but keep covered.

Uncover rice and mix with a wooden spoon. Arrange rice on a serving platter. Cover rice with sautéed ground meat (like a veil). Decorate with dry roasted almonds.

Note: To dry roast nuts, place in a single layer on a baking sheet and bake in a 325°F oven for about 5 minutes, stirring occasionally. Or toss carefully in a non-stick pan over medium heat for about 3 to 5 minutes. Be careful not to let them burn!

ali nazik kebab

Ali Nazik
Gaziantep

This dish is popular throughout Turkey, but it originates in Gaziantep. While Nur was growing up, her grandparents cooked and taught her the best recipes of the region, including this one, and she is forever grateful for the guidance they gave her. In this dish, smoky eggplant is blended with garlicky yogurt and ground beef. Leftovers can be heated by steaming the mixture. This dish is best when served with warm pita bread.

Serves 6 to 8

4 pounds (about 5 to 6) large eggplants
4 tablespoons extra-virgin olive oil
1½ pounds ground sirloin
2 large tomatoes, grated
Sea salt
Freshly ground pepper
1½ teaspoons red pepper paste
3 cups plain strained yogurt (p. 237), at room temperature
3 to 4 cloves garlic, minced with ½ teaspoon salt
1 tablespoon butter

Lay the eggplants directly onto coals in the grill, broil in the oven, or lay directly over the gas burner on a stovetop. Roast until the skins are completely blackened and charred and the inside flesh is creamy. Patience is the secret here; turn the eggplants every 5 minutes to ensure even cooking and be careful not to overcook! Remove from heat and let cool a few minutes. Peel off the charred skin. Finely chop the eggplant flesh and place in a strainer; drain for 3 to 4 hours to get rid of excess water.

Meanwhile, in a medium-size skillet, heat the oil and sauté the ground beef until the color changes. Stir in the grated tomatoes and season with salt and pepper to taste. Add the red pepper paste and cook, uncovered, over medium-low heat, 10 to 15 minutes (there should only be about 2 tablespoons of liquid left in the pan). Remove from the heat and set aside.

Place the yogurt and minced, salted garlic in a large bowl; mix well. In a skillet, heat the butter and the eggplant purée. Mix in the yogurt mixture. Spoon the mixture evenly onto a shallow baking dish. Cover with the cooked beef and serve warm.

kilis kebab

Kilis Kebabı
Kilis

The city of Kilis is famous for this local delicacy. Kebabs of eggplants and ground beef are skewered and sweated. This interesting technique yields a moist, flavorful dish.

Like other Asian eggplants, Japanese eggplants have a sweet, delicate flavor. They are longer and narrower than American eggplants, and have a bright green calyx. This dish is served with tomato sauce flavored with pomegranate molasses. It is especially lavish when served over a bed of rice.

Serves 6 to 8

2 pounds Japanese eggplants (preferably of equal size)
1 pound ground sirloin
1 onion, grated, and 2 onions, thinly sliced into half circles
½ teaspoon salt
½ teaspoon freshly ground pepper
½ teaspoon allspice
¼ cup olive oil
1 tablespoon butter
1 green bell pepper, seeds, ribs, and stem removed, thinly sliced
3 large tomatoes, diced into ¼-inch cubes or 1½ cups canned diced tomatoes, drained
1 tablespoon red pepper or tomato paste
Sea salt
Freshly ground pepper
1 cup hot water
2 tablespoons pomegranate molasses (or 2 tablespoons freshly squeezed lemon juice
    mixed with 2 teaspoons brown sugar)

Wash the eggplants. Cut off the stems and cut crosswise into 1-inch pieces. In a bowl, combine the ground sirloin and grated onion. In a separate bowl, combine the salt, pepper, and allspice; then season the beef with this mixture. Knead with your hands to mix well. Divide the mixture into walnut-size meatballs. Thread the meatballs onto flat skewers, alternating with eggplant pieces, and pressing the meatballs until they resemble the shape of the eggplant pieces.

Preheat oven to broil. Grill the skewers under the boiler for 3 to 4 minutes on each side. Remove from heat and set aside.

In large skillet, heat the olive oil and butter. Add the sliced onions and sauté for 3 to 4 minutes. Stir in pepper, tomatoes, red pepper paste, and salt and pepper to taste. Continue to cook for another 8 minutes. Add hot water and pomegranate molasses. Gently slide the meatballs and eggplant pieces into the sauce so the meat can sweat. Cover and bring to a boil, reduce heat, and simmer for 15 to 20 minutes.

baked leg of lamb

Dobo
Mardin

This typical dish of Mardin is usually served with fried eggplant and fried green cubanelle peppers. Mardin is a multicultural city that has recently become a popular tourist destination. The restaurants of the region offer a distinctive cuisine.

Serves 6 to 8

1 (about 5 pounds) boneless leg of lamb
7 to 8 garlic cloves
12 skinless almonds
Sea salt
Freshly ground pepper
3 tablespoons butter
2 tablespoons canola oil
1 cup hot water

Rinse the lamb and dry well with a kitchen towel. Cut large garlic cloves into thick slices and leave small ones whole. Using the tip of a sharp knife carefully cut enough slits into the lamb to hold all the garlic slices and the almonds. Push garlic and nuts carefully into the slits. Season lamb with salt and pepper.

Preheat the oven to 425°F. Heat the butter and oil in a Dutch oven large enough for the leg of lamb. Sauté the meat over medium-high heat, turning occasionally, until golden brown on all sides; be careful not to let it burn! Remove from the heat and stir in 1 cup of hot water. Cover and place in the oven. Cook for 10 minutes. Reduce heat to 350°F and bake for 1 hour and 40 minutes. Turn off the oven and let the pan sit for about 30 minutes before serving.

Arrange on a platter and serve with fried vegetables and rice.

quince stew with lamb

Ayvalı Tas Kebab
Gaziantep

In this dish, firm, tart quince accents the rich meat. Quince is often combined with meat in Turkish cooking. I had never had the pleasure of using quince until I met Nur. I remember our trip to a huge Chinese market where they were stacked on a produce table. We made quince jam, dessert, and compote; I could not believe what I had been missing all those years!

Serves 6

1½ pounds boneless leg of lamb, cut into 1-inch cubes
1 tablespoon canola oil
2 tablespoons butter
1 large onion, finely chopped
3 cups hot water, divided, plus more for soaking
4 quinces (about 2 pounds), peeled, halved, seeded, and cored, cut into 1-inch cubes
Sea salt
Freshly ground pepper
2 teaspoons brown sugar
1 tablespoon tomato paste
1 teaspoon red pepper paste
2 teaspoons pomegranate molasses (or 2 tablespoons freshly squeezed lemon juice
    mixed with 2 teaspoons brown sugar)
¼ teaspoon cinnamon

Rinse lamb, and drain on paper towel. Heat the oil in a 4-quart pot. Add lamb cubes, mix well, and cook, stirring until the color changes and lamb starts to release its juice, about 10 minutes.

Cook, uncovered, over medium heat until all the meat juices have been reabsorbed. Add butter, onions, and 1 1/2 cups of hot water. Bring to a boil. Reduce heat and simmer, covered, for 25 to 30 minutes.

Meanwhile, place quinces in a large bowl, cover with water and add a teaspoon of salt. Let sit 30 minutes, rinse and drain.

Uncover lamb after 25 to 30 minutes, season with salt and pepper to taste. Add sugar, quinces, and 1 1/2 cups hot water. Using the handles, shake the pan from side to side, cover, and simmer for another 25 to 30 minutes or until lamb and quinces are tender. Before removing pan from the heat, stir in the pomegranate molasses, taste, and adjust seasonings if needed. Sprinkle with cinnamon. Remove from heat and let stand, covered, for 10 to 15 minutes. Mix well, place in a serving bowl, and serve with rice.

zucchini with chickpeas and vegetables

Kabak Doğrama
Gaziantep

Here, zucchini are mixed with garden vegetables, chickpeas, lemon juice, and mint. Most people can never have enough zucchini recipes, especially if they grow it in their gardens. Also known as *courgette*, zucchini comes in a variety of colors ranging from green to grey, and yellow to almost black. It has a mild flavor and mixes well with a variety of other vegetables, herbs, spices, meats, and sauces.

The ideal size for zucchini is 3 to 6 inches long. Really large ones will have huge seeds and watery flesh. It is important never to overcook zucchini because they get mushy. As a variation, Nur likes to prepare this recipe using Japanese eggplants. This is a lovely vegetarian dish that can be made ahead.

Serves 6

1½ pounds pale green zucchini
¼ cup plus 2 tablespoons canola oil, divided
2 medium onions, finely chopped
1 green bell pepper, washed, with seeds, ribs, and stems removed, finely chopped
3 to 4 medium tomatoes, finely chopped
1 tablespoon tomato paste
Sea salt
Freshly ground pepper

1 cup hot water
¾ cup canned chickpeas, washed and drained
4 to 5 cloves garlic, minced
Freshly squeezed juice of ½ lemon
1 tablespoon dried mint
¼ teaspoon Aleppo pepper

313

Wash the zucchini and scrape the outer peel, making a striped design. Cut the zucchini into 4 lengthwise slices, then cut into 1-inch pieces crosswise, wash and drain.

In a large skillet, heat 1/4 cup of the oil, add the onion and green pepper and sauté for 5 minutes, stirring constantly. Add the tomatoes, mix well, and cook for another 6 to 7 minutes. Stir in the tomato paste and season with salt and pepper. Add zucchini and hot water. Mix well, and simmer, covered, for 15 minutes. Add chickpeas, garlic, and lemon juice, mix well, and cook another 7 to 8 minutes. Remove from heat.

In a small skillet add 2 tablespoons of oil; when it starts to sizzle, turn off the heat and add the dried mint and Aleppo pepper. Mix and pour over the zucchini. Serve with plain rice or a bulgur pilaf.

Variation: You can substitute 1 1/2 pounds Japanese eggplants for the zucchini. Alternatively, you can add 1 pound boneless leg of lamb to the recipe, diced into 3/4-inch cubes. Sauté the lamb with the onion, tomato, and tomato paste for 40 to 45 minutes or until tender. Prepare the zucchini or eggplant as per this recipe, and add to the lamb mixture.

purslane with beans, lemon, garlic, and mint
Pirpirim Aşı
Gaziantep

This is a one-dish meal that is light, rich, lemony, and garlicky. For Nur, it is the queen of the vegetable dishes. Her grandmother prepared it with dried purslane, which she re-hydrated. It may be hard to find purslane all year round but sometimes it is available from farmers' markets. If you cannot find purslane, spinach or Swiss chard leaves will work. Vegetarians will love this excellent main course. Nur serves it with thick, fresh, country bread.

Serves 6

⅓ cup extra-virgin olive oil
1 large onion, finely chopped
3 medium tomatoes, finely diced
1 tablespoon tomato paste
2 pounds purslane leaves and stems, washed, drained, cut into 1½-inch lengths
¼ cup coarse bulgur, rinsed
¾ cup water
½ cup canned chickpeas, drained and rinsed
½ cup canned black-eyed peas, drained and rinsed
½ cup green lentils, cooked
Freshly squeezed juice of 1 lemon
3 to 4 cloves garlic, minced
1 tablespoon butter
1½ tablespoons dried mint
½ teaspoon Aleppo pepper

Heat the olive oil in a 3-quart saucepan over medium heat. Add the onion and sauté for 3 to 4 minutes; stir in the tomatoes, mixing well. Continue to cook for another 7 to 8 minutes, and stir in tomato paste. Mix well and add purslane. Continue to cook for another minute or two until the purslane wilts.

Stir in the bulgur and water. Cover the pan and reduce heat to simmer. Simmer for 10 minutes or until the bulgur is cooked and the water has been absorbed. Stir in the chickpeas, black-eyed peas, lentils, lemon juice, and garlic. Mix well and cook, covered, for 4 to 5 minutes.

Meanwhile, melt the butter in a small skillet over medium heat. When it sizzles, turn off the heat and add the dried mint and Aleppo pepper, mixing well. Pour the butter mixture over the purslane in the pan and transfer to a serving dish.

grandmother fatma's grape pudding
Üzüm Peltesi
Gaziantep

This brightly colored pudding is made from red grape juice, which is unusual; most Turkish puddings are milk-based. After the harvest in late autumn, Nur's family received crates of grapes from their hometown of Gaziantep. Her grandmother always prepared grape pudding, which she felt would give the family lots of energy in their studies. She always chose ripe grapes to make this juice.

Serves 6

4 cups red grape juice
½ cup sugar
1 tablespoon freshly squeezed lemon juice
1½ cups water, divided
4 tablespoons cornstarch

Topping:
1 cup seeded red grapes, cut in half
2 tablespoons coarsely chopped pistachio nuts

315

In a medium-size pan, combine the grape juice, sugar, lemon juice, and 1 cup water. Whisk well, and bring to a gentle boil over medium heat, stirring constantly. In a small bowl, mix 1/2 cup water with the cornstarch. Reduce heat, and whisk the mixture into the pan. Continue to cook, stirring constantly, until the pudding thickens.

Divide the pudding into 6 individual cups and set aside to cool for a few hours at room temperature. Decorate the tops with grape halves, cut-side down, and sprinkle with nuts.

Variation: This can also be made with grape molasses. Instead of grape juice, use 1 cup molasses, 4 cups of water, 1/2 cup sugar, the juice of 1 lemon, and 4 tablespoons cornstarch. Eliminate the grapes and decorate with pistachios or walnuts.

nightingale's nest

Bülbül Yuvası
Gaziantep

This sweet, syrupy dessert is made with rolled, crinkled sheets of phyllo, which are coiled to resemble nests. For this recipe you will need an *oklava*: a long 1/2-inch rolling stick. You will also need eight to ten toothpicks. To serve this elegant and delicious dish, you may choose to place a scoop of ice cream in the center of each nest and sprinkle with ground pistachios.

Makes 8 to 10

Syrup:
2 cups water
2½ cups sugar
Freshly squeezed juice of ½ lemon

16 to 20 (13- or 14 x 18-inch or 12 x 17-inch) sheets phyllo, at room temperature
1¾ cups (3½ sticks) melted butter
1⅓ cups finely ground walnuts
¼ cup finely chopped pistachio nuts, for decoration
Ice cream (optional)

To Prepare the Syrup:
Place water and the sugar in a saucepan and bring to a boil. Reduce heat to medium and cook, stirring, until the sugar has dissolved, about 10 minutes. Stir in the lemon juice, mix well, and cook for another 5 minutes. Remove from the heat, let cool at room temperature, cover and set aside.

Preheat oven to 350°F. Lightly grease a jelly roll pan. Place phyllo sheets on a clean work surface and cover with a lightly dampened kitchen towel to prevent them from drying out. Place a sheet of phyllo on your work surface so the long side is parallel to you. Brush the sheet with melted butter and place another sheet of phyllo on top of it. Brush the second sheet of phyllo with melted butter and sprinkle 2 tablespoons of walnuts all over the top of the phyllo.

Place your *oklava* (or dowel) along the long edge of the phyllo. Fold the phyllo over the stick and carefully and gently roll until the sheet is completely rolled around the stick. Holding the rolled phyllo with one hand, gently remove the dowel with your other hand. Coil the phyllo into a nest (or pinwheel), securing the end with a toothpick. Place the nest on the prepared pan. Repeat until all the phyllo has been used.

Brush the tops of the nests with melted butter and bake for 30–40 minutes or until golden brown. Remove from the oven and carefully remove the toothpicks. Ladle the cooled syrup over the nests, turning them occasionally so that both sides can absorb the syrup. Sprinkle with pistachio nuts and serve with ice cream, if desired.

glossary of terms and ingredients

Aleppo Pepper: A dark red Syrian pepper with high oil content. It can be found in mild, medium, or very hot. The flavor is similar to paprika with an exotic flavor; it is sublime anywhere paprika is called for. A substitute for Aleppo pepper can be made by mixing 3 parts paprika to 1 part cayenne pepper or red pepper flakes, but if preferred, just paprika will do.

Arugula (rocket): A leafy green vegetable used with fish dishes and a main ingredient in salads.

Aşure: A popular Turkish pudding that is traditionally served on holidays and special occasions. The ingredients vary from recipe to recipe and can include grains, legumes, dried fruits, nuts, sugar, and spices. Aşure is often called "Noah's Pudding" because it is believed to have been made by Noah and his family using all the food that remained on the Ark. One traditional variety calls for forty ingredients, one for each day of the Flood of Noah.

Ayran: A refreshing drink made of yogurt (or milk) beaten with cold water and a dash of salt.

Bazlama: A thick, round, leavened flatbread, traditionally baked in a *tandır* (a clay oven) or between two thin hot iron plates.

Beyaz peynir: A popular Turkish medium-soft white cheese soaked in brine. Similar to Greek feta, it has a slightly coarse texture.

Black-eyed peas: Kidney-shaped beans that are named for the black spots that appear on each. They have a subtle savory flavor.

Boerek (börek): A popular pastry or pie. Thinly rolled pastry dough, often a paper-thin variety called *yufka*, is layered or filled with a variety of fillings. The most popular fillings are cheese, meat, spinach, and potatoes. The many varieties of boerek are fried, baked, cooked on a griddle, or broiled. If properly made, boereks should be light and crisp with no trace of excess oil. Traditionally, it was said that no girl should marry before mastering the art of making these pastries.

Bulgur: A cooked, dried, and partly debranned cracked wheat; the wheat grains are hulled and steamed before they are cracked and dried. Bulgur is available in different textures from fine to coarse. Usually used in pilafs, soups, *dolmas* (stuffed vegetable dishes), and salads like *tabouleh*, it is a popular ingredient in Central, Eastern, and Southeastern Turkey and throughout the Middle East.

Cherries: A fleshy fruit named after the Turkish town of Cerasus. Cherries date back to around 300 BC and are available in sweet and sour varieties; sour cherries are smaller and softer than the sweeter, firmer varieties.

Chickpeas (garbanzo beans): One of the earliest cultivated vegetables, chickpeas are almost-round, pale-yellow legumes that are slightly bigger than a pea. They are high in protein and have a firm texture and a mild, nutty flavor. Chickpeas are available dried or canned.

Collard greens: A relative of cabbage, these loose-leaf cooking greens are dark green in color, and resemble flat cabbage leaves. Their thick leaves are often used in Turkish soups and sautés and they are occasionally stuffed. Their center rib is frequently used in soups.

Çömlek: An earthenware pitcher with handles on both sides.

Cornmeal: dried corn kernels that are ground into a fine, medium, or coarse flour. Yellow and white varieties are available.

Cranberry beans: Not to be confused with pinto beans, cranberry beans are medium-large tan beans splashed with wine-colored streaks. They have a sweet flavor, similar to that of chestnuts. Borlotti beans are the most common variety of cranberry bean.

Cubanelle peppers (Italian frying peppers): A large thin variety of mild sweet pepper.

Daikon (or white) radish: Sometimes called Japanese radish, this long, thin, white radish has a sweeter flavor than the American red radish.

Dandelion greens: The slender green leaves of the dandelion plant, identified by their saw-tooth edges. They have a subtle bitterness, and taste best when young.

Dill: An herb with a slightly anise-like flavor that complements all types of salads, especially cucumber. It is an excellent addition to pilafs and sauces for fish, eggs, cheese, or vegetables.

Döner Kebab: Stacked slices of marinated lamb that are rotated and cooked on a vertical spit, then cut into thin slices and served with pita bread.

Dolmas: A variety of stuffed vegetable dishes that use anything from tomatoes to eggplants to cabbage to grape leaves. The vegetables are stuffed with a filling of minced meat, rice or bulgur and herbs (these are eaten hot) or rice and herbs (these are eaten cold).

Dry roasted nuts: Nuts that have been roasted in a non-stick skillet or pan without any oil. To dry roast nuts, heat a non-stick skillet or pan, add the nuts, and cook over medium heat for 5 to 7 minutes, shaking the pan so the nuts do not burn. Remove from heat and let cool. Roasting nuts makes them sweeter.

Fava beans (broad beans): Large, flat, light-colored beans about 8 inches long. Unless otherwise specified, you can use fresh, dried, or frozen fava beans for the recipes in this book. When cooking the delicate-skinned beans, add the water gradually to prevent them from falling apart.

Freekeh (firik): A nutritious grain—made by roasting green wheat—with an earthy, smoky flavor. Because it is harvested while it is still young, *freekeh* retains most of its protein, vitamins, and minerals. It is low in carbohydrates, high in fiber, and rich in probiotics. In Turkey, it is never cooked by itself, but rather mixed with other ingredients to mellow its strong flavor.

Golden potatoes: Firm potatoes whose skin and flesh range from buttery yellow to golden in color. Nur likes to use these instead of white potatoes, which she feels get mushy when cooked. Yukon Gold is a common variety.

Grape leaves: The leaves of the grape vine. They are most commonly stuffed. In Turkey, fresh leaves are used, but in most supermarkets they are available soaked in brine in one-pound jars.

Gözleme: Thin sheets of flatbread stuffed with a variety of fillings and traditionally cooked over a wood-burning fire.

Hellim (halloumi) cheese: More commonly known by its Greek name *halloumi*, *hellim* is a semi-hard, mild white cheese that is usually made from sheep or goat's milk and seasoned with mint leaves and soaked in brine. It is the traditional white cheese of Northern Cyprus, but it is popular throughout Greece and Turkey. *Hellim* has a pleasant flavor and a soft, springy texture. It retains its shape even when heated so it is very versatile to cook with.

Halva (helva): A sweet dessert usually made with semolina and milk, but there are several versions of halva that use a variety of ingredients. The name comes from the Arabic word *halwa* (sweet), and it is one of the oldest Turkish desserts. It came to Anatolia before the Turks, and is still very popular today. In Turkey, it is a symbol of good fortune, and served on special occasions such as Ramadan, Kandil, and other holy days, but it is also used to honor birth and death.

Kadaifi: A fine shredded pastry that looks like long strings of shredded wheat. It is made from flour, milk, and water, but it can easily be purchased ready-made and frozen. In Turkish cuisine, it is most commonly used to make desserts, which are often filled with nuts, cream, or unsalted cheese. Before using, it should thaw in the refrigerator overnight, then sit at room temperature for an hour.

Kashkaval cheese: A mild pale yellow cheese that is similar to pecorino Toscana. It is often grated and combined with feta and used to fill boereks.

Kebabs: Cubes of plain or marinated meat, or patties of ground meat (usually lamb), that are skewered—often with chunks of tomato, green pepper, and onion—and stewed or grilled over a charcoal fire. Almost every district in Turkey has its own kebab specialty.

Kibbeh: Shells of ground meat and fine bulgur that are stuffed with a variety of fillings. There are as many variations of this dish as there are ways to spell it. Kibbeh is popular throughout the Middle East.

Kofta: Dishes of finely minced or chopped meat combined with various ingredients (such as vegetables and spices) that are shaped and grilled, fried, broiled, or baked. Kofta are very popular in Turkey, and

and there are hundreds of varieties. Most are lemon shaped, but they are named according to their cooking method, shape, or ingredients. When plump, dipped in egg, and fried, they have the marvelous name of Ladies' Thighs (*Kadınbudu*). Sometimes they are cooked and served in sauce.

Mantı: Stuffed dumplings made with very thinly rolled dough. Similar to ravioli, *mantı* are believed to have been introduced to Turkey from Central Asia.

Maras red pepper flakes: These are moderately hot, full-flavored dried red pepper flakes. They are a tasty substitute for Aleppo pepper or paprika, and can be added to your food while it is cooking or sprinkled on the finished dish.

Mastic (gum arabic): The crystallized resin of the mastic or *Pistacia lentiscus* tree, which grows in six villages of southern Chios (a small Greek island). To quote Diane Kochilas, "It has a wonderful deep aroma and flavor, at once woody, earthy, and musky, like incense." Since ancient times, mastic has been known for its healing properties, especially for gastrointestinal ailments. To use mastic in cooking, the rock-hard, somewhat sticky crystals have to be pounded—usually with a little sugar to keep them from sticking to the mortar and pestle or spice grinder. You can find mastic in Middle Eastern, Greek, or Turkish markets.

Mezze: A collection of appetizers, traditionally served to awaken the appetite before the main meal. Now, mezze dishes are also served as snacks or with meals as side dishes. Examples include *pastırma*, hummus, eggplant dishes, and dips.

Mint: A fragrant herb that is used both fresh and dried in Turkish cuisine. It is most commonly used to flavor soups, salads, lamb dishes, fresh peas, or potatoes. Fresh mint is frequently used as a garnish, or to make tea. Dried mint is more common in Turkish recipes than fresh mint.

Mung beans: a popular health food that originated in Asia. Mung beans have small, light yellow leaves and a silvery white shoot. They are usually used in sprout form and have a subtle nutty flavor.

Oklava: A long, thin rolling pin—about 22 inches long and half an inch thick—often used in the preparation of flatbreads, desserts, Mantı, and boereks. Oklavas can be found in Middle Eastern or Turkish markets, but you can easily substitute a half-inch dowel from the hardware store.

Okra: Also known as ladyfinger, okra is the ridged, green, slightly fuzzy pod of the okra plant. It is thought to have originated in Ethiopia before making its way through North Africa and the Middle East, and finally, the Americas. With its unique flavor and texture, okra is a popular vegetable in Turkish cuisine. Its taste—somewhere between that of eggplant and asparagus—complements many other vegetables, especially tomatoes, peppers, and onions. When it is cooked, okra emits a juice that acts as a thickening agent, which explains its long-standing use in soups and stews.

Orzo: A pasta that is shaped like grains of rice and frequently used in Turkish soups and stews.

Pilaf (pilav): One of the most important dishes at a Turkish table, a pilaf is a grain dish, usually made with rice or bulgur and combinations of lentils, vermicelli, or vegetables such as eggplant, chickpeas, beans, or peas. In the past, pilafs were a course by themselves, but now are served as accompaniments to meat or chicken.

Pastırma: Turkish cured beef. The meat is salted, coated with spices, and dried in the sun.

Pekmez (molasses): *Pekmez* is most commonly made from grapes and sometimes from other fruits. It is often used to sweeten desserts.

Phyllo: A paper-thin dough used in many mezze dishes, pastries, and desserts, including baklava. The dough is made of flour, eggs, and water and rolled paper-thin, but it can be purchased ready made in most supermarkets (it comes frozen in packages of about 20 to 22 sheets or leaves). In Turkey it is available in a variety of thicknesses. For the recipes in this book, the sheets should be 12 x 14 inches or 12 x 17 inches. These must be defrosted before using.

Pide (pita bread): A round leavened flatbread that is traditionally prepared during Ramadan. Pide is sometimes topped with meat, cheese, or herbs to make a pizza-like dish.

Polenta: A dish made from boiled cornmeal. Occasionally, this is fried.

Pomegranate: A nearly round, red fruit with leathery skin and hundreds of seeds and a sweet and sour taste. Each seed is encased in a thin, edible membrane, surrounded by a white pith. Pomegranates are native to Persia, where they have been cultivated for thousands of years. They are one of the seven fruits mentioned in the Old Testament, and have become a symbol of fertility around the world. It is best to remove the seeds in the kitchen sink to prevent the juices from splashing.

Pomegranate molasses: A molasses made from pomegranate syrup and grapes or brown sugar.

Pomegranate syrup: The boiled, concentrated juice of sour pomegranates. This syrup is loaded with antioxidants. It is frequently used in salad dressings, and complements herbs like basil, mint, and cilantro, or spices like cumin, coriander, and orange zest in a chicken or meat marinade. Because of its high sugar content, pomegranate syrup can burn easily; when grilling meats or vegetables, brush pomegranate-syrup-based marinades on after cooking.

Pulse: A class of vegetables that includes the edible seeds of peas, beans, lentils, and similar plants that have pods.

Purslane: a plant with small yellow flowers, reddish stems, and a slightly sour, salty taste. The leaves can be cooked as a vegetable or used in salad, and can be used either fresh or dried.

Quince: A pear-like fruit that is a relative of the rose. Quinces are thought to have originated in the Fertile Crescent in Asia Minor, the cradle of civilization. Sometimes they are referred to as the golden apple, and many believe the apple spoken of in the Garden of Eden was in fact a quince. Uncooked they are dry and astringent but after cooking they become soft and flavorful, turning a lovely pink or red in color. In Turkish cooking, quinces are most commonly used in jams, desserts, or to flavor lamb.

Red pepper paste: A preserved thick paste made from skinned red peppers. It is most frequently used as a substitute for fresh red peppers (1 tablespoon red pepper paste equals one fresh pepper).

Ricotta salata: a salted smooth ricotta cheese, usually produced in Sicily, it is snowy white with a firm texture, somewhat similar to feta cheese.

Rosewater: A syrup distilled from fragrant rose petals and used to flavor a number of milk puddings, drinks, and syrups.

Semolina: Semolina is a meal consisting of the inner endosperm of wheat, a by-product in the manufacture of fine flour. There are two types of semolina: durum is yellow and made from hard wheat. It is used to make pasta, couscous, or bulgur. Soft wheat semolina is white and used for cereals and desserts. Semolina has a sugar-like consistency and a mildly nutty flavor. In baking, it is prized for its special texture as well as its thickening properties.

Spinach roots (bunch spinach): The reddish stems at the bottom of the spinach plant (not the roots that grow underground). Spinach roots are available from Chinese and Middle Eastern groceries.

Strained yogurt (Greek yogurt or *labneh*): Yogurt that has been drained of much its liquid. Strained yogurt can be found in many supermarkets, Middle Eastern Markets, or health food stores, but see page 237 for a recipe.

Sumac (sumak): A sour slightly peppery spice made from the burgundy-red fruits of the sumac shrub (a relative of the cashew tree). The fruits are dried and usually ground into a coarse, deep-burgundy powder, which is used for its strong, tart, lemony flavor. Sumac is available in Middle Eastern markets.

Swiss chard: a nutritious, leafy cooking green with white or red stems. The leaves can be used like spinach: cooked or served raw in salads. The stems are used in soups or stews, or they can be braised and used in other dishes. Swiss chard is very high in calcium.

Tahini: a thick paste made from roasted and ground sesame seeds. It is often used in making halva.

Tandır: A traditional clay brick oven used in the preparation of flatbreads and kebabs. They are often in the wall or ground, and are still common in rural areas of Turkey.

Tarator sauce: A sauce made from thick slices of white bread, garlic, salt, ground walnuts, olive oil, and lemon juice. It is often served with fried seafood or vegetables.

Tarhana: A dried pebble-like pasta, usually made from flour, tomatoes, red and green peppers, yogurt, semolina and herbs, but every region has its own variations. *Tarhana* is traditionally made in the summer, dried in the sun, and stored for use throughout the winter. A variety of soups are made from *tarhana*, because of its thickening properties.

Vermicelli: A thin pasta that is often used in soups and pilafs. It is most commonly available broken into strands the size of a straight pin.

Wheat berries: healthful, unprocessed wheat seeds (containing the whole grain). Wheat berries have a nutty flavor and a crunchy texture.

Yogurt: A cultured milk product that has been produced for over 4,500 years. Turkish yogurt is usually made with ewe's milk and served with almost everything.

Yufka: Paper-thin layers of phyllo pastry that are most commonly used to make boereks. If you cannot find *yufka* leaves, 2 sheets of phyllo dough can be substituted for each sheet of yufka.

suggested reading

Classical Turkish Cooking by Ayla Algar (Harper Perennial), 1991

Field Guide to Herbs & Spices: How to Identify, Select, and Use Virtually Every Seasoning at the Market by Aliza Green (Quirk Books), 2006

Field Guide to Produce: How to Identify, Select, and Prepare Virtually Every Fruit and Vegetable at the Market by Aliza Green (Quirk Books), 2004

Imperial Taste (Republic of Turkey, Ministry of Culture), 2000

A Mediterranean Feast by Clifford Wright (Wm. Morrow & Co.), 1999

Mezze Modern: Over 90 Delicious Appetizers from Greece, Lebanon, and Turkey by Maria Khalifé; photography by Stuart West (Interlink Publishing), 2008

The Ottoman Kitchen by Sarah Woodard (Interlink Publishing), 2002

Sephardic Holiday Cooking: Recipes and Traditions by Gilda Angel (Decalogue Books), 1986

The Sultan's Kitchen by Ozcan Ozan (Periplus), 2001

A Taste of Turkish Cuisine by Nur İlkin and Sheilah Kaufman (Hippocrene Books), 2002

Timeless Tastes by Semahat Arsel (DiVan), 1999

A Traveller's History of Turkey (5th edition) by Richard Stoneman (Interlink Books), 2009

Turkish Cooking by Ghillie Basan (Aquamarine), 2006

shopping guide

Adriana's Caravan
www.adrianascaravan.com
800 316 0820

Aphrodite Greek and Middle Eastern Imports
5886 Leesburg Pike
Falls Church, VA 22041

Asadur's Market
5536 Randolph Rd., Rockville, MD 20852
301 770 5558

Dayna's Market Online Ethnic Grocery Store
26300 Ford Road Suite 407
Dearborn Heights, MI 48127
313 999 1980

Elite Nature Organic Juice USA, Inc
www.organicjuiceusa.com

Kalustyan's
123 Lexington Avenue, New York, NY 10016
212 685 3451
www.kalustyans.com

Mediterranean Bakery Inc. and Cafe
352 S Pickett Street, Alexandria, VA 22304
703 751 1702

Lezzett Turkish Market and Cafe
1119 Nelson Street, Rockville, MD 20850
301 545 1688

Melissa's World Variety Produce, Inc.
P.O. Box 21127, Los Angeles, CA 90021
800 588 0151
www.melissas.com

Penzey's Spices
800 741 7787
www.penzeys.com

Sahadi's
187 Atlantic Avenue, Brooklyn, NY 11215
718 624 4550
www.sahadis.com

Shamra
2650 University Blvd.,
Wheaton, MD 20902
301 942 9726; fax 240 337 6468
www.shamra.com

The Spice House
1941 Central Street, Evanston, IL 30201
847 328 3711
www.thespicehouse.com

Sur La Table
1765 Sixth Ave. South, Seattle, WA 98134-1608
866 328 5412
www.surlatable.com

Tulumba
129 15th Street, Brooklyn, NY 11215
866 885 8622
www.tulumba.com

Turkish Taste
31 Downs Avenue, Greenland, NH 03840
603 661 5460
www.turkishtaste.com

Zabar's
2245 Broadway, New York, NY 10024
212 787 2000
www.zabars.com

Zamouri Spices
P.O. Box 65
Olathe, KS 66051
913 829 5988 or 866 329 5988

Zingerman's Mail Order
422 Detroit Street, Ann Arbor, MI 48104
888 636 8162
www.zingermans.com

index by recipe

329

330

ingredients index

(v) = Vegetarian option (substitute vegetable stock for chicken stock where needed)

334

338